The Good Metropolis

Alexander Eisenschmidt

THE GOOD METROPOLIS

From Urban Formlessness to Metropolitan Architecture

Birkhäuser
Basel

Layout, cover design and typesetting
Miriam Bussmann

Copy editing
Elizabeth Gregory, Polly Koch

Project management
Ria Stein

Production
Bettina Chang

Paper
Magno Volume, 135g/m^2

Lithography
bildpunkt Druckvorstufen GmbH

Printing
Beltz Bad Langensalza GmbH

Library of Congress Control Number: 2018966362

Bibliographic information published by the German National Library
The German National Library lists this publication in the Deutsche Nationalbibliografie; detailed bibliographic data are available on the Internet at http://dnb.dnb.de.

ISBN 978-3-0356-1632-3
e-ISBN (PDF) 978-3-0356-1635-4

P.O. Box 44, 4009 Basel, Switzerland

Part of Walter de Gruyter GmbH, Berlin/Boston

9 8 7 6 5 4 3 2 1

www.birkhauser.com

Contents

Introduction

The subject of this book is the productive tension between the city and architectural form. It seeks to reevaluate the relationship between these two realms in which architecture's inherent predisposition toward form is often matched only by the city's ability to avoid it. While design is defined by intention and deliberation, the urban environment frequently appears aimless and conflicted, even accidental, fostering a tendency to view urbanization as undermining and negating architecture's effectiveness. This book, however, traces an alternative discourse of architecture's relationship to the city. As the title "The Good Metropolis" suggests, I explore here the fascinations with the modern city expressed by the architectural avant-garde and beyond, revealing how the forces of urbanization often served as a stimulant for architecture's spatial imagination. It considers so far overlooked courses of action within architectural modernism and twentieth-century urban theory that are not predicated on tectonic functionalism, technological inventions or such like but instead on architecture's intimate relationship with the metropolis. I will argue that the city has been a predominant force (even if often unconsciously) within architectural discourse and that recognizing it as such will not only allow us to reconsider historical narratives but will also give us a better understanding of our current fascinations and anxieties in regards to urbanization.

While industrial cities of the nineteenth and twentieth century in Europe and the US were predominantly criticized as discontinuous, chaotic, irregular, and overwhelming—in other words, formless—this book examines positions that aimed to discover architectural intelligences in the city without form. The following chapters, therefore, attempt to open up a territory of connections that challenge the predominant historiography of architecture's position to the city. After all, the urban discourse of the avant-garde has often been viewed in a historical lineage that travels from modernist urbanism to postmodern non-planning—the former critiqued the terrain of the industrial metropolis that was in need of restructuring through architecture and planning, while the latter's acceptance of the existing or admiration of the historical city held modernist planning and architecture responsible for its failures. This historiography, however, cannot account for the continued fascination with urban formlessness throughout modernity, it cannot provide a coherent explanation of the emergence of a metropolitan architecture, and it gives us very few directives for understanding today's possible engagements with the world of extreme urbanization. The intention of this book is, therefore, to outline an alternative trajectory—one that complicates the apparent opposition between planning and non-planning, between critique and embrace of the city, between form and the informal, or better, between architectural form and urban formlessness.

The concept of the "formless city" will be instrumental here. It surfaced frequently in the architectural discourse of the last century, often appearing as part of a critique of "cities without form" and the "urban jungle"; yet the term's impact has to a large extent been overlooked or, at most, approached as an object of research by analysts seeking to represent these fluctuating conditions. Both positions are difficult to reconcile with the formless: one excludes an important and prominent theme in architecture, while the other seeks to demarcate a condition that by necessity evades certainty and definition. As Rosalind Krauss and Yve-Alain Bois have outlined in their use of Georges Bataille's concept of the *informe*, approaching the formless in art as "a pure object of historical research … would run the risk of transforming the formless into a figure, of stabilizing it."[1] In relation to the city, the "formless" points toward additional challenges, where continuous fluctuations are the only consistency in an increasingly complex world of urbanization. As a result, attempting to define, re-form, or configure the formless in the realm of the city does not only contest its conceptual underpinning but might even be unattainable. The latter is exemplified in the many unfinished attempts to fully understand and penetrate the metropolis. Projects such as Nicolas de la Mare's *Traité de la police* (1705–1723), Robert Musil's *Mann ohne Eigenschaften* (1921–1942), and, more recently, Harvard's *Project on the City* (initiated in 1996) are all efforts at documenting the complexities of modern urbanization as much as they are evidence that this very condition can only be approximated through a cumulative study of multiplicities that is ever-growing and in constant flux.

This list of projects undertaken centuries apart—each with a different strategy to engage the existing city's urbanization—is intimately linked to the trajectory of the metropolis, its population growth, increased complexity, and territorial takeovers. Speaking of the modern city, Lewis Mumford, for example, refers to its "giantism" and its unorganized, decentralized growth, in which the "form of the metropolis … is its formlessness, even as its aim is its own aimless expansion."[2] Of course, Mumford's pessimism sees little creative potential in the technologically saturated city of the recent past and points toward an earlier history before the metropolis became a universal problem of congestions (both horizontally and vertically). The following chapters have a different aim, but referencing the pre- and early-industrial city and its incorporation into the modern discourse is nevertheless valuable. After all, records from the late sixteenth century reveal that capital cities of provinces began to be named "metropolis" (from the Latin "metropolitanus" and the Greek "metropolis," or "meter-polis" the "mother-city"). Therefore, it should come as no surprise that modernist historian Sigfried Giedion described Pope Sixtus V as "the first of the modern town planners ... [since] he was aware of the city as complex organism."[3] Not only would population growth, regional connectivity, and the consolidation of nation states into centers of power begin to alter the makeup of the city (now a "complex organism"),[4] but this shifting terrain would equally impact its relationship to architecture. With the emergence of capital cities—in their utter difference from their agricultural surroundings yet connected far beyond as parts of a larger network of cities, culture, and Meccas for foreign travelers—came a decreased confidence in architecture's abilities to engage the scale of the city. New urban procedures and mechanisms were at work, surpassing the scale of architectural design and calling for the new practice of urbanism in an attempt to control and reform the ever-growing force-field of the metropolis.[5] In 1867, Ildefons Cerdà called this process "urbanization."[6] For him, as for many other architects, the city's condition was no longer comprehensible via conventional means of analysis, nor was it possible to engage its formlessness through previous techniques of design. The convergence of the desire to order the urban ground with the increasing rationalization of the city and urban life and the subsequent aestheticization of modern rationalization, marked the birthplace of the modern metropolis. By that time, the bond between architecture and the city had dramatically reconfigured.

An early project that unlike any other expresses the tension between the two territories is Giovanni Battista Piranesi's *Campo Marzio dell'Antica Roma* (*Campus Martius of Ancient Rome*, 1762).[7] Here, the viewer travels through an infinite city, configured by a maze of accumulative architectural fragments—a project that is as much a document and comment on an emerging urban disorder as it is a formulation of a potential architecture of the city. Interestingly, a few decades after Piranesi completed his etchings, Immanuel Kant defined the sensation of the sublime as it relates to "formless and endless environments," in his text on the *Kritik der Urteilskraft* (*Critique of Judgment*, 1790).[8] While for Kant the city was not a point of reference nor could "products of art" such as buildings exhibit the sublime (as they cannot be divorced from purpose or reason), his notion of "rude nature" indirectly approximates the increasingly incomprehensible scale and multiplicity of the city.[9] In this context, Kant's notion of the beauty of form versus the sublime of the formless provides a subtext to Piranesi's challenging urban landscape of kaleidoscopic

Giovanni Battista Piranesi, *Il Campo Marzio dell'Antica Roma*, frontispiece, 1762.

fantasy. While the accumulation and clashing of architectural forms negate the possibility of singularity, the form of the city disappears as well. Divided and structured only through the Tiber River, the map shows architectural derivations intersecting with one another and creating a heterogeneous field of difference. For Manfredo Tafuri, this was an image of the "struggle between architecture and the city, between the demand for order and the will to formlessness."[10] Architecture, the so-called "ordering element," was hopelessly overwhelmed by the urban environment that Piranesi rendered. But, with an apparent lack of formal autonomy, Piranesi not only hinted at a new city-architecture relationship but also outlined the possibility of engagement with the city by architecture. While absorbed by the city, the countless architectural pieces nevertheless seem to collectively form an architectural urbanism that renegotiates its position within overwhelming urbanization.

This contrast was also singled out in Heinrich Wölfflin's early art historical observations on the paradigm-shifting introduction of the Baroque. His juxtaposition of Renaissance and Baroque architecture identified a strict formal language versus a free, painterly, and formless architectural space respectively.[11] As Wölfflin's binary pairing of "linear and painterly" relates to concepts of form and formlessness, his description of Baroque architecture opens up additional readings of Piranesi's *Campo Marzio*. "In the painterly style," he wrote, "there is only an equilibrium of the masses, with no neat correspondence of the individual forms to each other."[12] And while these aspects leave Wölfflin "with a certain sense of desolation," his descriptions of the "elusive disorder," the "transitoriness," the "indefiniteness, limitlessness and infinity" of the formless Baroque are equally captivating imagery for the emerging modern city that Piranesi had drawn. There is undoubtedly no longer a sense of fulfillment, completion, or happiness therein but rather a constant anticipation, relentless tension, and contradiction. However, according to Wölfflin it is also this lack of definition with which the Baroque gives the viewer the impression of "unlimited potentialities."[13] Is that not the sensation we have when viewing Piranesi's *Campo Marzio*? The disorder, partiality, and incoherence of the city here turns into a generative terrain—an opening up rather then a closing down.

The use of the "formless" in Kant's philosophy of the sublime and Wölfflin's analysis of the Baroque shows the concept well established within modernity, and Piranesi's plan suggests that the emerging metropolis was one of its sponsors. It would play a key role in the imagination of eighteenth-century architectural and urban thought, exemplified by projects such as Pierre Patte's visionary collective monuments for Louis XV (1765) and Étienne-Louis Boullée's sublime projects for a metropolis (1781–1792). Nonetheless, with the growth of the city its turmoil also grew and, in turn, a desire to reorganize its various strata, which were threatening to spin out of control. In an effort to curb the disorder of large cities, Marc-Antoine Laugier's 1753 *Essay on Architecture*, for example, compared the planning of a city to carving avenues into a forest in the tradition of André Le Nôtre's garden art and yet he still found that "irregularity and disorder ... suits great cities so well."[14] The following century, however, would witness countless reports on the city as an "urban mess ... and the result of a gigantic accident."[15] The turmoil of the metropolis was increasingly viewed as problematic, which fostered consecutive investigations of the existing city, all with the aim to curtail its disorder. What transpired was the formulation of new disciplines that, unlike architecture, were now solely devoted to an understanding of the modern city—its development and its recalibration.

These ambitions resonated particularly in the urban climates of Europe, where historical cities had to be expanded beyond their obsolete fortification walls while simultaneously witnessing the growing divide between country and city. Nineteenth-century officials sought to address these conditions through the metrics of scale and growth, aiming to provide not only a linguistic differentiation between cities but also legal frameworks for the way large cities could engage their surrounds.[16] Terminologies such as *Großstadt*, *Grande Ville*, and Large Town came along with official definitions through which cities with a population greater than one hundred thousand could negotiate their expansion.[17] In this context, *Städtebau*, town planning, and *urbanisme* emerged as autonomous disciplines almost simultaneously during the second half of the nineteenth century, collectively aspiring to formulate a scientific investigation of the city that focused as much on its logistics and networks as on its configuration.

Three implemented city transformations of the mid-nineteenth century stand out: Baron Haussmann's counter-revolutionary axial avenues through the working-class districts of Paris; Ludwig von Förster's administrative military space of the Ringstraße in Vienna; and Cerdà's proliferating grid of services that expanded the city of Barcelona. While Cerdà's organizational logistics appear more scientific and are certainly less representational in comparison to the avenues of Haussmann and von Förster, all outlined an approach to the city that was devoted to the managerial distribution and control of population and resources. In the case of Haussmann, the widening of streets and the implementation of a catalog of façades was just as important as the construction of the sewer system and street lighting. For Cerdà and Haussmann, not the architect but surveyors, statisticians, and engineers were in command of reconfiguring and expanding the city.[18] Early theories of urbanism were drafted on the backdrop of these city expansions, in response to the urban pandemonium of Berlin and London, and with an increasing familiarity with the expansive grids of New York and Chicago. Cerdà had already included a short memorandum to his plan for Barcelona; and what he titled "A Theory of City Building" was in the following decades elaborated and negotiated by urban planners such as Reinhard Baumeister, Camillo Sitte, and Hermann Josef Stübben.[19]

Baumeister's search for a scientific discourse on the city that could coordinate urban expansion, was influenced by Friedrich Engels's critique of the industrial town and led him to projections of an exponential urban population influx that would further traumatize the metropolis.[20] These dystopian scenarios would become effective in propagating a new science of the city that aimed to find answers to urbanization, which was now clearly viewed as a problem. Baumeister's 1876 publication, with the telling title *Stadt-Erweiterungen in technischer, baupolizeilicher und wirtschaftlicher Beziehung* (City expansions in relation to technology, building policy, and economy), emphasized the value in "anticipating the disadvantages of [urban] growth" and focused on traffic as the main concern that was to be solved with rational means and occasional insertions of picturesque moments, within a newly ordered urban realm.[21] Ultimately, the city emerged in the planning literature by the end of the nineteenth century as the most pressing problem for humanity. Portrayed as a devastating condition, it apparently could no longer be resolved by the singularity of architecture but only through a technical, methodical, and systematic engagement with the city as an entity. Of course, Baumeister knew that a complete understanding of the city was an impossibility, as unfeasible as the desire for stabilizing the metropolis. While this presented a crisis for architecture's formal disposition, the new field of urban planning understood the dilemma as a never-ceasing mandate for research on the city.

Architects, in their diminished responsibility, had to position themselves in relationship to the overwhelming (ever-growing yet always incomplete) scientific evidence with which planners now approached the city. And, indeed, the statistical systematism of Baumeister and his allies figured into the work of architects such as Otto Wagner or Le Corbusier. Wagner's study of *Die Großstadt* ("The Development of a Great City") cites the economy of population densities and Le Corbusier's argument in *Urbanisme* (*The City of Tomorrow and Its Planning*) is seemingly based on the statistics of urban growth patterns. The historiography of modernist architectural visions of the city, therefore, focuses primarily on moments when architects have attempted to counteract the uncontrolled conditions of urbanization. This, however, gives little room to bridge the apparent divide between their architectural design and their urban plans. After all, how could the aggressive sensationalism of the Plan Voisin be reconciled with the urban sensibility of the Cité de Refuge, both of which Le Corbusier conceived only a few years apart for Paris? Or, how might the infinite grid of Wagner's layout for Vienna be related to his legendary tectonics? Perhaps, this is only possible if one is willing to detect in these works a simultaneous "horror and fascination" with the metropolis, a dualism that is less apparent in planning but that often becomes productive in architecture. Wagner, for example, presumed that most city dwellers take comfort in the anonymity of the metropolis, a reversal of the city's negativities into productive urban repercussions.[22]

This strategic reversal in attitude comes into play where architectural intelligences are discovered in the city without form. Simultaneously enthralled and traumatized by the turmoil of the metropolis, some figures began at the turn of the century to focus on the disordered, disjunctive, and anarchic moments of the modern city in an attempt to formulate an understanding of the discontinuities they found dominating. The term "formless city" was utilized early on in the German architectural discourse on the modern *Großstadt* during the end of the nineteenth and the beginning of the twentieth century in publications such as *Die Schönheit der großen Stadt* (The beauty of the metropolis) by the architect August Endell (1908), *Die Architektur der Großstadt* (The architecture of the metropolis) by the art historian and critic Karl Scheffler (1913), and *Der Städtebau* (City building) by the urban theorist Werner Hegemann (1911). In these texts, the concept was used to gain access to the city. Endell, for example, entirely reversed the negativities associated with contemporary urbanization and instead detected a new "beauty" within it; Scheffler employed the formless as a strategic device to reveal potentials of the metropolis; and Hegemann aimed to define and combat urban disorder, while unintentionally capturing the most complex image of the city. In all these works, the existing urban condition crystallized into an operative concept that, in turn, penetrated the architectural discourse.

The city of Berlin was at the center of attention in these texts. It had experienced one of the most rapid population increases in modern history, a surge that was not equally matched by new construction. As a consequence, Berlin witnessed unprecedented densities and aggressive territorial negotiations. While around 1800, the two largest cities of Germany (Berlin and Hamburg) competed for the status of the most populated, over the next seventy years Berlin would surpass Hamburg's population numbers by more then threefold. At the beginning of the nineteenth century, Berlin became the center of the Prussian Reforms, which initiated the modernization of government (guided by ideas of the Enlightenment), abolished serfdom (allowing peasants to travel and settle in towns), abandoned the monopoly of the guild system (encouraging free competition in industry), and reformed education (founding, for example, the University of Berlin in 1809). In 1871, Berlin become the capital of the German Empire and would acquire a more central position in cultural, intellectual, and social life.[23] By 1910, 60 percent of Germany's population lived in cities, of which Berlin was by far the largest with a population of over two million. Its growth had emerged from a unique combination of circumstances: advanced industrial activities, enormous building efforts, and a complex web of town councils, rural municipalities, and estates. This assemblage of multiple territories and constituencies, which were not unified until the Greater Berlin Act of 1920, inhibited town planning efforts across the entire city. It is, therefore, no coincidence that the lack of planning, absence of a coherent urban form, and randomness of urban implementation were recognized by many authors who were based in Berlin at the time. While the city reflected a specific constellation of influences, its exceptional commitment to metropolitan forces often provoked architects and planners to see Berlin as an indication of larger trends still ahead for other cities (with very different histories); and some channeled the specificities of Berlin's *"Planlosigkeit"* (lack of a plan) toward a different mentality concerning metropolitan conditions in general.

The following chapters will show how the discourse around Berlin was no isolated episode. Instead, an adjusted attitude on the existing city became a way of approaching different urban environments across the twentieth century. While more often than not architects aimed at imposing a new order, for the authors that are discussed here the very disturbance of the city's formlessness also opened up new conceptual territories, facilitated unorthodox readings of space and time, and upset common notions and preconceptions about architecture. Not always intentional, the disruptive and "uncultivated" nature of the city became for a number of architects a performative and constructive condition; even for some of the most uncompromising modernists. Ludwig Mies van der Rohe, for instance, observed in 1955: "We have to live in a jungle, and maybe we do well by that."[24] In view of a new territorial urbanization, Mies reevaluated the apparent urban negativity as a counter-site that could provoke unexpected creativities—urban inspirations and imaginings only heightened by the intensity of the city.

During the twentieth century, a number of architects formulated alternative urban theories that went beyond a binary of opposition to or acceptance of the existing city. In their works, one can identify a mentality that finds latent productivities in the turbulences of the modern world as part of an attempt to engage urbanization from within. In these theories and projects, the attitude toward the city radically shifts. This new mentality often arrives through altered ways of seeing and perceiving the city, through a frequent extrapolation of existing conditions in order to reach urban alternatives, and by consistently inventing new narratives to challenge conventions. Each of the following chapters focuses on one such trajectory, with the aim of illuminating architecture's particular relationship to the city. No attempt is made to account for completeness; rather, a selective reading of episodes follows strands of ideas, through different cities, and into the projects and writings by a range of figures.

The first chapter focuses on a change in perception of the metropolis, an analytical seeing that in particularly productive instances was first driven by scientific aesthetics and the psychology of form that impacted urban analysis. Endell's early re-reading of the city that utilized empathy theory and impressionist vision to discover latent "beauties" in the formless metropolis, influenced artists such as Umbo and László Moholy-Nagy, and guided designers and visual theorists such as György Kepes in the development of his *Language of Vision* (1944). With the search for a new outlook on the urban world came a new view of the city that eventually would haunt modernists such as Walter Gropius and foreshadow a mentality of seeing potential in the most unlikely places. These ranged from the freeways in Reyner Banham's Los Angeles to the parking lots and signs of Robert Venturi and Denise Scott Brown's Las Vegas. All the projects highlighted in this chapter deferred the urge to design the city in favor of a new urban "vision" that triggered a rethinking of design.

One of the clearest examples in which changes in perception of the city influenced design methods was the emergence of a "metropolitan architecture." A concept initially observed by Karl Scheffler in the warehouses, apartment buildings, and department stores of the metropolis, it would become a new paradigm through which the city challenged architecture to recognize new forms. Here, the forces of the metropolis had brought about (and literally shaped) new spatial and organizational conditions, which resonated in the ideas for an urban architecture carried forward by works that span from Ludwig Hilberseimer's *Großstadtarchitektur* to the Office for Metropolitan Architecture (OMA). In such projects, the second chapter detects an openness that rejects the dichotomy between outright resistance to, or unconditional embrace of, metropolitan forces and counters the rigid *Städtebau* mentalities at the time, as well as the modernism of the 1920s and 30s, and the modernisms that came after. Possibly the most stimulating contribution by this strand of architects and thinkers was the extrapolation of existing urban characteristics in order to create intellectual *Spielraum* (margin, room to play) for the invention of a new architectural urbanism.

Many of these projects tapped existing conditions through narratives in order to craft alternative realities. The third chapter investigates how these would disseminate and, ultimately, influence and "détourn" existing conventions and preconceptions. An analysis of Berlin's City-Building Exhibition of 1910 (the largest exhibition on urbanization and urbanism at the time) positions architecture's wish to fully comprehend the metropolis in relation to the city's constant avoidance of being pinned down. Hegemann, the exhibition's organizer, aimed to comprehend, critique, and combat the formless metropolis, yet his inclusive documentation of the city unintentionally generated an exceedingly intricate image thereof. While failing in regard to the curatorial mandate, the exhibition and the publication that would follow reverberated in decades to come, shaping Le Corbusier's urban project and informing Walter Benjamin's urban radio broadcasts. This chapter reads city narratives as vehicles of rhetoric that shift established conventions and, in turn, reposition architecture. The Situationist city *détournement* in the 1950s and 60s, followed by Constant's nomadic constructs and Bernard Tschumi's transcriptions of Manhattan and his subsequent explorations of cross-programming, are indicative of the constructive nature of urban narratives. These projects highlight the opportunistic use of the existing city as the springboard for alternative scenarios; not just in the imagination of the authors but also, and even more importantly, in the minds of the viewers, listeners, readers, and participants. Benjamin, for example, not only updated Hegemann's views on the city by utilizing Moholy-Nagy's discourse on the "new optics" through an explicit use of the "urban image" and of "transparency," he also implied a new urban future.

While the three parts are conceived as independent texts, each traversing the twentieth century, the topics, figures, projects, and locations discussed are closely related. As the chapters run parallel, the subjects can cross over, protagonists of one section might reappear elsewhere, and cities and urban locations may resurface as backdrops for multiple ideas. This facilitates at least two different kinds of readings: a sequential reading that exposes the trajectory of one topic carried by very different figures across time, and a non-linear reading that cuts across multiple chapters. The second one, for example, unearths the history of "metropolitan architecture," from Scheffler via Hilberseimer to OMA, but each part of that sequence also enables a cross-reading into other chapters, where Koolhaas's *Delirious New York* (1978), for instance, can be understood in relationship to Banham's *Los Angeles* (1971), Venturi and Scott Brown's *Learning from Las Vegas* (1972), or Tschumi's *Manhattan Transcripts* (1981). Intentionally, my argument relies not on a singular group of architects or theorists (although they will form a collective over the course of the book), but rather on the ideas and projects put forward by very different figures that coalesce into a modified discourse on the city. Some of the projects discussed here are well known while others are rather obscure, yet their relationship to each other exposes new insights. Well-known examples might in the end become unrecognizable, while projects that were largely forgotten suddenly appear strangely familiar.

However, this is not primarily an endeavor at revising history. My attempt is rather to at once: illuminate a topic fundamental to architecture yet too often misunderstood; expose architecture as a discipline deeply indebted to the potentials of the city; and detect an undercurrent of architectural urbanism that crosses scales from building to city. With that ambition, the book builds on Marshall Berman's provocation, that an appropriation of the modernities of yesterday "can be at once a critique of the modernities of today and an act of faith in the modernities ... of tomorrow and the day after tomorrow."[25] For the purpose of the following chapters, I expand Berman's call by relating the abstraction of "modernity" to the particular multiplicities of the city. I hope to show that metropolitan urbanization penetrated, stimulated, and defined the discourse of modern architecture and modernity itself. This investigation, then, seeks to demonstrate how concepts and conditions of the existing city became productive for the architectural discourse and, therefore, are essential for an understanding of tropes and dualities within modernity: order versus chaos, boundary versus *Spielraum*, emptiness versus saturation, purity versus multiplicity, and pure negativity versus potent negativity. Thus, appropriating yesterday's concepts of the formless city might give us the capacity for a constructive critique of the city of today as well as the necessary conviction to engage the city of tomorrow.

"*What is astonishing is that the metropolis, despite all its ugly buildings, despite its noise, despite everything that one can criticize, is, for those who want to see, a wonder of beauty and poetry.* **August Endell, *Die Schönheit der großen Stadt*, 1908**

To grasp spatial relationships and orient oneself in a metropolis of today, among the intricate dimensions of streets, subways, elevated trains, and skyscrapers, requires a new way of seeing. **György Kepes, *Language of Vision*, 1944**

Learning from the existing landscape is a way of being revolutionary for an architect. ... that is, to question how we look at things. **Robert Venturi, Denise Scott Brown, and Steven Izenour, *Learning from Las Vegas*, 1972**

1 Imagination

New Urban Optics and the Specter of a Beautiful Metropolis

In 1971, Denise Scott Brown published an unexpected plaidoyer in favor of "Las Vegas, Los Angeles, Levittown, the swinging singles on the Westheimer Strip, golf resorts, boating communities, Co-op City, the residential backgrounds to soap operas, TV commercials and mass mag ads, billboards, and Route 66," when she declared them "sources for a changing architectural sensibility."[1] For her, those new environments rendered previous forms of urban space obsolete and superseded conventional aesthetic preferences, functional paradigms, and formal typologies. While during the 1960s, most architects felt unsettled by the increasing suburbanization and decentralization of the existing city propelled by new technologies and mass media, for Scott Brown those conditions seemed inescapable. But, viewing the dramatic urban shifts as a given was only one prerequisite in the process of rethinking even the most problematic urban environments. Just as importantly, the new context called for a different way of seeing the city—an intentionally altered outlook on the world that allowed architects to recognize and utilize new potentials in urbanization.

Especially after the turbulence and revelations of the 1960s, this embrace of contemporary urbanization seemed unique and unprecedented. Yet, despite the apparent novelty, these ideas and mentalities participated in a modernist genealogy initiated in the late nineteenth century, when theories of vision intersected with the new optics of the metropolis. A new way of seeing emerged in that period, as an alternative to engagements with the city that commonly vacillated between idealistic planning and dystopian resignation. August Endell's small but influential book *Die Schönheit der großen Stadt* (The beauty of the metropolis; 1908) developed an aesthetic theory of the contemporary metropolis that promised a novel sensuality. Endell proposed not a restructuring of the urban environment through design but a rethinking of design through a new perception of the city. Influenced by modern psychology, empathy theory, impressionist ideas, contemporary sociology, and the literary circles of the day, Endell's argument ran counter to the anti-urbanist tendencies of the early twentieth century. His thesis surprised most readers: the city's center, he argued, lay in its marginal sites, and its lasting identity was captured in its fleeting moments. While the familiar form of the city had vanished, its new formlessness became the driver for an alternative urban imagination.

Although Endell never drew up encompassing city plans, did not participate in urban design competitions, and focused primarily on individual building projects, his most significant publication is devoted entirely to rethinking what constitutes the city. *Die Schönheit der großen Stadt* takes the reader on a journey through a metropolis that slowly reveals itself as Berlin. Throughout the book, Endell described urban scenes—of streets, plazas, and stations, as well as the margins of urbanity, such as the city's blank walls and outskirts. Armed with an unconditional openness to what he found in the contemporary metropolis, the descriptions set out to report on whatever the city had to offer. As such, the book is an early example of subverting the existing architecture and planning discourses by questioning the abilities of these disciplines to solve problems. Instead it attempts to re-calibrate attitudes toward the city. Seemingly naïve declarations like "The city is beautiful!" offer an alternative position that emphasizes the city's capacities rather than its failures.

This new urban outlook would eventually influence even the most uncompromising modernists and promote recognition of latent possibility in the most unlikely places. One such trajectory runs from the impressionist gaze of Endell in Berlin and Munich, to the abstracted vision of Wassily Kandinsky in Munich and the Bauhaus, to the psychological optics of László Moholy-Nagy at the Bauhaus and later in Chicago, to Reyner Banham's motorized lens of Los Angeles, and the cinematic pursuits of Robert Venturi and Scott Brown in Las Vegas. While it is important to recognize the different subjective effects that these various techniques and technologies produced, the modalities that these figures deployed all point toward a shared way of seeing existing conditions alternatively. This chapter tracks that lineage.

August Endell's Psychology of Form(lessness)

Endell's text enters the discussion of architecture's relationship to the city at an intense moment in urban history. Confronted with the vortices of the nineteenth-century metropolis saturated with new technologies, spatial and material effects, and a pulsating infrastructure, philosophers saw the vanishing of the "homeland"; sociologists searched for the role of the individual within an increasingly urbanized world; and architects and planners sought to understand and then redesign this urban landscape. A short paragraph in Friedrich Nietzsche's *Also sprach Zarathustra* (*Thus Spoke Zarathustra*) typifies the skepticism toward the contemporary city of his day. Approaching the gates of the metropolis, Zarathustra's companion and pupil characterizes it as a location where "you could find nothing

Viaduct of subway line (U2), Berlin, 1902. Photograph of the newly constructed train tracks that carved a new infrastructural space into the city near Gleisdreieck station.

and lose everything ... great thoughts are boiled alive [... and where] all great feelings decay."[2] For Nietzsche, issues of urban density, health, and the unequal distribution of capital were the inevitable outcome of the capitalist metropolis, so "there is nothing to better, nothing to worsen." And, he wished he could "already see the pillar of fire in which it will be burned!"[3] This view portrays the metropolis as mere tragedy, a condition in which modern stimuli and building forms, as well as market forces had voided all previous forms of urban life. The City, he wrote in 1882, had lost its "buildings and sites that would altogether give expression to the sublimity of thoughtfulness and of stepping aside."[4]

But architects of the late nineteenth and early twentieth century evinced more hope that the expansion of the metropolis and the problems that came with it could be addressed through redesigning urban environments. In the German discourse, the newly emerging discipline of *Städtebau* (city building) explored new approaches to analyzing the modern city and reining in metropolitan expansion. These thinkers aimed to once again form a coherent urban entity by reintroducing order to the metropolis that had seemingly spun out of control. Endell's publication takes account of both the philosophical and the architectural argument by acknowledging that the metropolis "has predictably always been the target of excessive attacks," where "wild hedonism, nervous haste, and revolting degeneration accumulate into a greyish chaos" and where the "unspeakable ugliness of cities is condemned."[5] Not only did Endell recognize the alienating conditions of the modern environment, its spatial and qualitative deficits, and the resulting longing for its annihilation, but he even shared a feeling of revulsion toward it. Describing Berlin and its belated but rapid modernization and industrialization as monstrous aligned Endell's accounts with the imagery that Nietzsche associated with the modern city.[6] These similarities were no coincidence. Endell, a philosopher and psychologist by training, not only had detailed knowledge of Nietzsche's work but in 1898 designed the cover for *Thus Spoke Zarathustra*, perhaps the first modern cover to signify the book's content.[7]

Despite Endell's alliance with Nietzsche's thinking, however, in his work as an architect he clearly felt compelled to find constructive moments of engagement within the contemporary metropolis, while at the same time remaining skeptical of the positivist practice of *Städtebau*. During the legendary Werkbund conference of 1914, for example, Endell delivered a passionate speech against the development of a universal strategy for designing cities, which he suspected played a part in *Städtebau*. Critiquing its "secretive aesthetics," Endell argued that architects must be alert to the difference between urban plans and pedestrian observation.[8] Between the two predominant strands of urban critique, Endell's work interjects a third directive that suspends Nietzsche's pessimism and *Städtebau's* optimism. The metropolis that Nietzsche wanted in flames and that *Städtebau* sought to rework, Endell asked architects to see with new eyes. Works such as *Die Schönheit der großen Stadt* articulate an altered mentality in which an aversion toward the modern world exists alongside a "passionate love for today and now."[9]

The writings of Georg Simmel and Rainer Maria Rilke assisted the development of this mentality. Simmel had already criticized Nietzsche's "bitter hatred ... against the metropolis" in his essay "Die Großstädte und das Geistesleben" ("The Metropolis and Mental Life") and offered an interpretation of the modern city as functioning to provide the space for contemporary struggles and reconciliations between "the atrophy of individual culture" and "the hypertrophy of objective culture." Simmel understands the problematic conditions of the metropolis as productive and even "pregnant with inestimable meanings for the development of psychic existence."[10] In this psychological reading of the metropolis, the horrors—the negative aspects of the modern city—are no longer reason to negate metropolitan urban life and its overwhelming stimuli. Instead these conditions emerge as vital for the metropolis and an opportunity.[11] In line with these ideas, the dreadful moments of the city are reinvestigated in *Die Schönheit der großen Stadt,* with an intuition of potential in the very conditions that are in conflict with common ideals of urbanity. Coming from outside the discourse and pursuing a new outlook at the city for architecture, Endell's conceptual framework registers in the literature of figures working in other fields.[12]

Rilke (whom Endell first met through the prominent intellectual circle around Lou Andreas-Salomé in the late 1890s) and in particular his 1910 novel *Die Aufzeichnungen des Malte Laurids Brigge* (*The Notebooks of Malte Laurids Brigge*) are important points of reference for Endell's unique dealings with the problematic conditions of the city as motivations for architecture.[13] Published only two years apart, the writing of Rilke's *Notebooks* and Endell's *Schönheit der großen Stadt* took place around the same time and their protagonists share very similar experiences: they discover the city and themselves through fantastic and traumatic experiences in the metropolis. Rilke's central character (synonymous with the author) confronts the turmoil of urban form, the multitude of people, the emptiness of plazas, the speed of traffic, and the brutality of everyday life, and is forced to see anew: "I am learning to see ... everything enters me more deeply and doesn't stop where it once used to." Later on the protagonist adds: "For the sake of a single poem, you must see many cities, many people and Things ..."[14] Here, the conditions of the metropolis propel a new way of seeing that requires the viewer to overcome preconceptions and allows for a refocusing of visual urban experiences. Just as Endell called for a new devotion (*Hingabe*) to visual impressions of the city, so did Rilke's protagonist experience seeing as something that penetrates—an act in which the world is "taken in" by the observer. The similarities between Rilke and Endell's notions of seeing the modern city anew show not only how Rilke's understanding of urban space and Endell's sensibility regarding visual explorations informed one another; they also illustrate the wide range of discourses that acknowledged the city as a source for creative potential. Observations of the city that for Rilke were existential led Endell to introduce to architecture a new focus on sensory experiences that revised attitudes toward the metropolis.

What Endell regarded as the "real" and "pure visibility" of the metropolis, was aided by concepts of scientific aesthetics and the psychology of form. He relied on the *Einfühlungstheorie* (empathy theory) of Theodor Lipps in defining what he called "the world of the visible." Investigating the relation between subject and object, Lipps wrote: "[t]he form of an object has always ... been formed by [the viewer's] inner activity."[15] In order to go beyond our habits of shaping the formal and practical appearance of what we see, Lipps argued that we would need to suspend our knowledge of the object and be absorbed into optical perception. He established his theory within the trajectory of nineteenth-century aesthetic thought, which included Robert Vischer's definition of empathy as an aesthetic delight that is experienced when projecting our feelings or emotions into objects, Konrad

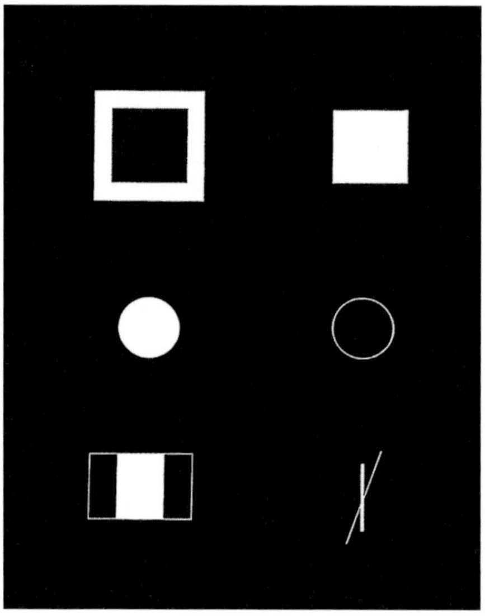

Theodor Lipps, *Raumästhetik und geometrisch-optische Täuschungen*, frontispiece (1893). Figure-ground depiction of geometric shapes, often used to illustrate optical illusions and later utilized in experiments by figures such as Wassily Kandinsky, Kazimir Malevich, and György Kepes.

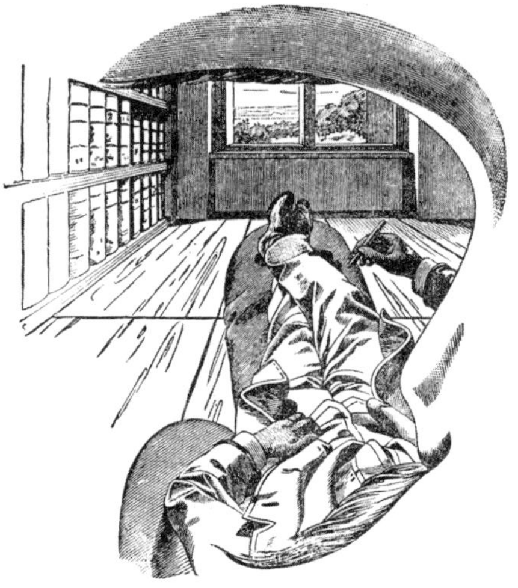

Graphic analysis of the act of seeing by drawing the view of a room in the perspective of one eye. From Ernst Mach, *Die Analyse der Empfindungen* (1902), 15.

Fiedler's proposal of a form of perception that drains all external references from the object observed, and Heinrich Wölfflin's explanation of the effects that forms evoke in their purest or most abstract sense.[16] While through these works, empathy would become a recognized concept in studies of art, Lipps developed a more general theory of experience that focused on vision, optical perception and recognition, as well as emotional response theory.

Influenced by Lipps's inclusive principles, Endell developed a concept of vision that distinguishes between orientation guided only by knowledge and a vision that relates to the individual's feelings or moods.[17] He considered the former an objective seeing and the latter a vision that goes beyond the object in an act of pure reflection. Already in his first major publication *Um die Schönheit* (Concerning beauty, 1896), Endell defined "pure seeing" as "a devotion to visual experience without associations and any extraneous thoughts [...that] would reveal an entirely new world."[18] The suspension of prior knowledge and absorption into pure optical perception would lead to a new abstract art and eventually a new city, "an art with forms that mean nothing and represent nothing and remind one of nothing, yet that will be able to move our souls so deeply, so strongly, as before only music has been able to do with tones."[19] What Endell here described has a history that is not limited to Lipps and Vischer but draws on early-nineteenth-century interrogations of the psychological and physiological underpinnings of vision.

Immanuel Kant in his *Kritik der Urteilskraft* (*Critique of Judgment*) had already associated pure judgment with exhibiting "free beauty" through artistic "form[s] ... that mean nothing in themselves; that represent nothing—[that are] no object under a definite concept."[20] Two decades later, Arthur Schopenhauer revised Kant's ideas by connecting scientific discoveries about optics with aesthetic discourses on vision and on making the modern subject fully aware of its aptitude for "pure perception."[21] As Jonathan Crary has shown, this was no longer understood as a transcendental condition but rather a biological capacity.[22] When Endell devoted his attention to architecture, his fluency in these ideas would facilitate the conception of a different kind of architecture and vision of the city at the turn of the twentieth century. Endell's introduction of scientific aesthetics and physiological psychology into architecture and urban analysis seemed strategic. It challenged architecture's traditional associations with form, proportion, and function and countered the quantifiable and value-based arguments of planning with aesthetic theory.

In the late 1890s, Endell wrote a series of three articles seeking to explain how certain visual forms resonate with the observer and suggesting psychological explanations.[23] He described, for example, how lines of altered thicknesses, lengths, and repetitions are perceived differently and, therefore, trigger unique emotions. In the second essay, Endell even tried to equate certain line configurations with degrees of feelings over time. And, in the last essay, he included drawings of building fronts, which he claimed would have various effects on the viewer. Highly unconventional, to the point where even the editors of the journal that published the articles distanced themselves from these findings, the theory clearly seeks to challenge traditional forms of architectural style by arguing the effectiveness of elementary forms and their variation. For this reason, Nikolaus Pevsner in his *Pioneers of Modern Design*—one of the first efforts to formulate an interpretation of twentieth-century modernism while it was still in the making—argued that Endell contributed much more to modernism than to *Jugendstil* or Art Nouveau, the period to which he seemingly belonged.[24] But, what was even more unique than Endell's attempt to formulate architecture as an abstract art was that his aesthetic theory was a rethinking of form-making just as much as it re-envisioned the perception of existing conditions. The latter would become crucial for engagements with the contemporary metropolis.

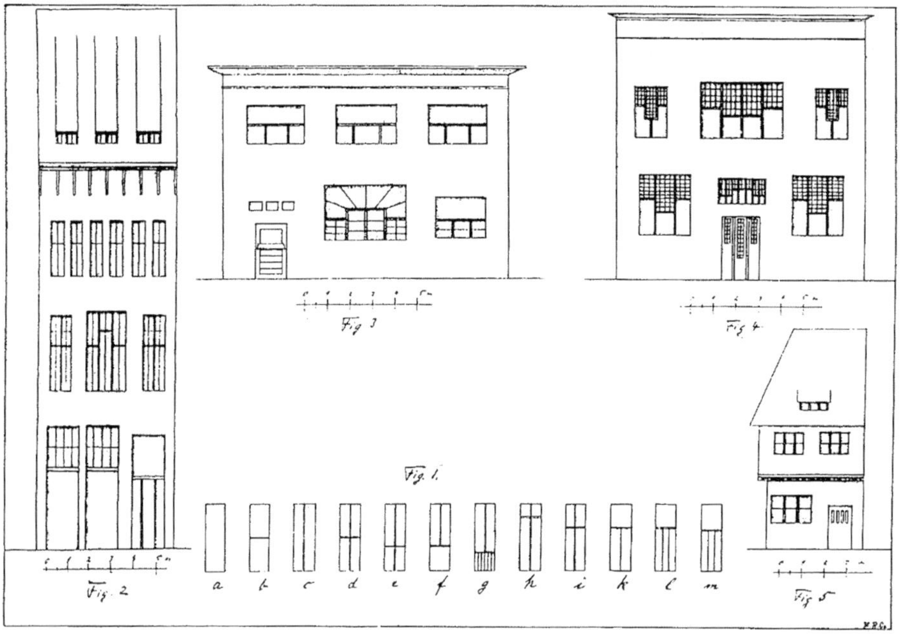

August Endell, Building proportion study, in "Formschönheit und dekorative Kunst," *Dekorative Kunst 2*, 1898: 122. Nikolaus Pevsner writes about this illustration: "The shape of the first-floor windows and the flat roof are again almost 'misdatable'."

What his studies in aesthetics and psychology formulated as a new way of seeing was deployed in *Die Schönheit der großen Stadt* to discover a "new" metropolis. He criticized the romanticization of nature and history (valued in contrast to the relentlessness of the metropolis) and posited instead a way of seeing able to recognize within the contested realms of the modern city aesthetic potentials that "[lie] exposed before everyone's eyes and yet [go] barely noticed."[25] Paraphrasing from his earlier essays, Endell called for a new visual dedication to the city in order to detect what he described as "countless wonders."[26] The psychological "pure vision" of empathy theory is here directed toward urban imagery, which is dissociated from the object of associations (in this case the totality of the city) and in its place focuses on forms of pure impression (isolated urban locations). In fact, Endell wrote, "the city is without form and *Gestaltung* (layout, shape) ... [since] there is no correlation between house and street."[27] In line with the conventional reading at the time that portrayed the metropolis in all its fractured, inconsistent multiplicity, Endell spoke of the modern city as a "heap of stone" and its buildings as

Gleisdreieck railway intersection under construction, Berlin, 1901. For Endell, Gleisdreieck visualized the metropolitan collision of forms and juxtaposition of speeds.

"flat, dull, and formless."[28] And yet it was exactly in this formless pile of urbanization that he found a new urban aesthetics, and even "beauty."[29] While the metropolis could no longer be understood as an object per se, nor had it any overarching representational value, localized impressions of the metropolis could distil intense urban conditions that described a different kind of city altogether.

In *Die Schönheit der großen Stadt* the city is not examined through its iconic buildings, historic monuments, picturesque parks, or choreographed plazas, but through the so-called "ugly" moments of the city. Endell wrote: "I will talk only about the modern city whose form, with ever fewer exceptions, is abominable."[30] While the city had lost its form—its urban unity, symmetry, and coherence—the locations of metropolitan formlessness would become the primary sites for a new visual experience of the city. For example, by studying the new rail lines that carve through the metropolis, including its bridges and stations, Endell discovered a new technological monumentality. While the complexity and multiplicity of these sites could not be fully grasped or taken in by any one viewer, these were also conditions hinting at a new kind of urbanity. He described the infrastructural concoction of Gleisdreieck (the railway intersection of three major branches of Berlin's public transit system), for instance, as "enormous" and intensely disruptive with its "great arches of the triangular junction" that are in "a strange contrast to the slender, bizarre forms of the iron construction."[31] Gleisdreieck, the ultimate expression of the city without form, was viewed as a new spatial parameter indigenous to contemporary urbanization. The conceptual framework of empathy theory shifts here from the abstract notion of form to a specific vision of urban imagery within metropolitan formlessness.

Endell's "pure seeing" no longer sought to understand the metropolis in its entirety but detected isolated urban conditions, which, removed from all pragmatic consideration, revealed a different urbanity, saturated with colors and forms. Taking the reader on a journey, the book centers on locations in Berlin, where Endell set out to reveal aesthetic conditions within the formlessness of modern urbanity by collapsing the sites with natural phenomena, the movement of the city, and modern technology. He described how the play of light and shadow, color, rain and sun transformed the city that had grown so rapidly that its overcrowded housing, rising factories, and developed infrastructures made it into a prototypical industrial metropolis. Atmospheric and spatial effects, however, transform the modern cityscape into a differentiated play of forms that have a "life" of their own. For example, fog makes modern urban space readable by filling endless straight streets, shadows transform large urban forms into fantastic motifs, and modes of infrastructure morph into animated shapes.[32] While clearly enjoying the vagueness of certain associations, Endell's new optics also expanded the concept of the metropolis through its accounts of visual effects that previously were not part of the urban discourse.

For Simmel, the modern world no longer granted the observer views of the whole, but single details could be assembled in order to approximate a new urbanity. While planners and urbanists were deeply dissatisfied by their inability to view the city in its totality and continuously sought to gain access to more elevated vantage points, Simmel's visual sociology articulates the impossibility of grasping the metropolitan totality and Endell's project entirely depends on a perspective based in the midst of the city.[33] This penetration through details from within the metropolis gave the flâneur of the nineteenth century a new knowledge of the city and revealed to Endell a new way of seeing. Charles Baudelaire had already recognized in the sketches of Constantin Guys a new form of observation that positioned the viewer in the "midst of things;" he described the painter as "see[ing] the world, [being] at the center of the world, and yet ... remain[ing] hidden from the

László Moholy-Nagy, *Blick vom Berliner Funkturm*, Berlin, 1928. Inaugurated in 1926, the Radio Tower provided Moholy-Nagy with elevated views of its surroundings for a series of photographs.

Umbo (Otto Umbehr), *Unheimliche Straße I*, 1928. In the same year that Moholy-Nagy took photographs from the Radio Tower, Umbo shot a series of pictures of street scenes from above in which the shadows cast by the evening sun put the orientation of the viewer into question.

world."[34] Similarly, Simmel's act of analytical viewing at the turn of the century is no longer a removed act of the thinker but an embedded observation that selects moments of interest within the abundance of everyday experience. Since Endell attended some of the lectures that Simmel gave on this topic after 1901 at the University of Berlin, it comes as no surprise that Simmel's concept of the *Moment-bild* (snapshot) as a fleeting image in the mind of the viewer also animated Endell's optical vision of the modern city. For both, the central position from which the observer chooses the perspective toward the "fragmentary images" is not arbitrary. Simmel's *"soziologische Ästhetik"* (sociological aesthetics) describes this perspective as necessarily an aesthetic one—a perspective that reveals the significance of conditions through a deep involvement with them, rather than a distanced, abstract view. Then, "[e]ven the lowest, intrinsically ugly phenomenon appears in a context of color and forms, of feeling and experiences that bestow upon it a fascinating significance."[35]

Taking reference from Simmel, Endell's theory focuses on ordinary urban conditions and an intensely direct reading of effects that expose these locations to new qualities of the metropolis. At one point, residues of rain are described as they color the ground: "The light grey asphalt becomes a rich brown; the outlines become harder, the air becomes more visible, depth appears deeper; everything receives definiteness, massiveness."[36] What Endell observed and sought to communicate in his writing was vividly depicted in the photographic experiments of the 1920s. Moholy-Nagy, in his views from Berlin's Radio Tower, for instance, shows an urban territory that was both familiar and estranged. The heightened depth that Endell had previously articulated becomes a large crater that seemingly breaks a plaza open. A figure-ground reversal that was part of Lipps's aesthetic discourse and that Endell introduced into the analysis of the city, would become paramount for artists such as Moholy-Nagy and Umbo. It accounts for the interrelatedness of the work of this period as much as it underscores the limitations of language for communicating the complex visual optics that Endell had in mind. What the discourse of psychological aesthetics sought to communicate through writing was visualized in the experiments of the avant-garde a decade later.

Endell, however, would still rely on impressionist works as the only illustrations in his book since they came closest to a "pure seeing ... [as t]hey no longer painted people, bridges, and towers but instead the strange phenomena that air, light, dust, and reflection had made out of them."[37] His choice of Claude Monet's paintings of *St.-Germain-l'Auxerrois* and *Flußufer*, as well as Max Liebermann's *Kanal in Leyden* as the only illustrations in *Die Schönheit der großen Stadt* comes, therefore, as no surprise; especially as they were utilized to convey a concept of seeing the city that goes beyond an associative recognition of objects. After all, impressionism owed much to the metropolis—its new construction materials, like glass and steel, its urban and industrial spaces, and its visual stimuli in general.[38] In fact, along with the appearance of the industrial metropolis, experiential conditions of architecture and the city had already received great attention and were incorporated into concepts of urban design. Camillo Sitte's "artistic principles" and Hendrik Petrus Berlage's "impressionistic architecture" are only two examples that reveal an increasing interest in impressionist ideas throughout European architectural culture at the turn of the century.[39] Yet Endell reversed the impressionist lens, aiming it back at the city to make new visual discoveries by conflating it with empathy theory. While Sitte made the psychopathology of modern urbanity responsible for the emergence of phobias such as *"Platzscheue"* (agoraphobia), Endell inverted that widely circulating wisdom and proposed a different kind of seeing through which the city (even its empty plazas) would become a space filled with effects rather than a terrifying empty void.[40] In essence, Endell acted as a kind of psychoanalyst whose aim was to "teach them [the inhabitants] to see their city genuinely for once."[41] The metropolis was no longer the purely negative mechanization of an "artless world"; it came to be seen as an accumulation of fantastical aesthetic moments.

What Endell was unable to see, however, was that his psychological reading of the city was less related to late-nineteenth-century impressionism than to the coming generation of the avant-garde. Already in 1912, painters such as Franz Marc explored an abstract art that went beyond any particular phenomenon—a project that was influenced by theories of art set forth in books such as *Abstraktion und Einfühlung* (*Abstraction and Empathy*) by the art historian Wilhelm Worringer.[42] Even earlier, Endell's text on a new abstraction had a profound impact on the development of artists such as Kandinsky, who in 1912 and together with Marc would publish *Der Blaue Reiter Almanach* (*The Blue Rider Almanac*). As Peg Weiss has shown in her book on Kandinsky's formative years, his intersection with Endell in Munich at the turn of the century proved to be highly productive and would, ultimately, set the stage for much of Kandinsky's abstraction.[43] Endell's call for an art of forms that bypasses the intellect and affects the viewer directly, reverberated throughout Kandinsky's work, just as the analysis of the relation between abstract lines and points in space and the correlating emotional response called forth in the viewer would be taken up by both.

In 1910, Kandinsky completed a manuscript that addressed psychological methods of color analysis and in 1914 began to work on his later Bauhaus publication *Punkt und Linie zu Fläche* (*Point and Line to Plane*).[44] Echoing Endell's theory,

Wassily Kandinsky, *Punkt und Linie zu Fläche*, cover (1926). The book is organized according to the geometries that Kandinsky announced on the cover and concludes with a fifty-page appendix of graphic experiments that incrementally grow in complexity and terminate in Kandinsky's painting *Kleiner Traum in Rot.*

Kandinsky speculated on the effects of different geometries on the viewer, expanded on the relationships between lines, points, and surfaces, found examples in the world to illustrate these ideas, and explored their deployment for art. Endell's writings are a constant point of reference for Kandinsky, who described two forms of urban observation: a street viewed from behind the window or from the midst of the city. Of course, Kandinsky advocated an embedded observation, in which the pulsations of urban movement, color, and sound would not be muffled and could be actively experienced. Once the viewer enters into the speed of the metropolis, he argued, "a play of horizontal and vertical strokes and lines" appear.[45] But only to the observer who can be fully immersed in the city. Endell's ambition to develop a new visual experience of the city was taken by Kandinsky as a starting point and directed toward painting. The forms that Kandinsky would analyze in detail had already appeared as *Jugendstil* ornament on Endell's first architectural work, the Photo-Atelier Elvira in Munich (1897).[46] It should, therefore, come as no surprise that Endell's concepts resonated in later visual experiments in art and photography in particular.

For Endell, engaging the formless city was an act of simultaneous deep embeddedness and intentional remoteness. On the one hand, it meant to delve into the city and proceed through the middle; on the other, thoughts of intellectual association were to be held at bay. Therefore, the project is based on the existing metropolis at the same time that it escapes from it. As such, Endell's project outlines not only a new urbanity but also a different kind of "visionary," one that is less about forecasting the new and, instead, is contingent on a new optical vision of the existing city. Here, the delirium of the formless metropolis becomes an array of individualized forms and colors that do not form a whole again but produce kaleidoscopic urban imagery. Of course, the technique indulges in visual games, which Zeynep Çelik Alexander recently analyzed as a practice able to manipulate the observer through kinaesthetic stimuli rather than placing the viewer squarely in front of the modern world.[47] At the same time, however, the project's contribution to architecture and urbanism is as much based on its commitment to the existing metropolis and search for its latent potentials as it is based on an outlining of a new aesthetic analysis beyond the pragmatics of the city. As such, Endell's spatio-aesthetic study of urban conditions is far removed from statistical practices such as planning. While planning intervenes in the measurable actualities of the city, Endell's optical aesthetics reposition architecture's view toward the city, establishing an alternative analytics that relies on a visual rethinking, made nonetheless accountable by tapping the realities of the metropolis.

László Moholy-Nagy's Urban Optics

Moholy-Nagy's urban photography was influenced by Endell (through the work of Kandinsky) but, more importantly, his photographs confirm Endell's observations and in many ways demonstrate the dissociation that Endell had previously theorized. The abstracted vision of the metropolis would in the crosshairs of Moholy-Nagy's camera crystallize into specific urban imagery. The Hungarian-born artist settled in 1920 in Berlin, exhibited in 1922 in the gallery *Der Sturm*, and was invited in 1923 to teach at the Bauhaus, where Walter Gropius had hired Kandinsky just one year prior.[48] During these years, Moholy-Nagy formulated what he called a "new vision," aided by the camera's technology. He literalized through the viewfinder of his camera what Endell had argued through descriptions of urban situations. The camera, Moholy-Nagy felt, allowed one to "see the world with different eyes."[49] His formulations echoed closely the sensational rhetoric of his precursors. In the Bauhaus book *Malerei, Fotografie, Film* (*Painting, Photography, Film*), he noted how the apparatus of photography enabled an "impartial optic, which our eyes and their rules of associations cannot perform."[50] Clearly, for Moholy-Nagy the camera was far superior to the human eye. While the photographs come close to what Endell described, Moholy-Nagy's rhetoric had a much more objective tone. Camera-seeing was now to provide an unbiased view of the world, which would enable a heightened reality and in some cases a total penetration of the object—a transformation of vision that recorded both at the scale of the microscope and of the telescope, encompassing a range of perspectives, from aerial photography to X-rays. Moholy-Nagy's catalog of images documents a photographic record of the existing world as much as it is a reworking into a surreality.

Walter Benjamin, familiar with Moholy-Nagy's photography via Sigfried Giedion's book *Bauen in Frankreich, Bauen in Eisen, Bauen in Eisenbeton* (*Building in France, Building in Iron, Buildings in Ferro-Concrete*), would detect in photography a strange kind of vision different from that of the naked eye, "if only because an unconsciously penetrated space is substituted for a space consciously explored."[51] For that very reason, the potentials of photography for urban analysis seemed to be of particular relevance. Moholy-Nagy ventured into the city to capture the banal and the engineered realities of modern life; Giedion illustrated his book (designed by Moholy-Nagy) with many of these photographs in order to tap new architectural ingenuities driven by metropolitan technology; and Benjamin's fascination with urban photography (by Moholy-Nagy in particular) is based on its capacity to reveal hidden details through techniques of close-ups, blow-ups, zooms, and crops. Photography became understood as something that could pierce through the complexity and multiplicity of the modern world and, by doing so, bring into view sections and fragments that were previously illegible or lost in the haze of modernity. "The camera," Benjamin noted, "introduces us to unconscious optics as does psychoanalysis to unconscious impulses."[52]

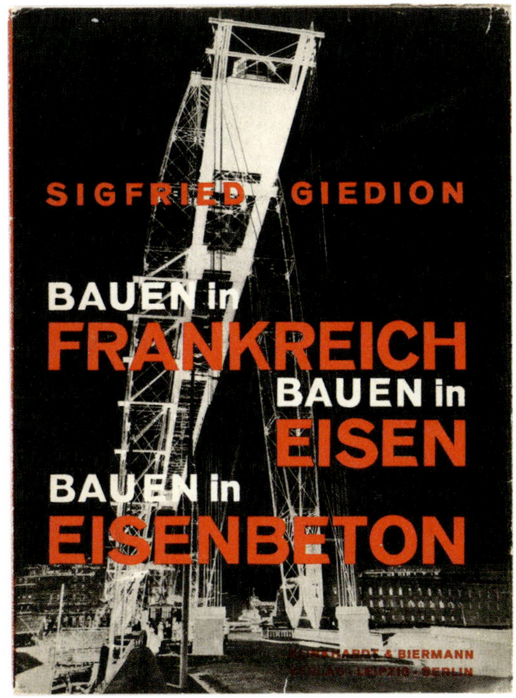

Sigfried Giedion, *Bauen in Frankreich, Bauen in Eisen, Bauen in Eisenbeton*, cover (1928). László Moholy-Nagy designed the book with a cover that shows the Pont Transbordeur spanning the industrial harbor of Marseilles, a structure that for Giedion signaled a new spatial experience.

While Benjamin's unconscious optics strips away the very aesthetic impressions that Endell depicts, both aim at a new way of seeing existing form—explorations that Moholy-Nagy's photographs connect. In the late 1920s, photographing Berlin's Radio Tower and the Pont Transbordeur in Marseilles, Moholy-Nagy was mesmerized by their engineering, but even more so by the unparalleled views of the city that they provided. He had previously photographed the Eiffel Tower in Paris (1925) by looking upwards through the girders and into the sky. For the Berlin

László Moholy-Nagy, *Berliner Funkturm*, Berlin, 1928. Photograph of the terrain surrounding the base of the Radio Tower, with partial views through the structure.

Film stills from László Moholy-Nagy, *Impressionen vom alten Marseiller Hafen (Vieux Port)*, Marseilles, c. 1929. At midpoint in the three-minute film, the camera documents the activities and moving parts of the Pont Transbordeur and follows passengers on their ride across the water.

(1928) and Marseilles (1929) series, however, he climbed the structure and pointed his camera toward the city. While for planners, the high vantage point was a position from which to survey and to gain an overall understanding of the city, for Moholy-Nagy, the elevation of the Radio Tower presented through the optical vision of the camera a different kind of city—one that was abstract, visual, and kaleidoscopic. Here, evenly spaced chairs would turn into graphic patterns, different materials into shades of grey, and pathways into swirling ornaments. These photographic visualizations of the city transformed concrete objects into geometries, outlines, and fields, removed from the conventional associations of the city and hinting instead at a new kind of surreal spatial graphics. This seeming opposition between the realities of the city and the surreal visualization through the camera was not only an abstraction of the metropolis but aimed at detecting the magical in the banal. Benjamin addressed this issue most directly in his 1929 essay on "Surrealism," arguing that "we penetrate the mystery only to the degree that we recog-

"Cantilevered roof for sunbathing," in László Moholy-Nagy, *Von Material zu Architektur* (1929), 224. The photograph shows the appropriation of the entry canopy of the Scala Theater in Berlin as a raised terrace for performers to relax, just above the city's traffic, c. 1925.

nize it in the everyday world, by virtue of a dialectical optic that perceives the everyday as impenetrable, the impenetrable as everyday."[53] Ultimately, Moholy-Nagy became what Benjamin would call a "type of illuminati."

Activating this "dialectical optic," Moholy-Nagy viewed the city through the iron lattices of these massive structures, which created an auxiliary lens that visually cropped parts of the metropolis. Modernist painters such as Robert Delaunay had already depicted the buildings adjacent to the Eiffel Tower as a fractured and reflected cacophony of forms, seemingly shattered by the tower's light-weight members. While Delaunay's work hinted at a new spatial condition that questioned the solidity of architecture and the opposition between interior and exterior, the mobility of Moholy-Nagy's camera stitched these fragments into a new order through shifting points of view—an effect only surpassed by his use of film. His early movie *Impressionen vom alten Marseiller Hafen* (*Vieux Port*) (Impressions from the old port of Marseilles) from 1929, for example, shows how not only the structure of the Pont Transbordeur reconfigures parts of the city but also how the moving parts of the elevated ferry act in themselves like a roll of film—cutting and splicing sections of the city. Together, the lens of the camera and the lens of engineered form assembled a new world. Giedion had one year before proposed that "in the steel limbs of a *pont transbordeur*," one experienced an aesthetic where "through the delicate iron net suspended in midair[,] stream things, ships, sea, houses, masts, landscape and harbor."[54] For Giedion as for Moholy-Nagy, the optics of this newly seen city implied a new kind of architecture as well as a new urbanism that embraced the complexities of space, the intermingled simultaneity of infrastructures, the range of different speeds, and the multiplicity of materials.

Moholy-Nagy famously concluded his second book for the Bauhaus series, *Von Material zu Architektur* (*From Material to Architecture*, later translated as *The New Vision*), with a double-exposure photograph by Jan Kamman of the Van Nelle

Factory in Rotterdam designed by Brinkman & van der Vlugt, which predicts the next generation of glass architecture, and which he described as the "illusion of spatial *Durchdringung* (penetration)."[55] While the concept of *Durchdringung* had already been theorized by Giedion, who used it to question the established norms and limits of architecture, it was not simply a concept born out of artistic ingenuity but emerged from optically aided observations of the city. Endell's mandate for a new vision is expressed in Giedion's and Moholy-Nagy's treatment of urban environments that are far removed from conventional idealizations of the city and instead champion an urban climate of overlaps, saturation, multiplicity, and complexity. Urban formlessness was celebrated as a new spatial montage that collapsed an array of metropolitan conditions into a single moment. Moholy-Nagy, for example, published a photograph of sunbathing dancers occupying the cantilevered roof over the entry of Berlin's Scala Theater and noted that this prefigures the use of rooftops for gardens and airplane landing strips. As a result of the contrast between light and shadow, the photograph can equally be misread as a floating surface above the sidewalk or as a carpet-like incision into the midst of traffic. Through these images, everyday appropriations of the city became understood as radical modes of spatial invention.

"Overlapping traffic," in László Moholy-Nagy, *Von Material zu Architektur* (1929), 210. This photograph of an infrastructural node in San Diego, c. 1925, celebrates the saturation of metropolitan traffic and the spatial complexities of movement.

One striking image that Moholy-Nagy sampled from the newspaper *Der Weltspiegel*, shows a layered infrastructural node, where air travel, train lines, vehicular movement, and pedestrian traffic converge at a singular moment in time and space. This urban montage was both exemplary of the unprecedented complexities of the metropolis and instructive for a new kind of urbanism. The latter would be set in motion through principles of montage that took lessons from the metropolis, or what Giedion called the "raw material" of the contemporary city that reveal "possibilities for how our cities may later be designed."[56] But whereas Giedion saw instances of montage in the images of the Eiffel Tower and the multi-level urbanism of industrial landscapes, for Moholy-Nagy, ordinary metropolitan conditions revealed as much as specialized locations. For him, the dynamics of the metropolis provoked a kinetic architecture in which static forms are replaced by dynamic structures. Ideas represented through his *Lichtspiel* (*Light-play*) film from 1930, and addressed again in the 1947 book *Vision in Motion*, would find parallels in Giedion's *Space, Time and Architecture* (an exploration of the effects of the fourth dimension on architecture and urbanism).

Most of these ideas, however, are already well developed in Moholy-Nagy's work of the 1920s.[57] The highly original filmscript "Dynamik der Gross-Stadt" (Dynamic of the metropolis), for example, reveals that he already contemplated the forces of the metropolis in 1921. The scenario was a precursor to Walter Ruttmann's *Berlin – Die Sinfonie der Großstadt* (*Berlin: Symphony of a Great City*, 1927) and was even more abstract than Dziga Vertov's *Man with a Movie Camera* (1929), both of which appeared several years after Moholy-Nagy's script. But "Dynamic of the metropolis" also differs radically from these later city symphonies. As Edward Dimendberg noted, "[r]ather than depict the unities of time and place, Moholy-Nagy pursues a mode of metacinematic exploration that takes the modalities of perceptual and cinematic responses to the metropolis as its subject matter."[58] While the film was never produced, the script articulates that Moholy-Nagy meant to steer clear of the ethical dilemmas of the metropolis and to focus instead on its potentials for film, art, and architecture: "... not to educate, nor to moralize, nor to narrate; but only to have visual impact."[59] This not only resonates with Endell's statement almost fifteen years prior, but foreshadows a mentality on the subject of the metropolis that would participate in the modernist debate on the city, and influence strands of thought in mid-century architectural discourse. For the first scene of the film, for instance, Moholy-Nagy envisioned an array of moving points and lines that slowly would morph into the metal skeleton of a massive zeppelin under construction. The points and lines that Kandinsky explored with the assistance of Endell's theory return now full circle to the discussion of the city, as these elements were propelled by the whirlwind of the metropolis—an image only possible to conceive through a renewed position toward the modern city and seen through the optics of the photographer's lens.

The architectural discourse is clearly impacted by the new reading of the formless metropolis in the lineage from Endell, via Kandinsky, to Moholy-Nagy

L. MOHOLY-NAGY:
DYNAMIK DER GROSS-STADT

SKIZZE ZU EINEM
FILMMANUSKRIPT

Alle Rechte, insbesondere das Recht der Verfilmung und Übersetzung, behalten Autor und Verlag sich vor.

Das Entstehen einer Eisenkonstruktion.

Erst Tricktischaufnahme von sich bewegenden Punkten, Linien, welche in ihrer Gesamtheit in einen Zeppelinbau (Naturaufnahme) übergehen.

Kran bei Hausbau in Bewegung.
Aufnahmen: von unten
von oben

von schräg

Ziegelaufzug.
Wieder Kran: in Kreisbewegung.

116

Großaufnahme.
Die Bewegung setzt sich in einem Auto fort, das nach links saust. Man sieht ein und dasselbe Haus dem Auto gegenüber in der Bildmitte (das Haus wird immer von rechts in die Mitte zurückgezogen: dies ergibt eine starre, ruckartige Bewegung). Ein anderes Auto erscheint. Dieses fährt gleichzeitig entgegengesetzt, nach rechts.

Diese Stelle als brutale Einführung in das atemlose Rennen, das Tohuwabohu der Stadt.

Der hier starre Rhythmus lockert sich langsam im Laufe des Spiels.

Ein Tiger kreist wütend in seinem Käfig.

TEMPO TEMPO TEMPO

TEMPO
TEMPO
TEMPO
TEMPO

Häuserreihe auf der einen Seite der Straße, durchscheinend, rast rechts durch das erste Haus. Häuserreihe läuft rechts weg und kommt von rechts nach links wieder. Einander gegenüber liegende Häuserreihen, durchscheinend, in entgegengesetzter Richtung rasend, und die Autos immer rascher, so daß bald ein FLIMMERN entsteht.

Der Tiger:
Kontrast des offenen, unbehinderten Rennens zur Bedrängung, Beengtheit. Um das Publikum schon anfangs an die Überraschungen und Alogik zu gewöhnen.

Ganz klar – oben hoch – Bahnzeichen:

(Großaufnahme)

Alle automatisch, au-to-ma-tisch in Bewegung

auf auf ab ab AUF Auf AB Ab ab

1 2 3 4 5
1 2 3 4 5
1 2 3 4 5

Rangierbahnhof.
Ausweichestellen.

1 2 3 4 5

László Moholy-Nagy, "Dynamik der Gross-Stadt," 1921–1925, in László Moholy-Nagy, *Malerei, Fotografie, Film* (1927), 116–117. In this script, the tempo and aggressiveness of the metropolis are highlighted through graphic and photographic means.

and Giedion. In contrast to the common understanding of the modernist view of the city as a counter-terrain needing to be reformed, this lineage reveals a close proximity between the formless city and avant-garde architecture and urbanism. It runs counter to the well-rehearsed rhetoric of Le Corbusier's *Urbanisme* and the early Congrès internationaux d'architecture moderne (International Congresses of Modern Architecture, CIAM), but its repercussions are far more intensely felt and lasting. Even figures like Gropius would during the postwar era declare that "the designer must learn to see; he must know the effects of optical illusion, the psychological influence of shapes, colors and textures [and] the effects of contrast."[60] These sentences participate in a larger discourse that sought to define a perceptual framework that would ultimately guide design. When Moholy-Nagy, Gropius, and their protégé, and later colleague, György Kepes escaped the Nazis first to England and then to the US, the idea of a "modernized vision" was carried into the cultural and urban ether of these countries.

Kepes's widely read *Language of Vision* (1944), was one such carrier, for it channeled the ideas of Endell, Kandinsky, Moholy-Nagy, and Giedion in an effort to interrupt the long-standing system of perspectival representation and launch a mode of vision supported by the new technologies of photography and film (from micro to macro). Kepes—who had worked in Moholy-Nagy's office in Berlin and London and also taught at the New Bauhaus and the Institute of Design under the directorship of Moholy-Nagy—initiated in 1947 a program on visual design at MIT, which had profound impact on his colleagues in architecture and planning.[61] While Kepes emphasized Gestalt theory in his explorations of visual communication and representation in an attempt to distinguish himself from Moholy-Nagy and Giedion, like them he also spoke of the contemporary city as an environment that demanded a new vision. For Kepes, a new way of seeing was of "utmost importance in the chaos of our formless world" in order "[t]o grasp spatial relationships and orient oneself in a metropolis of today."[62]

Clearly, his theories swerve toward a totalizing organizational system of visual language that was to reconfigure the formless city in order to once again make sense of the contemporary world—a tendency especially pronounced in his paper for the 1946 conference "Planning Man's Physical Environment" at Princeton University. According to Reinhold Martin, this paper extends the framework of the book into the scale of the city.[63] It foreshadows Kepes's collaboration with Kevin Lynch on the research for *The Image of the City* and links the effects of visual interpenetration to conditions of transparency, as developed in Colin Rowe and Robert Slutzky's seminal essay, "Transparency: Literal and Phenomenal," and, by extension (and affiliation) in *Collage City*, by Rowe and Fred Koetter.[64] In contrast to these more totalizing regimes of vision, however, the visual and aesthetic theories from the first half of the twentieth century would also come into the orbit of architects, theorists, and historians who by the 1960s sought engagements with the city that were less concerned with a new framework of vision than with utilizing a new urban optics for discoveries within the formless city without demanding its regulation. Once these visual and aesthetic theories connected with postwar urbanism, they ignited a new conception of the contemporary city. This altered perception of urban terrains resulted in interpretations vastly different from common readings of the city.

The travels of Venturi and Scott Brown to Las Vegas and Banham's explorations of Los Angeles, and their resulting publications, produced a new reading of the city that owes much to the psychology of vision utilized previously. For example, the strategies and methods of Banham, Venturi, and Scott Brown were deeply impacted by Moholy-Nagy's optical vision and the influences of speed on perception and urban space. Just as the earlier theories proposed a new mentality with respect to the metropolis through new perceptions of conditions like the industrialized urban climate of Berlin, so would the studies of Las Vegas and Los Angeles find potentials in exactly the terrains that are commonly perceived as detrimental. While decades apart and based in very different environments, the earlier and later group utilized similar mindsets with reference to the city. Even the enemy lines seem to have shifted only slightly; the former targeted the universalities of *Städtebau* and the latter critiqued centralized planning. Of course, the politics of planning as well as the makeup of the cities that it engaged had dramatically changed; and with this shifted the ideological ground underneath architectural projects that engaged the city. After the traumas of war and the implementation of massive reconstruction efforts, generational shifts, technological developments, and amplified transportation and communication networks, a new frame of mind began to question the predominance of standardization, the science of planning, the morals of conservation, and the arguments of rationalist thought.[65] Architectural culture saw a growing skepticism toward modernist postwar reconstruction and the functional city of the Athens Charter, a reservation that coincided with an emerging interest in urban vernaculars and the social realities of present-day life.

Reyner Banham's Motorized Lens

In 1959, the year that saw the demise of CIAM, Banham challenged zoned urbanism by combining the Situationist psychogeographic drift with his love for Los Angeles. His essay "City as Scrambled Egg" effectively produced a new urban image and introduced a new outlook on postwar modernization, communication, and leisure.[66] The radicalization of contemporary life proposed by the young generation resonated in images of the city as decentralized, free, and in motion. While Le Corbusier had compared the city to an egg with demarcated zones and boundaries, Banham argued that motorization and telecommunications had long scrambled the city; "I don't just mean in Los Angeles. A large part of the population of Europe already lives conurbatively."[67] The entire region between Amsterdam and Rotterdam was already one conurbanized arena, effectively formulating an early definition of the megalopolis. Unlike CIAM's city of the urban core with designated outskirts, the center was now seen to be everywhere. For Banham, this was the terrain of contemporary urbanization that needed to be understood by holding prejudgments at bay and instead doing, what he called, "leg-work on the territory."[68]

For his research on what would become the book *The Architecture of the Well-Tempered Environment*, Banham visited the US in 1964 and 1965, and it was during this time that he stayed for the first time in Los Angeles. He would return frequently in the late 1960s, would learn how to drive a car, and photograph and film the city during countless excursions to many corners of this sprawling mega-

Reyner Banham, *Los Angeles: The Architecture of Four Ecologies*, cover (1971). Banham saw David Hockney's work on the environments of LA as unparalleled and chose his painting *A Bigger Splash* (1968) as the cover image for the first edition.

city. Because of its lack of coherence, of traditional urban forms and of planning; because of its excess of sprawl, its roadside architectures, and its car-obsessed lifestyle, the majority of literature to that point set in or about Los Angeles had a strongly dystopian view of the city. From the Los Angeles of the Great Depression in John Fante's *Ask the Dust* (1939), to Los Angeles as an ecological disaster in Peter Blake's *God's Own Junkyard* (1964), the spectrum of accounts of the city as a problem-ridden and unrepentant urban climate far exceeded the few works that found Los Angeles at all intriguing. In 1950, the British journal *Architectural Review* published a special issue on US cities, entitled "Man Made America." It focused on the visual chaos of urbanization while simultaneously seeking a middle ground in evaluating its potentials. Chicago is associated with the City Beautiful movement and Los Angeles is referred to as "city un-beautiful," yet roadside architecture, petrol stations, drive-in cinemas, and shopping malls are also described as a new expression that the authors seek to account for.[69] In this atmosphere, Banham's book, *Los Angeles: The Architecture of Four Ecologies,* offered a different kind of analysis of the city, not so much countering predominant views as providing a new urban and architectural history. For Banham, the city was not the disastrous outgrowth of modern urbanization and not even a forecast of future urban developments. *The Architecture of Four Ecologies* portrays Los Angeles as a unique constellation of urban conditions, "an extraordinary mixture of geography, climate, economics, demography, mechanics and culture."[70] Banham was clearly taken by the city and in 1972 even débuted in the short BBC documentary about his work *Reyner Banham Loves Los Angeles*.

While he recognized its "splendours and miseries," he somehow found in all these conditions an "unrepeatable and unprecedented" quality—a quality in which he was determined to discover potential.[71] The motorized culture, which for many was the origin of Los Angeles's doom, was for Banham the representation of a new "mobile metropolis." As Anthony Vidler has noted, this thesis was influenced by the German urban geographer Anton Wagner, whose 1935 dissertation on Los Angeles describes at length the dynamism of the city—from geological fluxes to transit networks.[72] Interestingly, Wagner's city of comparison is Berlin. Twenty-seven years after Endell's publication, Berlin's previous expansiveness and dynamism were surpassed by this much younger city in California; a development that could only be understood through a study of its continuously shifting urban forces and related modifications. [73] For Banham, Wagner's was the only research that achieved a "comprehensive view of Los Angeles as a built environment," foreseeing an architecture of movement.[74]

In the fast pace that dominated the city—from the freeway urbanism that foreshadowed a new monumentality to the flimsy and easily deployable architecture that was always ready to move on—Banham detected an unparalleled technological self-confidence. It comes into sharp focus when considered in relation to his earlier prophecy that technological culture will progress with or without architecture. More than ten years prior, Banham's *Theory and Design of the First Machine Age* had already positioned modern architecture in relation to and as conditioned by technological progress. He not only introduced Futurism into the modernist canon but also gave an original interpretation of Endell's work, which had been, as mentioned previously, first introduced into the writing of architectural history by Banham's mentor Nikolaus Pevsner. Endell's radical structure for the horse racetrack in Berlin of 1910, was reexamined in *Theory and Design of the First Machine Age* as a prelude to later technological developments and called "a rare and early approximation to a true space-frame structure."[75] In this publication, Banham concluded that an architect who decides not to "run with technology ... may find that a technological culture has decided to go on without him."[76] Whereas Endell and the Futurists deployed technology for architectural innovation, Banham found in Los Angeles a "naively nonchalant reliance on a technology that may not quite exist yet."[77] In other words, Los Angeles was one of the few instances in which technological progress had to catch up with what the city had stimulated. Therefore, understanding the dynamics of Los Angeles was for Banham a way to identify the productivities of motorized urbanism as well as the architectures that came with it.

Banham deployed a hands-on research that he had already admired in Tom Wolfe's writings on Los Angeles and Las Vegas. Wolfe had introduced literary techniques into journalism that advocated a more involved way of investigating and writing in contrast to a reporter's detachment and objectivity. His 1963 essay "Kandy-Kolored Tangerine-Flake Streamline Baby," which two years later would become the book title for a collection of writings that Banham reviewed, observed the customized car scene in Los Angeles. Wolfe credited that scene with having its own style, worth investigating because of their "great sophistication that adults have not been even remotely aware of."[78] These treatments of urban conditions were of particular interest to Banham, as they intentionally suspend conventional value judgments, zoom-in on popular urban culture, and connect with the subject matter through personal experience. The latter is what Banham described as "walk[ing] the territory in detail."[79] He acknowledged at the outset that his book *Los Angeles* was no conventional historical monograph; and, taking clues from Wolfe, his prose frequently shifts from historical insights to personal experience and references from popular culture. The rhetorical inclusivity aids his view of architecture as including a range of works, from the designs of architects to the structures produced by amateurs, to the residues of the city. The latter, architecture in response to the ecology of urbanization, was at the heart of *Los Angeles*. To broaden the definition of architecture, to include hamburger bars and freeways, Banham connected these spatial and logical experiments with the larger territory of the city—an approach he first tested in radio broadcasts in the late 1960s.

While Banham mentioned the uniqueness of Los Angeles in articles as early as the late 1950s, it was only after his extended visits to the city and during the four consecutive radio broadcasts for the BBC's Third Programme in 1968 that he systematically outlined what in the book would become three of the four ecological tropes and the definition of an alternative architecture. In the first broadcast, "Encounter with Sunset Boulevard," Banham announced that he felt "at home in Los Angeles," a city so vastly different from London and yet very similar in its structure. The second appearance was titled "Roadscapes with Rusting Rails" and was his tribute to the freeway system and the experience of driving. The third talk addressed the isolation of certain neighborhoods. In "Beverly Hills, Too, Is a Ghetto," Banham noted that the district's population seems to have a "total indifference to the needs of all communities except one's own," a view he both criticized and described as "irresistibly attractive."[80] The latter view is related to the topic of his final broadcast, which examined Los Angeles's culture of "doing your thing"—a notion that in Banham's eyes had remarkable effects on artistry and the built environment.

From surfboard decorations to the home-made architecture of the Watts Towers by Simon Rodia, Banham detected a frame of mind that gives no importance to precedents, indulges in its own interests, and caters more often to notions of the bizarre than to the useful. In the chapter on the architecture of the "fantastic," he speaks of the Watts Towers as a "self-absorbed and perfected monument ... unlike anything else in the world."[81] The home-made experiment of the soaring structures of cement, steel, and colored pottery that was constructed over a thirty-three year period, was understood as an expression of originality and creativity that is able to

Simon Rodia, Watts Towers, Los Angeles, 1967, in Reyner Banham, *Los Angeles: The Architecture of Four Ecologies* (1971), 130. The Watts Towers is depicted three times in the book: a street view (displayed here), a detailed view of the towers, and in a neighborhood view of Watts.

unfold in a culture of "doing your thing." Rather than focusing on the creativity of the builder, Banham sees the origins of ingenuity in the unique culture of the city that is conducive to the development of "objects [that] may appear grotesque, ludicrous, stimulating or uplifting" but that, nevertheless, "fit into an established local pattern of architectural invention that reaches deep into the city's history and style of life."[82] Yet to detect these ingenuities and to recognize them as valid contributions to architecture and urbanism required an altered way of viewing the city—a mentality that Banham perceived in the paintings of David Hockney and the photographs of Ed Ruscha, which would become guides in the discovery of a new architectural ecology.

Hockney, also from England, settled in Los Angeles one year before Banham's arrival and declared that he had found "the world's most beautiful city."[83] To his surprise, no one had so far painted Los Angeles; in fact, for Hockney nobody even knew how the city looked. In retrospect, he recalled how after seeing a massive

Ed Ruscha, "Donovan & Seamans, 5760 Wilshire Blvd.; Wilshire Miracle Professional Bldg.; Prudential employees lot, 5700 Wilshire Blvd.; California Federal multi-level, 5670 Wilshire Blvd.," in *Thirtyfour Parking Lots in Los Angeles* (1967), re-published in Reyner Banham, Los Angeles: *The Architecture of Four Ecologies* (1971), 85. Ruscha's deadpan delivery of the image caption echoes the straightforwardness of the photograph.

freeway under construction, it occurred to him, "this place needs a Piranesi; Los Angeles could have a Piranesi, so here I am."[84] Hockney's paintings of backyards, swimming pools, and modern homes report on the city's leisure culture. The iconic painting *A Bigger Splash*, which Banham chose for the cover of his book, shows the emblematic lifestyle with a flat blue sky, tall palm trees, an explicitly modern house, a director's chair, and a pool. The splash in the cobalt blue water suggests that someone had just jumped from the diving board to cool off from the dry heat in the yard. In Banham's eyes, Hockney got Los Angeles right and he even exaggerated his role as the chronicler of the city, knowing quite well that Hockney portrayed a very particular California. And, while the private luxury in Hockney's painting hardly represented most of Los Angeles, the straightforward flatness of the work becomes for Banham essential for giving form to a lifestyle of "doing your thing." The straight-faced documentation of different surface conditions neither celebrates nor

"Chaos on Echo Park," in Reyner Banham, *Los Angeles: The Architecture of Four Ecologies* (1971), 22. With this first photograph, Banham announced the tenor of the book.

accuses the apparent superficiality on display but simply documents it as a color palette, with remnants of inhabitation.

Whereas Hockney records the atmospheres of California weather and its fascination with water, Ruscha's photographs take stock of the building types that make this kind of lifestyle possible. According to Banham, there was still no better way to engage the typical buildings of Los Angeles than through the documentations of Ruscha.[85] The series *Thirtyfour Parking Lots* signaled for Banham a refusal of town planning morals, as they are selected "for doing their parking lot thing."[86] The straightforwardness of these photographic works (*Twentysix Gasoline Stations* in 1963, *Some Los Angeles Apartments* in 1965, *Every Building on the Sunset Strip* in 1966, and *Thirtyfour Parking Lots* in 1967) was perception-altering in that they plainly document buildings and streets that were thought to have no artistic or aesthetic value.[87] And, indeed, Ruscha even suggests that he depicts the environment "like it is," through books of photographs that show exactly what the titles state. Yet, of course, these works are not free of value judgments; they do present the work in a format that enables a rethinking of what is photographed. By adding no explanation to the series of photographs that are all similar in scale and tone, Ruscha removed the importance of the single structure and drew attention to the urban typology of the petrol station, the apartment home, the entertainment strip, and the parking lot. When Banham made a selection from Ruscha's parking lot series to illustrate his book, he, in turn, set out to develop his own series of images that gave access to a new inclusive view of architecture.

The visual engagement with the city (in the documentation of typologies by Ruscha and of lifestyle by Hockney) had a large impact on Banham's readings of the city as well as on his research, the use of images in his publication, and his own use of the camera. The latter became a means to access scenes of architectural and urban innovation that had not been properly understood as such. His book, with over one hundred photographs, makes this very clear by juxtaposing photos taken by Banham himself with drawn maps, images by architectural photographers, archival illustrations, images from popular sources, and photographs and paintings by artists. The frequent adjacency between the different media seems to be intentional. For example, the introduction begins with his photograph of drive-in restaurants with large signs at Echo Park, followed by a historical image of Los Angeles as a pueblo settlement, a map of early Spanish and Mexican ranchos drawn by his wife Mary Banham, a photograph of St. Vincent's Church by Julius Shulman, and another map showing early railroad and water distribution systems. In fact, a longer repetition of illustrations from one source only happens in two of the thirteen short chapters: "Architecture I: Exotic Pioneers" and "Architecture III: The Exiles." But, even then, Banham seems to make every effort to intersperse other imagery in order to diffuse conventional readings. An aerial photograph of the massive parking lot around the Dodger Stadium by Ruscha, for example, is used in "Exotic Pioneers" to emphasize the scale shift between the built work and its surrounding landscape, while in "The Exiles" Banham used one of his own shots to contrast architectural masterpieces.

These visual inserts add integrally to the book's written argument. The photographs, maps, and paintings of *Los Angeles* form a visual essay that revises our understanding of the city. They do not simply illustrate the writing but stand on their own as visual communications of the city's architectural climates. Printing all of the different images at low resolution and in black-and-white binds them together, but their diverse origin and content articulates the uniqueness of the city in all its multiplicity and contrast. The imagery of this photo-documentary communicates an idea of architecture in the broadest sense of the term—an architecture driven by the forces of Los Angeles.

In the context of Banham's use of photography, it is worth recalling once again Moholy-Nagy's books, for both rely on the camera to see the world with different eyes. Indeed, Banham's fascination with the work of Moholy-Nagy long predates his attraction to Los Angeles. The last seven pages of his final chapter in *Theory and Design in the First Machine Age* are devoted to Moholy-Nagy's publication *Von Material zu Architektur* (*The New Vision*). About seeing that text for the first time, Banham recalled: "Words cannot convey the impact made on the eye by the original edition of this book," which was in particular the result of the use of photography in the publication and "the range of its illustrations."[88] Banham was fascinated by the choice and variety of imagery and went on to explain how one felt the influence of the popular culture of magazines on Moholy-Nagy, who utilized these origins to formulate a new notion of visual culture. For Banham, Moholy-Nagy's use of imagery and text presented an openness toward current developments that was different from the dogmatism of other modernists and defined, instead, a new "kind of non-Deterministic Functionalism" that was "built on more liberal foundations" and, therefore, was more open for interpretation.[89] It seems that early on Banham identified in Moholy-Nagy's optical vision a model that not only gave access to a different kind of modernism but, more important for the purpose of this chapter, projected a visual theory that facilitated a different way of seeing; one that Banham utilized in his new vision of Los Angeles.[90]

To access the city's motorized urbanity, Banham's research coupled the photographic exposure of the city with the required mobility of the car. Just as Moholy-Nagy described a *Vision in Motion* in 1947, where "speeding on the roads and circling in the skies has given modern man the opportunity to see more,"[91] Banham utilized the car in order to gain access to the ecology of connections between the city and architecture. Or as Moholy-Nagy put it, "'vision in motion' is vision in relationships"; by which he meant that the increased speed of movement can give exposure to the complex networks of the contemporary world.[92] In this light, Banham's excursions through Los Angeles, armed with his camera and behind the wheel of his American car, gain significance, not just as a unique terrain to be investigated by a historian, but as a different kind of research on the city. He understood freeway driving as the key to engaging Los Angeles. After all, the efficiently calibrated interstate freeways of the 1950s had effectively replaced the parkways of the 1930s in a city that once claimed the largest streetcar system in the US.[93] What many saw as having destroyed the traditional city Banham viewed as a lens into a new form of urbanism. Dominated by freeways and boulevards, sprawling for miles in each available direction, and with very little public transportation, the city could only be accessed through driving, which Banham compared to a local language that he had to learn "in order to read Los Angeles in the original."[94]

With this newly acquired expertise, Banham observed up-close how the Angelenos not only spent a large part of their lives on the freeway but how commut-

"Freeway signs," in Reyner Banham, *Los Angeles: The Architecture of Four Ecologies* (1971), 218. The photograph illustrates the fourth ecology, which Banham poignantly titled "Autopia."

ing itself took on mystical proportions. The "freeways become a special way of being alive," he noted, one that couples "a strange and exhilarating mixture of long-range confidence and close-range wariness."[95] The territory of the car, between tarmac and signs, reaches lyrical dimensions in the fourth ecology, the "Autopia," which for Banham was impossible to avoid and in itself a complete way of life. The highway offers no longer simply an infrastructural organization and the car not just a mode of transport. Banham considered the freeway as an extension of driveways in front of countless individual homes and the car as another kind of interior. Driving down the off-ramp and slowing down the car, Banham observed girls tidying their hair, which he took to mean that "coming off the freeway is coming in from outdoors."[96] In this scenario, the transplanted domestic act as a routine at the freeway's off-ramp signals a new spatial configuration of the motorized metropolis that is no longer bound by the static confines of the traditionally zoned city. What emerges in its place is a mobile metropolis, for which Banham already imagined computerized automation for self-driving cars in its next stage of development.

For the time being, however, driving the freeway was at once a private experience and a public and communal event, which Banham even idealized as democratic urban transport. Obviously, what captivated him was the freedom of movement, smoothness of connectivity, and possibility for technological extrapolation. But the public domain of the freeway, though shared by many, was not quite as democratic as Banham wanted the reader to believe. After all, mobility comes with affluence, and Banham's excitement over car travel seems to willingly omit that car-based individualism was not granted to all. One fellow affluent traveler on Banham's cruise through the city was the heroine of Joan Didion's novel *Play It as*

Joan Didion, photograph by Julian Wasser, 1968 (above) and Reyner Banham in film still from *Reyner Banham Loves Los Angeles*, 1972 (below). Didion is leaning on her Corvette Stingray and Banham on his rental car. LA's car culture and freeway driving fascinated both.

It Lays, a fictional character for whom the freeway becomes a rare act of autonomy. The book follows the protagonist in her compulsive freeway driving as a kind of remedy for an otherwise unfulfilled life. "She [had] to be on the freeway by ten o'clock ... If she was not she lost the day's rhythm, its precariously imposed momentum."[97] Didion's novel, with a title that resembles Banham's favorite mentality of "doing your thing" and published one year prior to *Los Angeles*, gives clues as to what Banham might have meant when referring to "a state of heightened awareness that some locals find mystical."[98] Perhaps Banham had Didion or her character Maria in mind when he spoke of locals and their spiritual connection to freeway driving. In fact, Didion later made a distinction between driving the freeway—something anyone can do—and participating in it: "Actual [freeway] participation requires a total surrender, a concentration so intense as to seem a kind of narcosis, a rapture-of-the-freeway. The mind goes clean. The rhythm takes over."[99] Clearly, Banham was in Didion's orbit, which she made explicit when citing from his book about the freeway's capacity to expand one's feeling of being alive.[100] And, when Banham talked about the ability of locals to find a heightened mystical awareness in driving, Didion answered: "Indeed some locals do, and nonlocals too."[101] If one believes Didion, then Banham captured the exhilarating immersiveness of freeway driving correctly.

Possibly encouraged by Didion, Banham even utilized the metaphors of driving for the structure of his book, by placing the first and last chapters in the "driver's seat." Entitled "In the Rear-view Mirror" and "Towards a Drive-in Bibliography," the first looks backward at ways of writing history in order to be able to move forward, while the last appears to look forward as it proceeds through an annotated bibliography. But the ultimate expression of the all-encompassing nature of driving comes with his TV appearance in the BBC documentary that spelled out

Film stills of Reyner Banham and Julian Cooper, *Reyner Banham Loves Los Angeles*, 1972. The image on the lower left shows Reyner Banham in conversation with Ed Ruscha.

why and how *Reyner Banham Loves Los Angeles*. The 1972 film, a guided tour through Los Angeles by Banham himself, allows the movement of the car and the photographic imagery of the camera to coalesce. The film revisits the neighborhoods that were covered in the book, he meets artists like Ruscha who before provided illustrations, and interviews Angelenos who "do their own thing" and embody the freedom that Banham relished. For much of the film, Banham appears behind the steering wheel, guiding the car from location to location and in dialogue with the fictional "Baede-Kar"—a tribute to Karl Baedeker's early travel guides—that in the film appears in the form of a recorded narration through the car's stereo. Here, the architectural historian is the *Man with a Movie Camera*, to quote a much earlier Russian cinematic experiment in which the cinematographer was shown equally often in front of the camera and behind it. Similarly, Banham—who sometimes films and at other times is seen filming—constructs a cinematic essay; a testimony to the "vision in motion" that enabled him to access the city that he "love[d] ... with a passion that goes beyond sense or reason."[102] This introductory sentence to the film puts the final scene into perspective. As Banham cruises toward the ocean at the end of the day, the travel guide gives one last piece of information, namely that the spectacular colors in the sunset come from the pollution in the air. "Enjoy it! The best of it doesn't last long," the gentle voice on the cassette tape says and Banham adds that this plastic fluorescent spectacle is "the greatest exit line any city could ever have."[103]

With Banham's *Los Angeles*, the passionate confidence in conditions of the existing city reached new heights of optimism. Yet, he made no attempt at intentionally suppressing the negativities of the city, but rather engaged in an intense search for its potentials that could offer a revised mentality about urbanization and a new directive for urbanism. Los Angeles provided the terrain in which Banham tapped new ways of thinking about the city—ideas that emerged explicitly from the forces and dynamics of contemporary urbanization and were highly critical of planning. The movie, for example, follows Banham from an overlook on Wilshire Boulevard to a lecture at the University of Southern California, where he declares that Los Angeles breaks all the rules of planning and yet it works. On the one hand, Banham agreed with conventional planners in their belief that Los Angeles could not have survived without planning; on the other hand, he asserted that "conventional planning wisdom certainly would destroy the city as we know it."[104] For Banham, planning had failed the contemporary city and a new attitude toward urbanization (rather than design of the city) was needed. He found this frame of mind in Los Angeles's frequent and blatant cancelations of planning and in the urban ingenuities that emerged from those; a frame that he would bring back to the UK and utilize in one of the most provocative assaults on this young profession.

Non-Plan was a collective effort, in which Banham joined the architect Cedric Price, the urban planner Peter Hall, and the editor of the social affairs magazine *New Society* Paul Barker in the formulation of a manifesto that opposed top-down, State-directed urbanism and controlled, bureaucratic planning. The group's hostility against planning tapped into a larger postwar rethinking of modernist tendencies that questioned imposed ideas of organization and ideal scenarios of a city's workings. Instead, many protagonists had become deeply invested in existing conditions rather than in how urbanism envisioned cities to best function. Early on, the British Townscape movement studied and embraced the heterogeneity of historical city centers through visual analysis of buildings, contexts, and urban fabrics that took clues from eighteenth-century picturesque theory and applied it to the city. By the end of the 1940s, the journal *Architectural Review*—with Nikolaus Pevsner as editor, Gordon Cullen as art director, and Hubert de Cronin Hastings as publisher—became the primary vehicle for disseminating ideas on Townscape.[105] The optical appeal of everyday urban conditions and vernacular forms, or what the writers of Townscape would call "anonymous architecture," became the basis for a reconfiguration of urban analysis as well as a transformation of the architect as a "visual planner." One article from 1949 calls on architects and planners to delve into "the vast field of anonymous design and unacknowledged pattern which still lies entirely outside the terms of reference of official town-planning routine."[106] One year later, the issue *Man Made America* rehearsed Townscape mentalities in the US context. These ideas further developed through the anthropological tendencies of Team 10 and the urban pluralities celebrated by Jane Jacobs in *The Death and Life of Great American Cities* (1961), published in the same year as Cullen's anthology *Townscape*. In 1964, Bernard Rudofsky cited vernacular works as sources of inspiration in the exhibition and publication *Architecture Without Architects*.[107] During the 1950s and 1960s, existing urban contexts became increasingly viewed as generative for design exploration and worth protecting from postwar redevelopment efforts.[108] In the US, these shifts in mentality can be observed in publications such as Bernard Frieden's book *The Future of Old Neighborhoods* from 1964 as well as in legislative measures like the National Historic Preservation Act of 1966.

Published in *New Society* on March 20, 1969, "Non-Plan: An Experiment in Freedom" pushed the limits of this international debate. It followed Banham's insights on Los Angeles and issued the provocation: "what would happen if there were no plan?"[109] The authors proclaimed that the conservatism of planning, disguised as good intentions, made decisions for how other people should live on the basis of preconceived value judgments. As Barker would later recall, "we wanted to startle people by offending against the deepest taboos."[110] To this end Banham, Hall, and Price each took a section of the British countryside and imagined it as extensions of Los Angeles, with low density, automobility, advertisements, and sprawl. A mentality that Banham first detected in views of local Californians toward Los Angeles, now played out on the other side of the globe: "let it swing and see what happens."[111] The emblematic terrain of Los Angeles provided lessons for a new kind of self-guided and hands-off urbanism.

While all authors were credited for the entire text, Banham's writing focused on the so-called "Constable Country," named after the Romantic landscape painter John Constable and known for its old coach villages, rolling farmland, and ancient woodlands. Banham described it as the "most sacred of English sacred scen-

Illustration of a new Constable Country, in Reyner Banham, Paul Barker, Peter Hall, and Cedric Price, "Non-Plan," *New Society* (1969), 439. In this collaborative piece, Banham wrote the text on Constable Country, where he envisioned the picturesque countryside of this area taken over by signage, malls, and motels, one of which is called "Constable Motel."

ery," because its idyllic nature served as a reminder of Britain's pre-industrial past. Deploying the Non-Plan mandate and envisioning the lifting of planning restrictions in this area, led Banham to a scenario that would upset the established order through the introduction of the frenzied landscape of entertainment and commerce of Los Angeles. He imagined how the tall trees in the region would absorb massive one-story commercial buildings that are only announced through large signage. Banham was clearly intrigued by the dramatic juxtaposition of rural countryside and commercial buildings and signage that simultaneously questions established norms and invents a new urban ecology. In fact, this new terrain of large buildings, individual homes, and signage amongst the rolling woodlands hovers between conventional forms of city and suburb—a quality unsurprisingly similar to the conditions in Los Angeles. While previously, this "countryside and its villages ha[d] ... the perfect ecology for retired officers and gentlemen," Banham's projection densifies the region, so that one can imagine how single homes would sit next to big signs that float above tall trees, which, in turn, surround parking lots that front the commercial buildings in the "rolypoly countryside."[112] The introduction of these utterly different architectures into the protected and picturesque landscape was partially inspired by Wilshire Boulevard and its business towers, inserted into a sea of suburbia.

The short manifesto of the Non-Plan, however, is no simple importation of a foreign scene as a vehicle to intensify the countryside, but rather the result of the extrapolation of tendencies that existed already but were currently held back by planning. Understandably, this scenario received mixed reactions. By proposing to resist the bureaucracy of planning and to free up local economies, the deregulating proposals of Non-Plan came with a host of problems, not the least of which was the euphoria with increased mobility and the apparent free rein of economic drivers. This distrust in planning and openness to the market is part of a longer lineage of ideas. After an early critique of planning mechanisms by figures such as Endell, far-reaching skepticism toward planning made itself heard immediately after the Second World War. Karl Popper's philosophical critique in *The Open Society and Its Enemies*, for example, targeted teleological historicism as well as collectivist planning and economy because of their affinities to totalitarian ideology. For Popper, "... using a blueprint of society as a whole, ... demands a strong centralized rule of a few, and ... therefore is likely to lead to a dictatorship."[113] His ideas came under the auspices of preserving individual freedoms, but they also set the stage for an embrace of free-market libertarianism as promoted by Friedrich von Hayek in *The Road to Serfdom* and the later *The Constitution of Liberty*.[114] Indeed, the two ambitions—market deregulation and the proposed abandoning of planning—came dangerously close to one another in their shared efforts to free environments of constraints (trade, on the one side, and urbanity, on the other). And yet, it is also important to remember what in each case was to be deregulated and what was the ultimate goal of each intervention. To that extent, Non-Plan's emphasis on local economies and regional trends is revealing.

As Simon Sadler has pointed out, many of these ideas provoked a reinvention of culture by uprooting established symbols and ways of life.[115] For the members of Non-Plan, generating a revolutionary momentum after the events of modernism was no longer an option. Yet transgression within urban culture provided a way to engage existing urban dynamics, by canceling established norms and extrapolating selective currents from within. While the anarchic tendencies of the Non-Plan are often seen as an encouragement to the laissez-faire economics that take over when rules of planning are suspended, Banham seems to envision a new kind of architect as the producer of an environment that in its surreal radicalism rivals the schemes of most avant-gardes of the 1960s. Similar to his observations on Los Angeles, his scenarios in the UK focus on existing conditions (the city that is) to extrapolate from, and to project beyond utopian dreams.

In many ways, Los Angeles made Banham see the contemporary city and architecture anew. Or, more precisely, he found what he was looking for all along—"a sympathetic ecology for architectural design," which "behoves the world's architects to find out why."[116] The most significant condition in the urban climate of Los Angeles, was a "sense of having room to manoeuvre."[117] This is the very space in which everyone in Banham's Los Angeles is "doing their own thing" and in which new architectures are waiting to be discovered. While the book detects this *Spielraum* (room to maneuver, to move, and to play) in the urban ecologies of Los Angeles, Non-Plan deploys this newly found freedom to question planning strategies and envision a different engagement with the city—one propelled by a mentality supportive of existing urbanization. In his reading, the quintessential formless city does not result in more chaos but provides *Spielraum* for the discoveries of new and untapped potentials. "This sense of possibilities still ahead is part of the basic life-style of Los Angeles,"[118] which for Banham makes experiments such as the Watts Towers possible and that, injected into the British countryside, makes room for the emergence of a new kind of architectural urbanism.

Robert Venturi and Denise Scott Brown's Cinematic Vision

Banham's section in the "Non-Plan" article is illustrated by an image of a town saturated with signage that hints as much at Los Angeles as it suggests the imagery of Las Vegas. And, the final page of their manifesto against planning reads as follows: "The monuments of our century that have spontaneity and vitality are found not in the old cities, but in the American West. There, in the desert and the Pacific states, creations like Fremont Street in Las Vegas or Sunset Strip in Beverly Hills represent the living architecture of our age."[119] Whereas for Banham the urban multiplicity of Los Angeles by far outpaced Las Vegas, he did highlight the well-tempered environments of the hotels and casinos along the Strip. By the end of the 1960s, Banham wrote, that if measured on the architecture of fantasy, "Las Vegas has been ... a marginal gloss on Los Angeles," but the "pure environmental power, manifested as coloured light" makes a visit to the city in the desert mandatory.[120] Here, Banham identified a crucial moment of transition, in which architecture was modified "from forms assembled in light to light assembled in forms."[121] Of course, this strayed far from early modernism. But even more significant was that the technological self-confidence that he saw in Los Angeles expressed in the urban forms and logistics of the city, turned in Las Vegas into an ethereal architecture through the electric spectacle of light.

Venturi and Scott Brown, while similarly fascinated with the nocturnal environments of the city, expanded Banham's reading through a semiotic analysis of architectural and urban forms as seen through the windshield of a car while driving. Their mandate to detect architectural and urban intelligences in Las Vegas was at the time even more outlandish than Banham's observations of Los Angeles. While only a small portion of his book focused on buildings by well-known architects, in Los Angeles, at least, one could find some of these. Las Vegas, on the other hand, was despised by the high culture of architecture, for its consumerism and seemingly uncultivated spatial organization. Banham wrote in 1975 that "Las Vegas appeared to be an indistinct and undesigned formlessness composed of elements that fell below the threshold of architectural attention."[122] Of course, for Banham, this kind of formlessness was a challenge to the status quo and, therefore, a condition that gave a sense of possibilities for future exploration.

Eleven years earlier, Las Vegas had briefly surfaced on the architectural radar through an article by Tom Wolfe, "Las Vegas (What?) Las Vegas (Can't Hear You! Too Noisy) Las Vegas!!!"[123] To the surprise of most readers, Wolfe's analysis of the mass culture of casinos, hotels, motels, and drive-ins identified in these typologies the new landmarks of Americana. From the muzak in the air (and even underwater in swimming pools) to the skyline of signs (not of buildings), Las Vegas was understood as a true expression of American popular culture that displayed its confidence through the architectural consistency across the city. As such, Wolfe termed it "the Versailles of America" and "America's first unconscious avant-garde!"[124] For the introduction of his collection of essays in the following year, Wolfe asked: "[W]hat do we know about these signs, these incredible pieces of neon sculpture, and what kind of impact they have on people?"[125] Venturi and Scott Brown listened most attentively to this call for further study on the aesthetics and perception of the popular city of Las Vegas.

In its unique constellation of commerce, entertainment, climate, and technology, Venturi and Scott Brown found in Las Vegas the most dramatic and pure manifestation of the sprawling urbanization that dominated many cities in the US. As such, it stood against the widespread contempt that the architectural and urban discourse harbored toward these conditions. They aimed to understand Las Vegas's new form of urbanization, devoted to shopping, entertainment, and hotels, and accessed by car. While most architects were not able to accept the dramatic urban shifts that transformed the contemporary city, Scott Brown and Venturi were more than willing to suspend moral judgment over these conditions in favor of affirming the existing context and expanding the role of architecture. They argued that any "city [even Las Vegas] is an archetype rather than a prototype," in turn suggesting that lessons can be derived even from the commercially driven hyper-urbanity of Las Vegas.[126] In fact, they contended that especially in these seemingly un-designed and unplanned environments, one could tap the typical urbanism that approximates the archetype of the postwar American city. While not designed by architects, Las Vegas was far from un-designed: the city's casinos, hotels, and parking lots demonstrated a different kind of spatial expertise, not yet part of architecture's repertoire. Even as other architects could not decipher any organizational pattern in the constantly fluctuating heterogeneity and apparent formlessness of the city, Venturi and Scott Brown suspected otherwise.

Their 1972 publication *Learning from Las Vegas*, addressed the most extreme form of automobile-oriented, billboard-based, and entertainment-driven environment that urbanization had yet produced.[127] The aim was to reveal direct evidence of a new urban and architectural intelligence in Las Vegas. In order to make these productivities visible (to be able to detect, analyze, and represent this new city), however, they would no longer rely on established typological analysis but introduce new forms of observation and methods of representation through the use of the camera and of film. The procedures deployed for the study of Las Vegas as well as the photography of Scott Brown point back to the practices of Moholy-Nagy and Kepes.

At the same time that Wolfe published his essays on the city and Banham cruised through Los Angeles, Scott Brown moved to California and visited Las Vegas for the first time in 1965.[128] While trained in architecture and planning, her photography provided a lens to expose previously unidentified aspects of the built world. She had photographed popular and marginalized urban spaces, first in South Africa, where she grew up, and later in London and the US. These photographs already indicate a fascination with spaces of contemporary cities that are outside the architectural discourse—snapshots of everyday urbanism that would inform her mentality toward the city's actualities, her doubts about ideal planning, and, ultimately, the survey of Las Vegas. As Martino Stierli has pointed out, her photographs of American cities are already "mobilized views," often shot through the window of a moving car.[129] Of course, this would become the perspective through which much of Las Vegas was to be understood once Scott Brown and Venturi launched the "Learning from Las Vegas Research Studio" at Yale University in fall of 1968.[130]

Two years prior, Scott Brown had invited Venturi to visit her in Los Angeles, from whence they traveled together to Las Vegas. Already during their first joint visit to the city, some photographs seem to intentionally reveal the dashboard of the car, so as to simultaneously document the city as well as the vehicle that pro-

Denise Scott Brown, The Las Vegas Strip, looking southwest, 1966. Photograph by Scott Brown on her first joint exploration of Las Vegas with Robert Venturi—a trip that led to the essay "The Significance for A&P Parking Lots, or Learning from Las Vegas" (1968) and the Las Vegas research studio at Yale University that same year.

moted it. Furthermore, these images not only hint at the motorized urbanism of Las Vegas but also at the car's crucial role in the study of the city. The vehicle's front row seats, from where Banham previously gained access to the car-based urbanism of Los Angeles, were now becoming integral to the photographic documentations of the Las Vegas Strip. During the research trip in 1968, which produced the evidence for the publication of *Learning from Las Vegas*, Venturi, Scott Brown, and their collaborator Steven Izenour, would drive miles across the city. Scott Brown with a hand-held camera hunted for snapshots that reveal the ingenuities of popular urbanism while their students mounted cameras on the hoods of rented cars and on dashboards in order to sequentially document the conditions of the city's street-lined signage, parking, and buildings.

Ultimately, these experiments became the basis for a visual construction of Las Vegas that was intimately linked to the automobile and photography. In addition, it gave the authors some distance from the subject at hand; a distance that was essential, for it placed emphasis on the architectural and urban repercussions of the entertainment-driven commercial city and not on the dubious ethics of this urban model. Venturi's book *Complexity and Contradiction* had already outlined a critique of utopian impulses in modernism and *Learning from Las Vegas's* intentional avoidance of the city's economy and politics became in itself a political stand. Venturi and Scott Brown were now able to focus the conversation on the potentials of the city. The authors, therefore, declare early in the book: "Just like an analysis of the structure of a Gothic cathedral need not include a debate on the morality of medieval religion, so Las Vegas's values are not questioned here. The morality of commercial advertisement, gambling interests, and the competitive instinct is not at issue here."[131] The obvious negativities of the city are deliberately suspended in order to make room for discoveries of its latent possibilities for architecture.

In an effort to formulate techniques that would withhold judgments of the city for as long as possible in order to allow new insights to emerge, Venturi and Scott Brown developed what they called a "dead-pan" view of Las Vegas. Analyzing the city through "dead-panning," however, did not exclude intentionality on the part of the analyst-architect. In fact, Venturi and Scott Brown's motivations were not only spelled out, they also registered in the documentation of the city. The intention was to suspend preconceived notions in order to invent a new study of the city through new ways of looking at what was commonly regarded as taboo. In their research on Las Vegas, a deferral of biases was of the utmost importance for alternative views of the city to develop. For Scott Brown, the technique aimed at the most straightforward—almost clinical—representation of the material at hand, letting the city speak for itself. They aimed, as she wrote in 1970, "to avoid being upstaged by our own subject matter."[132]

For that to materialize, the work of Ruscha would become even more instrumental for *Learning from Las Vegas* than it had been for Banham's analysis of Los Angeles. Scott Brown first used Ruscha's photographs to illustrate her article "On Pop Art, Permissiveness, and Planning," and the book even emulates the techniques developed by the artist. The street elevation photography that Ruscha devised for his 1966 artist's book *Every Building on the Sunset Strip* became the precedent for "An 'Edward Ruscha' elevation of the Strip" in *Learning from Las Vegas*. As the clearest instance of a "deadpan" representation of the city, Scott Brown saw Ruscha's photographic work as "a new vision of the very imminent world around us."[133] Ruscha's unfolded views of the Sunset Strip and other streets in Los Angeles across several decades were neither an ironic statement nor a simple embrace of what exists. Rather, they generated a document of a city that revealed a new aesthetic. Combining historical representational techniques of street elevations with urban photography, Ruscha's experiments augment new readings of contemporary urban conditions.[134] By giving no emphasis to any particular building and showing each consecutively, *Every Building on the Sunset Strip* abstracts the individual objects

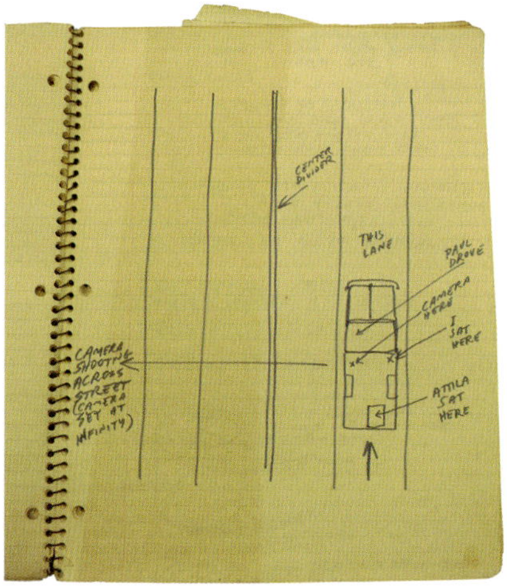

Ed Ruscha, Sketch from Notebook "Motorized Photographs, Sunset Blvd. and Other L.A. Streets," 1973. Starting in 1966, Ruscha documents the logistics of the project in several notebooks that include fuel receipts, schedules, and measurements, as well as sketches for the setup of his drive-by photography. Some are taken in preparation while others are recollections of past events, as when he remembers "PAUL DROVE" and "[he] SAT HERE."

Robert Venturi and Denise Scott Brown, Las Vegas research studio, Detail of "An 'Edward Ruscha' elevation of the Strip," 1968. Published in *Learning from Las Vegas* (1972), 28–29. The image caption continues: "Tourist maps are made of the Grand Central and the Rhine showing the route lined by its palaces. Ruscha made one of the Sunset Strip. We imitated his for the Las Vegas Strip."

almost beyond recognition and invents a way of viewing the city closely related to the perspective of the driver. While Ruscha wanted these experiments to be pure documentary views of the city, it is also clear that the linear unraveling of the street reveals an urban visual with an aesthetic appeal that is difficult to overlook.

During the field trip in 1968, Scott Brown and the students stopped in Los Angeles to visit Ruscha's studio, an indication of the importance of his work to *Learning from Las Vegas*. Once the group arrived in the gaming capital in the desert, the lessons and techniques of Ruscha were immediately implemented. For an analysis of Las Vegas, Ruscha's roadside photography was the technique to document the city with the aim to extract architectural and urban intelligences from the building typology of the casino, its relationship to parking, and the exuberance of the sign. Indeed, Venturi and Scott Brown's elevation of the Las Vegas Strip clearly shows the low-profile buildings, the scale of signage along the street, and the urban dispersion of casinos behind parking lots. In its linearity, this representation of the city even exaggerates these conditions, but (just like in the case of Ruscha) it also creates a new urban landscape that had not been seen by architects. The original publication in 1972 shows over three miles of the Strip, a distance that spans from the airport to the Sahara Hotel, with the former being the last conventional architecture that one encountered on the way to the city. "Beyond this piece of architectural image, impressions are scaled to the car."[135] Only from the driver's perspective was the new urban order perceivable, an order that remained obscured in conventional maps or pedestrian views.

The city's frenzied visual condition is described multiple times, approximating previous excursions into the "formless" while careful to acknowledge the difference between a lack of visual order and an absence of inherent urban form: "The image of the commercial strip is chaos,"[136] they noted, and yet, the street elevations were able to hint at a different kind of order—one that is complex, car-oriented, multi-colored, and multi-layered. While the individual photographs of scenes along the Strip (often shot by Scott Brown) communicate the impossible multiplicity of elements that a single photograph could capture at any given moment and in almost any direction, the unraveled street elevation presents a new image of the city. The formlessness that one experienced on foot and in individual photographs was given a new order through the act of driving and the pace of the car. Suddenly, the image sequencing of *Learning from Las Vegas* suggests a new, complex order, one that never fully overcomes the formlessness of the city, never establishes a total stability. Instead, *Learning from Las Vegas* seems to suggest that this order was always latent within the complexity of the car-based city, waiting to be discovered. The authors wrote: "It is not an order dominated by the expert and made easy for

Robert Venturi and Denise Scott Brown, Las Vegas research studio, "The order in the landscape is not obvious," 1968. Published in *Learning from Las Vegas* (1972), 30. Photographing the sidewalk between the parking lot and the road underneath the Stardust sign became a means to document the visual chaos one confronted while walking, in contrast to the experience while driving.

Preparation for *Las Vegas Deadpan* film shoot, Las Vegas, 1968. Photograph by Steven Izenour during the Las Vegas research studio field trip that allocated two days for filming, during which students mounted a camera on the front of a car in order to document the sequential views of a driver. The first film was *Las Vegas Deadpan*, with a duration of twenty-one minutes.

Film stills of *Las Vegas Helicopter Ride*, Las Vegas Strip, 1968. The last film that the Las Vegas research studio shot viewed the Strip from the air and focused predominantly on signage.

the eye. The moving eye in the moving body must work to pick out and interpret a variety of changing, juxtaposed orders..."[137] Emerging from the forces of the city (steered by the economics of the casinos, the predominant modes of transportation, and its linear urban typology), this new order, detected in the commercial strip, holds for Venturi and Scott Brown a key to accessing and engaging contemporary urbanization. The intricate pandemonium of elements, colors, and movements form in the gaze of the driver a new logic that one could understand as a moiré that crystallizes new imagery.

Already in 1944 Kepes's *Language of Vision* sought to detect visual orders in the chaos of the modern environment. His quest for a new way of seeing "the chaos of our formless world"[138] finally materialized in *Learning from Las Vegas*. Indeed, the Gestalt theory that Kepes introduced into urban analysis through his collaboration with Kevin Lynch and their study of "The Perceptual Form of the City" greatly influenced Venturi and Scott Brown.[139] Of more importance for the purpose of this chapter, however, is that Kepes as well as Lynch sought new perceptual conditions through which to analyze American urban sprawl. While Kepes described this typical urban environment as "visual disorder" that is only comprehended via the car, Lynch urged the reader to "learn to see the hidden form in the vast sprawl of cities."[140] But, whereas, Lynch's influential book *The Image of the City* frequently returns to concepts of the traditional European city in order to derive perceptual frameworks and methods of evaluation, Venturi and Scott Brown saw the conditions of contemporary Las Vegas as a place of no return. This difference had repercussions in the way each of the authors saw a possible engagement with the existing city. Lynch proposed to make the image of the American city legible once again while Venturi and Scott Brown accepted the city as it was. Lynch dismantled the disorder of contemporary urbanization in order to reveal a hidden "imageable" picture, whereas *Learning from Las Vegas* aimed at a new way for architects to see the city.

Invested in the visual tension between the chaos of the formless city and the hidden orders within it, both sides experimented with cinematic image sequencing.[141] While Lynch utilized it to distill an image of the city, Venturi and Scott Brown aimed at articulating a new car-based optics. Already the Ruscha-like photographic elevation studies of the Strip imply movement—a movement that is thematized in the different films by the Las Vegas Studio.[142] Those cinematic experiments operate within the lineage of the new optical vision of the metropolis (from Endell, via Kandinsky, to Moholy-Nagy's *Vision in Motion*). At the same time, they also capitalize on the modernist project in search of forms that could withstand the modern city. After all, the repercussions of traffic onto architecture and urbanism were part of the modernist rhetoric as early as the 1900s. The 1914 Werkbund conference on the topic, for example, became a platform where Endell analyzed the impressions of a street on the viewer and Peter Behrens called for simplified architectural forms in response to the new pace of the metropolis.[143]

Learning from Las Vegas develops this mentality. But, in contrast to modernist conventions, Venturi and Scott Brown did not urge architects to invent new forms in response to a changed urban climate but found that the city had already produced an architecture that one needed to learn from. As they drive up and down the Strip with the camera mounted on the car, a new city of signage, parking, and low-rise architecture emerges that in the cinematic record of movement along the Strip is revealed as a new kind of urbanism. For Venturi and Scott Brown, it showed "the value of symbolism and allusion in an architecture of vast space and speed ..." and it comments on "old clichés and inclusion of the everyday."[144] Venturi and Scott Brown's films of the Strip highlight most clearly the importance of the sign. That element of great consequence for the architectural oeuvre of the two designers here moved to the foreground. The movies, while intended as dead-pan, are not only analytical documents that stress the importance of the sign in the car-based city; they also give indication of Venturi and Scott Brown's vision of architecture as sign. In one movie filmed from a helicopter, Scott Brown's hand-held camera zooms as close as possible into the tall signage at mid-air, appearing dangerously close and revealing her fascination.

Allan D'Arcangelo, *The Trip*, 1965. The painting—published in *Learning from Las Vegas* (1972), 4—was for Venturi and Scott Brown a brilliant evocation of the contradictions of contemporary driving at cloverleaf intersections.

In his book on Los Angeles, Banham had already remarked on the peculiarity of the sign that "must be believed." He noted that "it seems incredibly bizarre when a sign directs one into the far left lane for an objective clearly visible on the right of the carriageway."[145] Nonetheless, one complies, and arrives as predicted. Venturi and Scott Brown would add that "the driver has no time to ponder ... he or she relies on signs for guidance,"[146] a paradoxical condition they illustrate with Allan D'Arcangelo's painting *The Trip*. Both books acknowledge the sign as part of the way-finding system and both see a split between orientation and representation, where the complexities of traffic have outpaced the abilities of comprehension. The driver will find the way while getting lost. Yet, *Learning from Las Vegas* seems to be more invested in the iconography of the sign than its navigational capacity. Wolfe's 1964 article on the city had already pointed out that "signs have become the architecture of Las Vegas," which owners do not coordinate in accordance with their building, rather they construct "the building to support the biggest sign."[147] A constellation that was absurd for most architects, was identified as

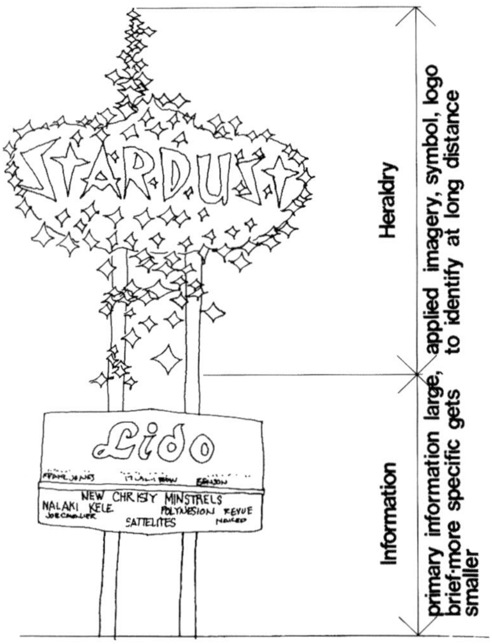

Robert Venturi and Denise Scott Brown, "Physiognomy of a typical casino sign," in *Learning from Las Vegas* (1977), 67. Graphic analysis of the sign attuned to communicate to drivers at multiple speeds and distances.

productive by Wolfe, Venturi, and Scott Brown, since it hinted at a new kind of architecture. In combining Gestalt theory and semiotics, the sign becomes in *Learning from Las Vegas* an architectural device for urban communication in the space of the city, which on the Strip emerges clearly in relation to distance and speed. With that in mind, the authors utilized diagrams to point out how the upper part of the sign communicates over long distances while the lower parts offer specific information, only decipherable when close by. All of this, of course, points to an environment conditioned by the car, which effectively replaced spatial constructs of architecture with the surface messages of the sign.

Mitchell Schwarzer, in his study of the impact of transportation and camera technology on the perception of architecture, explored new modes of expression in "buildings that communicate to drivers and that convey the commercial messages of commodity culture" and came to the conclusion: "Buildings have become like signs, another form of media."[148] Indeed, Venturi and Scott Brown's analysis of the sign deploys visual, spatial, and architectural tools to investigate an element outside the architectural discourse, documenting a seemingly unprejudiced view but also elevating the sign to the status of architecture. More precisely, an element of popular culture is analyzed with the intensity that is usually reserved for works of art. But in *Learning from Las Vegas*, this detailed analysis provides no pretext for passing judgment on the artifact's quality or content, instead offering a sensibility of openness regarding an aesthetic of what is commonly viewed as ordinary and even ugly. Aron Vinegar has already drawn connections between concepts of the ordinary and skepticism, a train of thought that is worth expanding upon.[149] After all, the famous imagery of the juxtaposition of the "duck" ("building is sign") and the "decorated shed" ("big sign—little building") can be traced along the contours of what Venturi and

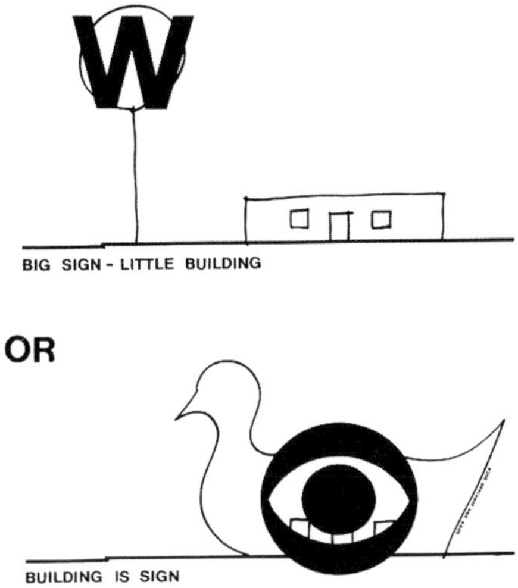

Robert Venturi and Denise Scott Brown, "Big Sign—Little Building, or Building is Sign," in *Learning from Las Vegas* (1972), 12. Diagram of Las Vegas's building culture as Venturi and Scott Brown understood it: either it blends "sculptural symbol and architectural shelter" or it separates its fronts and turns them "perpendicular to the highway as big, high signs."

Scott Brown described in the second half of the book as the "ugly and ordinary."[150] While the authors never spell out the alignment of terminology (of the ugly duckling and the ordinary shed), and instead use the final pages as a critique of modernism and a promotion of their own practice, their language and analytics of popular roadside signage point toward a unique mentality. The commercial city, exhibited in its highest form in the Las Vegas signs, is here viewed as an aesthetic visual experience. What is commonly viewed as failure and malfunction of culture, Venturi and Scott Brown turn around and exhibit as a significant architectural and cultural contribution.

They saw the city "as an aesthetic phenomenon ... not in terms of beauty, but in terms of the degree of artifice ...," or what Susan Sontag would call "Camp."[151] Sontag had already articulated a new sensibility that she witnessed in cultural products outside the realm of established value judgments, in her essay "Notes on 'Camp'"—a project very much in line with Wolfe's article on Las Vegas and written in the same year. For Sontag, "Camp" is a "depoliticized—or at least apolitical" way of looking at the world and finding pleasure not in high culture but its opposite. "There exists," Sontag wrote, "a good taste of bad taste," which she insists, "can be liberating."[152] For Venturi and Scott Brown it clearly was. At the very beginning of *Learning from Las Vegas* they declare that the values and morals of the city are not the focus of attention, and by the end they paraphrase Sontag and rhetorically ask the reader: "If [Las Vegas] is all bad, why is it so inspiring?"[153] For the authors, the answer to this question lies with a new architectural language inherent in the everyday city, the sign as a spatial language, and the suburban edge as a source of symbolism. While this is instructive for understanding their architectural project, Sontag's essay is a reminder that a certain outlook is needed in order to see the world with "campy" eyes. For her, it is this attitude and way of seeing that "has the power to transform experience. ... That turns its back on the good-bad axis of ordinary aesthetic judgment [and offers] art (and life) a different—a supplementary—set of standards."[154] In other words, "Camp" and "Learning from Las Vegas" are not totalizing concepts that void previous assumptions; instead, they add a way of looking at the world with more inclusive eyes.

The list of objects, books, films, plays, and places that Sontag associates with "Camp" is long, ranging from Tiffany lamps and *Swan Lake*, to the Brown Derby restaurant on Sunset Boulevard in Los Angeles—a list that always remains incomplete and that easily expands to the signs in Las Vegas and the casinos on the Strip. The photos by Scott Brown and, most poignantly, the self-portraits of her and Venturi in the desert with views of the Strip in the background, can be understood as visualizations of a supplementary lens that here comes in the form of her camera. Seeing Scott Brown's smile (she unlike Venturi looks into the camera), one can almost hear her say, "So bad it's good." Similar to their famous cartoon in which the speech bubble above the most generic building spells out, "I am a monument," Sontag's final and "ultimate Camp statement" reads: "it's good because it's awful."[155] While this statement has sometimes been interpreted as ironic, Venturi and Scott Brown's fascination with Las Vegas could not be further from it. Soliciting Sontag's concept for a second reading of *Learning from Las Vegas* reveals that Venturi and Scott Brown felt no cynicism, only compassion toward the Strip. "Camp taste," Sontag wrote, is "above all, a mode of enjoyment, of appreciation—not judgment," a mentality that Venturi in retrospect formulated as advice to architects: "pay special attention to what turns you on."[156]

With that in mind, Venturi and Scott Brown's fascination with Las Vegas and the sign in particular no longer appears as straightforward mining of architectural intelligences from the formless contemporary city. Instead, Sontag's notion of "Camp" crystallizes Venturi and Scott Brown's approach as a passionate pursuit of bad taste in the architectural successes of Las Vegas's urban failures. In other words, in the visual formlessness of Las Vegas's Strip they found accomplishments of architecture, only visible through an altered lens of perception. This new way of seeing the city becomes a prerequisite for a rethinking of, and a change in attitude with regard to, urbanization. What this chapter has described as an altered optics toward the city is clearly aligned with a particular sensibility (to use Sontag's term). Namely, to view the formlessness of the existing city as a condition that does not always require a new order, but for architects necessitates a rethinking through an altered way of viewing the world, an attitude that begins to see potentials in the most improbable environments.

Denise Scott Brown and the Las Vegas Strip as seen from the desert, November 1966. Photograph by Robert Venturi, who also posed at this location but turned his back to the camera, appearing as dark silhouette while Scott Brown visibly smiled.

What Venturi and Scott Brown make explicit in their acknowledgment of spatial and cultural productivities in things that the architectural discourse commonly resists or seeks to eradicate, is equally apparent in the work of Banham, Moholy-Nagy, and Endell. The figures discussed in this chapter all deploy a recalibrated visual lens to extract potentials from territories in the city that span from the ugly to the ordinary. Across the twentieth century they constructed a visual aesthetics in which conditions of the formless city were no longer seen as problematic but came to be understood as fruitful. From Endell's impressionist gaze at the margins of the city, to Moholy-Nagy's photographic exploits of the sped-up metropolis, to Banham's motorized lens along the freeway, and Venturi and Scott Brown's cinematic pursuits of "bad taste" in signs, these works question and sidestep the definitions of architectural culture through new ways of seeing. Here, imagination is linked most clearly to acts of perception and observation of the existing city, and, consequently, less to mental images of foresight and more to advanced concepts of eyesight. The search for new ways of viewing urbanization, however, performs in all these works a mode of observation that challenges conventional views and aims to communicate and visualize an alternative perception of the city. Therefore, finding productivities in the existing city should here not be understood as affirmation of what exists but rather as radical imagining of a different kind of city.

“ *Only the metropolis can be the location for the struggle toward a new building art.* Karl Scheffler, *Die Architektur der Großstadt*, 1913

Metropolitan Architecture ... is born out of necessity and driven by objectivity and economy, materials and construction, and economic and sociological factors. Ludwig Hilberseimer, *Großstadtarchitektur*, 1927

Manhattan ... keeps the illusion of architecture intact, while surrendering wholeheartedly to the metropolis. This architecture relates to the forces of the Groszstadt like a surfer to the waves. Rem Koolhaas, "Delirious New York," in *S, M, L, XL: Office for Metropolitan Architecture*, 1995

2 Extrapolation

Urban *Spielraum* and the Project of a Metropolitan Architecture

The first decade of the twentieth century witnessed a definition of architecture that would challenge the conventional relationship between city and building, and haunt architects for decades to come. Introducing the concept of a "metropolitan architecture," the critic and theorist Karl Scheffler set out to define an architecture born from within the metropolis. Not only was this concept of building intimately related to the modern city, but the city's spatial, programmatic, logistical, and commercial pressures propelled it forward. What Scheffler saw most vividly expressed in the warehouses, apartment buildings, and department stores of his hometown Berlin would become the driver for his investigations into a new architectural paradigm and a new relationship of architecture to the city. To him, the forces of the metropolis had brought about (and literally shaped) novel spatial and organizational conditions that architects until then had failed to recognize. The building types of the modern city, unique to the current urban condition, announced a new architecture of the metropolis, which he called "*Großstadtarchitektur*" (metropolitan architecture). While acknowledging the direct relationship of this evolving architecture to the commercial and industrial circumstances of the modern city, and the problems that came with it, he saw architectural innovations in locations that by many were viewed at best as mere residues of the modern city and in building typologies that were often deemed harmful to architecture. In his rejection of an outright resistance to, or unconditional embrace of, metropolitan forces, one can detect an openness that counters both the rigid *Städtebau* (city building) mentalities of the time and the more definitive modernisms of the 1920s and 1930s.[1] But rather than being merely transitional, his engagement with the metropolis offers an alternative to the categorical discourse of modernity as well as a tactical device instructive for architects to come. After all, these insights not only fueled the thoughts of critics and architects in his immediate vicinity, but also resonated in the ideas of an urban architecture that would captivate later generations: from Ludwig Hilberseimer's *Großstadtarchitektur* to the Office for Metropolitan Architecture.[2] By beginning with Scheffler's theories, this chapter presents an alternative trajectory within architectural modernism and beyond, one that is not predicated on the narratives of tectonics, functionalism, or technology, but on architecture's profound relationship with the modern and contemporary city.

Construction at Museum Island, Berlin, 1911. Photograph of excavation works revealing existing networks and historical layers of the city.

Karl Scheffler's Metropolitan *Spielraum*

Berlin was the stage on which Scheffler saw the tensions of modernity play out. As a city of asymmetry, difference, and multiplicity, Berlin was self-conscious about its potentials, unsentimental in its attitude toward culture, obsessive about technology, unapologetic in its taste for progress, ironic about its lack of history, and uncritical yet passionate in its optimism.[3] "Nowhere," Scheffler further argued, "is the character of modern building art—in positive and negative terms—more instructive."[4] *Berlin – ein Stadtschicksal* (Berlin – destiny of a city), his first book to focus entirely on the modern city, appeared in 1910 during a time when Berlin's new metropolitan culture was becoming accustomed to a recently constructed modern environment. As Scheffler recalled in retrospect: "Never was Berlin more loved for its lifestyle and more hated for its cultural irresponsibility as in these years."[5] Cultural irresponsibility was for Scheffler a highly problematic yet unavoidable trait of metropolitan urbanity. In fact, the book detects in Berlin's recklessness the origins for its urban modernity. Torn between the problems and productivities of the modern city, Berlin embodied a dualism that he viewed as its destiny, "condemned always to become and never to be."[6] The never-ceasing incompleteness of modernity was for Scheffler most clearly expressed in Berlin's imminent and always pending urbanity. He saw this city that "overnight" had become a metropolis as the incubator for all things modern. Here, the quintessential conditions of modernity, which Charles Baudelaire defined as "transitory, fugitive, and contingent,"[7] joined a formless urban maelstrom that was in a perpetual state of advancement, persistently striving toward culmination without the possibility of ever reaching it.

When describing Berlin as "an accidental configuration, which unlike other cities can only with difficulty be understood as a whole,"[8] Scheffler recognized a core problem for architecture's engagement with modern urbanity. With the emergence of the metropolis, the city as a coherent entity ceased to exist, which called into question historical forms of urban analysis and design. To position architecture and urbanism in relation to the modern city, a place that may never again form an entity, would become Scheffler's most daunting task. His deep-seated skepticism of the formless city rendered any attempts to accept the urban condition impossible, yet rejection of the existing state of urbanization was equally unfeasible.[9] His work, therefore, remained continuously suspended in the tension between the tribulations and promises of the modern city. For similar reasons, placing Scheffler's work in relation to conventional readings of modernity has proved to be challenging.

Late-twentieth-century interpretations of Scheffler's frequent analysis of the incompatible elements of modernity reveal a longing for synthesis and an attempt to formulate a new (and ultimately problematic) historical continuity. The critical histories of Manfredo Tafuri and Francesco Dal Co, for example, cite Scheffler's alleged "optimism," reading him as protégé of the capitalist metropolis; Massimo Cacciari saw Scheffler as an urban romantic who sought a new synthesis; and Julius Posener interpreted him as "*Anbeter der Macht*" (an admirer of power).[10] Scheffler's writings on the metropolis, however, rarely resolve any of the incompatibilities he identified—the one between architectural form and urban formlessness, for example, remained dynamic. On the contrary, Scheffler's ideological dilemma manifested in the constant tension between irresolvable dichotomies. The writing always oscillates between dualisms, such as order versus chaos, emptiness versus saturation, purity versus multiplicity, boundary versus margin. In this regard, even as others sought to resolve the tension between modern urban dichotomies, they remain dynamic in the writings of Scheffler. It is this conceptual dynamism that enabled his reevaluation of these urban conditions and with it the formulation of a highly original interpretation of the metropolis. For Scheffler, an effective engagement with the modern city demanded new forms of analysis that departed from common notions of urban coherence and instead had to arrive at an understanding of seemingly accidental and fragmented urban environments. His study of the city became an effort to achieve an unobstructed view of urbanization by disclaiming notions of common aesthetic values.

Georg Simmel's influential essay "Metropolis and Mental Life" is instructive here. Just seven years before Scheffler's book on Berlin appeared, Simmel had called for a new study of the modern city in which "the process of the currents of life, whether their individual phenomena touch us sympathetically or antipathetically, entirely transcend the sphere for which the judge's attitude is appropriated.... [I]t is not our task to accuse or to pardon, but only to understand."[11] Unlike most of his contemporaries, Simmel in his analysis of the metropolis and of modernity itself never resolved the conflicts that he identified between objective and subjective spirit, between individualism and individuality, and between class struggle and urban high culture. On the contrary, he saw it as impossible to synthesize these concepts and instead interpreted modernity as a continuously evolving landscape of contrast and difference. The dialectics between the contrasting themes of the modern city, he argued, are never solved—becoming instead the characteristics of an environment that one could no longer approach through common judgments. Both theories, Simmel's urban sociology and Scheffler's metropolitan history, understand the modern city's condition of formlessness and turmoil as historically given. But whereas for the sociologist "understanding" was the aim of urban analysis, Scheffler sought to expose not only the city's current condition but also its destiny. This meant investigating tendencies within the modern city in order to identify trajectories for new urbanisms to come.

Studying the map of Berlin and noting its "*Formlosigkeit*" (formlessness), Scheffler commented on "the lack of any clear structure."[12] What August Endell had identified as a city without form reappears in Scheffler's work as an un-designed urban territory. Siegfried Kracauer later described it as a city coming into being "wherever the distinct interests of masses of stone and streetscapes collide... [moments that] doze through time unconcerned about their image."[13] Seeing the city as influenced by the formless, Simmel observed "a struggle of life against form itself" and noted "the moralists, those who praise the old time, and the people with strict convictions for style are correct when they complain about the increasing 'formlessness' of modern life." But, he was quick to reply, "they do overlook that what happens is not only the negative breakdown of traditionally transmitted forms, but that a rather positive urge for life is discarding these forms."[14] Here, the breakdown of traditional forms is both problematic and life-affirming, a position that Scheffler had already incorporated.

Introducing terms such as "*instinktiv*" (instinctive), "*offen*" (open), and "*zufällig*" (by chance)—terms that suggest an urbanity that is unplanned, un-designed, and unfinished, a "formless" conglomerate created by dispersed forces—helped Scheffler formulate a theory in opposition to traditional idealizations of the city. He was equally fascinated by the formless as an expression of the plasticities of modernity in all their fragmented, all-encompassing, and constantly morphing nature. Even more dramatically, he defined the city as indifferent, a "lax and faceless me-

Map of the city center, Berlin, 1910. Published in the same year as *Berlin – ein Stadtschicksal*; Scheffler likely referred to such a map when speaking about Berlin's irregular layout.

Bülowstraße 70, Berlin, 1905. The photograph captures the moment when an elevated train drives through a housing block.

tropolis (*physiognomielos*)" with a "willingness to receive everything that is new—whether it be good or bad."[15] But in Scheffler's eyes, it is exactly this indifference that allowed Berlin to become a paradigm for modernity. On the one hand, indifference created an undefined urban image for Berlin that lacked the sophistication of older cities, while on the other, it fostered unconditional openness toward modern inventions. In other words, Berlin's carelessness about its appearance was a prerequisite for its total devotion to everything modern. As the city "without physiognomy" grew exponentially, so "grew its formlessness into something fantastical."[16]

The unplanned, tumultuous, and ever-changing metropolis was not only propelled by modernization, but also served as the source of a new kind of architecture. In fact, for Scheffler, architectural inventiveness occurred not in spite of the formless metropolis, but "especially because urban formlessness created *Spielraum* (room to maneuver) for unlimited possibilities," making the city the essential springboard for spatial and organizational imaginings.[17] Just as Walter Benjamin would later find that the "decay of the aura in works of art is matched by a huge gain in the scope for play [*Spiel-raum*],"[18] so did Scheffler hope to find new possibilities in the metropolis. Associating the term "formlessness" with "*Spielraum*" (the latter literally translating as "room for play" but also understood as leeway, margin, scope, elbow room, or room to move) opened new possibilities in the terrains of the modern city.

Already by the end of the nineteenth century, art historians such as August Schmarsow and Heinrich Wölfflin had made use of the term to stress the importance of bodily experience for the sense of space in architecture.[19] In 1912, Adolf Loos and the journalist and playwright Karl Kraus expanded on the term by calling for recognition of a difference between art and utilitarian objects, saying that "it is this distinction above all that provides culture with *Spielraum*."[20] According to Kraus, their practice was entirely devoted to identifying this alternative space. For them, *Spielraum* was an essential component of urban and architectural culture, without which the environment would be swallowed by either the artistry of *Jugendstil* or the rationalism of the Werkbund. Faced with Germany's increasing militarization and rationalization of urban life, critics sought to counter these tendencies, troubled by the demands for predictability and order. For the poet Karl Wolfskehl, an early acquaintance of Endell, room needed to be given to possibilities and accidents in an ever more rational world. Wolfskehl wrote: "The elimination of chance ... [and] the creation of order ... destroys the true *Spielraum*. No, no, it is certain: without a trace of the 'unexpected,' life cannot exist."[21]

What all of these uses of *Spielraum* have in common is their intimate relationship to *Denkraum* (room to think) and *Bewegungsfreiheit* (freedom to move)—terms that in essence liberate traditional thinking and movement, suggesting the possibility of discoveries within a newly gained space. Film historian Miriam Bratu Hansen's analysis of theories on early cinema already identified in *Spielraum* an "intermediary zone not yet fully determined in which things oscillate among different meanings, functions, and possible directions." And for that, it holds "an interval of chance, imagination, and agency."[22] Therefore, the introduction of the concept of *Spielraum* into urban theory comes as no surprise. It designated a realm in which to account for new forms of metropolitan space. The "*planlos*" (unplanned), inarticulate, and varied sites of the city became the zone in which alternative conditions could develop and where architectural paradigms could emerge. As much as the formless city was problematic, associating it with an expansion in *Spielraum* made the metropolis the very source for a new kind of architecture—one that developed in the latitudes of the modern city. Here, the crisis of urban form enabled architecture's reevaluation through an intentional shift in attitude that sought to discover potentials in the existing metropolis. The idea of the city swung from negative to prospective, and engagement with the city moved from oppositional to opportunistic. Forces of the metropolis, previously seen only as frightening, now held the possibility for an architecture sparked by the provocations of the metropolis.

The understanding of the existing city as essential for architecture set this particular modern project on a course very different from that of more well-rehearsed models. Unlike in the work of Hermann Muthesius, for whom modern expression was first and foremost a tectonic understanding of purposeful forms, modern architecture became deeply rooted in the modern city. In an article in *Die Neue Rundschau*, Scheffler announced that "the spirit of the metropolis will build a new body of architecture," making the modern city not an end in itself but the beginning in the development of a new form of building.[23] To develop this alternative trajectory, theorists who engaged the productivities of the modern city outside the discourses of architecture and city planning, which were primarily concerned with solving the so-called metropolitan problem, were highly influential.

Walther Rathenau in his ironically titled essay "Die schönste Stadt der Welt" (The most beautiful city in the world, 1899) had provided an oblique yet productive reworking of Berlin's "problems" that resulted from the city's particular modernity. Arguing that modern "Berlin did not grow but transform," Rathenau suggested that the city had not organically evolved over time, but rapidly mutated into a construct driven by modern forces of mechanization and spectacle.[24] The essay pairs harsh criticism of matter-of-fact urbanity, architecture, and culture with a determined affection for progress. Rathenau, himself a product of the modern me-

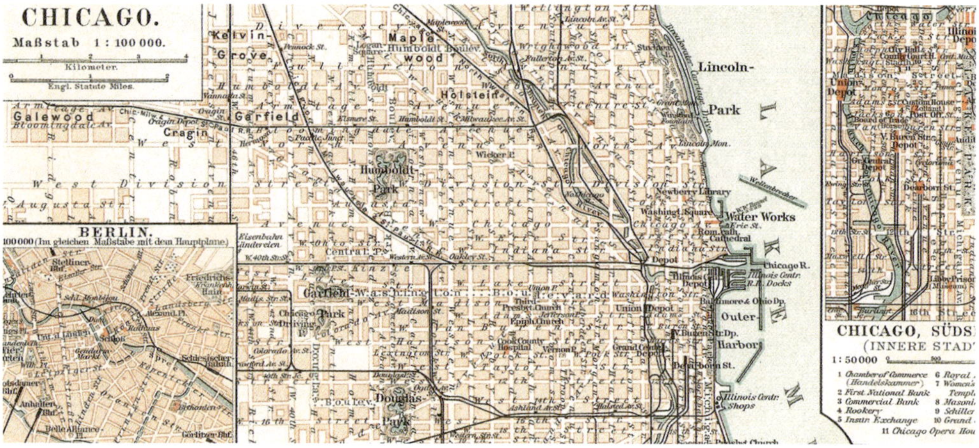

Map of Chicago with added comparative map of Berlin, printed by Meyers, Leipzig, Germany (1900). To German travelers on their journey through Chicago, the map acted as a constant reminder of the affinities between the two cities.

tropolis (an industrialist, politician, and later statesman), complicated common debates on matters of urbanity by arguing that a "city can be beautiful ... even if entirely without beautiful building-art." He added, "Berlin, after all, makes use of this right."[25] Here, Berlin is understood as a new kind of city lacking conventional beauty but possessing an intense urban environment that captivates nevertheless. To communicate the city's unique condition, Rathenau presented Berlin as the most American of all European cities and summarized it with the now famous words: "Athens on the river Spree is dead, yet Chicago on the Spree is rising."[26] A new Berlin had emerged that no longer conformed to traditional European conventions. Instead, the American city, and Chicago in particular, became the comparative model for grasping Berlin's development that otherwise remained mysterious.

A decade later but with equal drama, Scheffler criticized "Berlin's Americanism" by describing the city as "the capital of all modern ugliness" and noting its willing embrace of modern economy, industrial culture, and fast-paced urbanity.[27] This echoed Rathenau's descriptions of Berlin as "the first Americanized city in Germany and the most rigorous in Europe."[28] While many were surprised that the quintessential American metropolis could be the model for Berlin, the turn of the century had seen insiders and outsiders alike presenting Chicago as a city through which to better understand the German metropolis. Visitors from the US such as Mark Twain, who knew Berlin from descriptions in books, recognized Chicago when arriving in the capital. For Twain, "Berlin had disappeared" and reemerged as the "European Chicago." The two cities competed in their flatness, swiftness, constant growth, and newness—with Berlin the victor in the last measure. Twain wrote that Berlin was "the newest city [he] has ever seen," making "Chicago seem venerable beside it."[29] In Berlin, the streets were wider and straighter than anywhere else, buildings were "architectural Gibraltars," and the bureaucratic organization was unmatched. It was as though Twain were outlining an architecture of the metropolis.

Burnham & Root, Drawing of the Monadnock office building, Chicago, 1889. The architects envisioned the building volume to stand in sharp contrast to the surrounding, low-rise structures.

Both Twain and Scheffler hinted at the construction of an alternative city driven no longer by history, culture, or form, but by the acceleration of metropolitan forces. This condition brought about an entirely new urbanity—one that the cultural and urban critiques of sociologists such as Werner Sombart, Ferdinand Tönnies, and Max Weber addressed.[30] After traveling to the US as delegates at the Congress of Arts and Science, organized in conjunction with the World's Fair in St. Louis in 1904, their observations on the "monstrous city" of Chicago gave way to predictions on how Berlin might develop.[31] Tönnies, in particular, dwelled on the city's lack of an extensive urban history, which, unlike in most European cities, made an embrace of modernization possible.[32] In fact, local architects within Chicago had already summarized the productivities of this apparent lack of urban history. John Wellborn Root, of Burnham & Root, spoke during a lecture of an "America [that is] free of artistic tradition." He went on: "Our freedom begets license, it's true. We do shocking things, we produced works of architecture ... irredeemably bad; we try crude experiments that result in disaster. Yet somehow in this mass of ungoverned energies lies the principle of life."[33] The lack of history was associated with a freedom that encouraged the surpassing of established norms and conventions. Chicago's urban climate became a zone where metropolitan pressures had suspended artistic and stylistic traditions. For Root, this made a new simplicity and monumentality possible in buildings such as the Monadnock—an architecture driven by the forces of the metropolis.

Scheffler's theory on the capacities of these new conditions soon followed, arguing that the metropolis had brought about spatial organizations, programmatic tensions, and material conditions that fostered the emergence of new architectural paradigms. Influenced by Tönnies's analysis of a "Chicago without history," Scheffler linked Berlin's alleged deficits (having a past but no history, a society but no community, and an industrial culture but no works of art) not only to the youthful cities in what he called the "New World" but also to a metropolitan urbanization that prompted a similarly new architecture. Berlin's lack of history in particular conditioned its "true modernity."[34] After all, the city had catapulted into the metropolitan limelight in record time, growing from a small urban conglomerate in the mid-nineteenth century into an industrial center that by 1871 had become the capital of the German Empire.[35]

The general consensus in the cultural and urban discourse was that Berlin was dramatically different from more established German cities like Munich or Dresden. Scheffler extrapolated from these ideas by viewing Berlin's Americanism as a form of "instinct toward the future." He added: "While, on the one hand, the lack of tradition creates disorder, so it is, on the other hand, responsible for abolishing many harmful historical hindrances and generates absolute freedom of movement (*Bewegungsfreiheit*)..."[36] What the city was lacking—history, traditional culture, and urban form—instead of a deficit became a kind of freedom from these very forces, making room (*Spielraum*) for new experimentation. Berlin became part of the rhetorical comparison that Sombart had previously drawn by referring to the utter difference between Nürnberg and Chicago, only this time Scheffler saw Berlin as having everything in common with the American metropolis.[37] The conflation of the two cities (looking at the metropolis in the US to see what the future might hold for Berlin) enabled Scheffler to predict what he understood to be the city's destiny—a kind of hyper-urbanism fueled by what many viewed as "harmful" urban conditions. The laboratory of the American metropolis enabled the visualization of an accelerated urbanity that forecasted Berlin's very own metropolitan traits.

The population of Berlin doubled between 1871 and 1895, from 820,000 to 1.6 million. As new construction efforts on the outskirts of Berlin failed to accommodate the influx, population density reached its all-time high in 1900 when an average of 29,750 individuals lived on one square kilometer—making Berlin the most densely populated metropolis in Europe. The enormous urban pressures resulted in rapid construction fueled by developers' self-interests. Scheffler rejected the new developments, driven by economic speculation rather than urban consideration, but his intuition suggested that modern urbanity might lead to unexpected ingenuity in new building forms. In his article "Ein Weg zum Stil" (A path to style), he already detected in the apartment buildings of the city a typology that was uniquely attuned to modern life; a standardized floor plan suitable for a more restless metropolitan population was beginning to formulate a new architectural uniformity.[38] His book *Moderne Baukunst* (Modern building art, 1907) similarly records new architectural typologies in the newly built districts, industrial complexes, and infrastructural hubs. At stake was to situate the architectural paradigms that emerged from within the modern city as developments toward a modern architecture.[39] Three years later, Scheffler reiterated this idea in *Berlin – ein Stadtschicksal* by giving historical context to the term "*Großstadtarchitektur*" (metropolitan architecture), which by 1913 had found its way into the title of his book *Die Architektur der Großstadt* (The architecture of the metropolis).

As proof of the architectural power of the modern city, he observed the uniformity, legibility, and emergent typology of apartment buildings under construction and not yet adorned by ornamentation; the straightforwardness of industrial warehouses that seemingly related only to the needs of production and infrastructural conditions; and the department store as a new building type giving expression to commodity culture. With this interrogative dissection of a new metropolitan environment, the work participates in a much larger cultural enterprise. Émile Zola's record of the Parisian department store in *Au Bonheur des Dames* (*The Ladies' Paradise*) in 1883 or Henry B. Fuller's depiction of Chicago's first skyscrapers in *The Cliff-Dwellers* ten years later are examples of the vast body of writing in which new building types carry significant weight—to the point where both novels' characters and plots appear as mere backdrop to the city. The literary realism and naturalism with which these novels explore the new urban world is closely linked to Scheffler's subsequent identification of new building forms and his search for the underlying forces that created them. He began to understand the warehouses, apartment buildings, and department stores as the products of metropolitan trading systems, population surges, urban density, and the spatialization of commodity culture—speaking simultaneously to the formless city and the formative capacities of architecture. This field of relationships, set up between the urban realities of the metropolis and its new architectural paradigms, was later theorized as modernity's creation of "normativity out of itself."[40]

Scheffler, unlike architects of the time but in line with the period's literary figures, intentionally avoided the urge to tame the metropolis and instead worked

Rental housing ensemble, Berlin, c. 1905, in Karl Scheffler, *Die Architektur der Großstadt* (1913), 34. The image captions read: "Rental housing group in Charlottenburg" and below "Bare building frame in Schöneberg, Martin-Luther-Straße."

to associate urban conditions with spatial, programmatic, and material ingenuities that so far had remained unrecognized. In one of his key arguments, he presented two illustrations of large apartment complexes. *Mietskasernen* (rental barracks), as Berliners had termed the tenement housing because of its monotony and inhospitable living conditions, comprised the city's most notorious building fabric. They were responsible for much of Berlin's growth—fostered by rampant speculation, a spike in urban population, and a building code that encouraged this typology. Scheffler used the statistic that more than 150 people often occupied one of these houses, originally cited in Werner Hegemann's *Der Städtebau* (City building), to emphasize the density that caused this housing to resemble military quarters. He called upon the city to implement codes reining in the aggressiveness of investors that dominated urban growth. Here, Scheffler both echoed Hegemann's argument for a new form of civic city building and simultaneously found a new urban language for engaging with architecture.

His admiration for the uniformity of these complexes when still unadorned by stucco and ornamentation was not simply a call for modernist simplicity. More importantly, it was a reevaluation of a building type that dominated the urban landscape largely without the discursive impact of architecture. Viewing these homogeneous apartment buildings as a raw mass led to the conclusion that the entire urban block should be considered as one, and the massive apartment buildings merged in Scheffler's analysis into even larger ensembles. To visualize the possible coherence of an entire urban block, Scheffler used the image of a warehouse in Hamburg—a structure driven by the loading and unloading of material, the logistics of storage, and the technologies of distribution.

Storage houses, Hamburg, c. 1905, in Karl Scheffler, *Die Architektur der Großstadt* (1913), 36. The image caption reads: "Hamburg, the old storage houses at Admiralitätsstraße in Fleeth (as test for a unified façade constellation)."

Heinrich Tessenow, Row house, Hellerau, Germany, 1912, in Karl Scheffler, *Die Architektur der Großstadt* (1913), 168. The image caption reads: "Worker's row house for a family in Hellerau."

While it clearly participated in the functionalist rhetoric that figures such as Otto Wagner promoted, Scheffler's argument started with observations of the existing city and only afterward extrapolated from these conditions to possible futures for architecture. The anonymity of the metropolis (as witnessed in apartment buildings) within what Simmel would call "objective culture" had provoked a yet undiscovered architecture. It is no coincidence that Wagner at the very same time, in a lecture at New York City's Columbia University, spoke of "city dwellers who today prefer to vanish in the mass as mere numbers on apartment doors."[41] Scheffler was at the center of this debate, formulating a definition that many architects had been waiting for. The anonymity exposed in the new typologies would soon become a driver for a new urban architectural form, expressed in the department stores of Alfred Messel; the factory buildings of Peter Behrens; Endell's urban villas;

the public institutions of Ludwig Hoffmann; Muthesius's houses; the monuments of Hermann Obrist; and the homes of Heinrich Tessenow. Scheffler attributed to these structures a particular engagement with the metropolis even as the architects themselves were often unaware of how their buildings changed the makeup of the city and the role of the architect within it.

At first sight, Heinrich Tessenow's single-family homes (all situated at a distance from the modern city, either in the country or in the early garden city) have little in common with metropolitan architectural characteristics. If anything they appear as antidotes to the turmoil of the city. Yet the austere building surfaces, starved of ornamentation, were also one of the most extreme answers to the tumultuous and inhospitable world around them. The radical blankness of these structures stood against what Tessenow understood to be the lack of form in the metropolis, a condition no longer governed by human intention but merely the result of massive metropolitan interactions.[42] For all his skepticism toward the metropolis, he believed that architecture would soon be more closely linked to the modern city. In an autobiographical note, Tessenow described how by 1902 he had become increasingly convinced "that the architect's profession is tied to the big city and requires a predisposition and character also tied specifically to the big city."[43] Both the forms of architecture and the forms of practice were to change—a challenge that Scheffler directed back at Tessenow by stating: "One is eager to know how the artist [Tessenow] will master the tasks of a metropolitan building art."[44] While anticipating the appearance of Tessenow's work in the metropolis, these projects would be less an example of modern architecture's need for rigorous reduction and more a reiteration of the notion of an architecture that might be able to withstand the modern city without preconditioning its formlessness. The houses of Tessenow stand as clear markers in the quicksand of modern urbanization.

Alfred Messel's Interior Superblock

If Tessenow's homes provided Scheffler with a glimpse of a metropolitan architecture, it was in the work of Alfred Messel, the Wertheim department store in particular, that Scheffler found the most vivid expression of architecture's intimate relationship to the modern city and its spatial and commercial pressures. Designed by Messel and built between 1897 and 1906, the Wertheim department store was one of the largest in Europe. A place for the transient, theatrical, and fantastic experience of commerce, it became a key project for understanding the new architectural paradigm. It represented not only a new building type for a society of consumers but also a new relationship to the city. As the Wertheim store grew more massive and uniform in its different building phases, the store internalized the city, prompting Scheffler to develop his notion of the urban block as a productive extrapolation of the metropolis. While the evolution of the store linked it to the commercially and industrially driven modern city, the spatial outcome was surprisingly inventive.

The department store was a new building type in Berlin.[45] While New York had witnessed the installation of the first passenger elevator in a store on Broadway and Broome Street in 1857, and the iron and glass atrium of Bon Marché in Paris had fascinated customers since 1887, the department store arrived late in Berlin when the Wertheim consortium opened its store on November 15, 1897.[46] Georg Wertheim (one of the brothers who led the commercial endeavor) used the German term "*Warenhaus*" for the new flagship store—literally, a "house of goods"—a word closely related to the English "department store," which denotes the agglomeration of many stores into a single building.

Messel had already designed two shops for the company and saw this development as an opportunity to create a new kind of architecture. In the first building phase, Messel designed a massive glass façade that extended the shop windows over multiple floors and thus visually joined the turmoil of the metropolis with the tumult on the different retail levels. By giving form to the spatial (urban turmoil), economic (commodity culture), and material (glass and iron) forces of the metropolis, Messel had effectively constructed an interface between the metropolis and architecture. The complex spaces of layered shopping floors, connecting bridges, and high courtyards developed as an urbanism of the interior.

Posener's magnum opus on Wilhelmine Berlin and Frederic J. Schwartz's work on the Werkbund point out how Messel's store "was seen as both the architectural event of the decade and as a definitive solution to the problem of developing a representative architecture specifically for new retail institutions."[47] But the opening of the Wertheim store was the event of the decade not just for its importance in architecture; it also introduced an urban construct that would alter the formation and perception of the metropolis from within. As a new urban institution that gave a large number of individuals access and provided them with all essential aspects of urban life, it became a world of its own. From shops, via galleries, to restaurants and photo studios, the Wertheim store imported what metropolitan urbanity had to offer, condensing these different worlds into one spatial amalgam. Emil Claar, a contemporary observer, writer, and poet, described this collision of different environments as "*Die Welt im kleinen*" (A world in miniature), the same phrase that Benjamin cited from the *Illustrated Guide to Paris* when speaking of that city's arcades.[48]

Aerial view of Leipziger Platz and Leipziger Straße, Berlin, c. 1930. The Warenhaus Wertheim is at the center of the photograph, with its façade along Leipziger Straße and turning the corner into Leipziger Platz.

The typology—a product of the nineteenth century, a time when new production quantities coalesced with an accelerated consumer culture—had no explicit forerunners, and yet these large interiors did not arrive overnight. Benjamin, in his unfinished *Passagen-Werk* (*Arcades Project*), famously elaborated on the evolution of the department store from the shop in the arcade to become a realm in which consumers began to consider themselves as part of the mass. From the city as a landscape to the city as a room, "the department store ... puts even flânerie to use for commodity circulation."[49] Modern shopping was closely associated with such nineteenth-century forces as urban population growth, the proximity of public and commercial space, the mass production of goods, the division between producer and consumer, and the use of new materials. Streets lined with shop windows had already amplified the spatial effects of commodity culture in the city, where one no longer had to enter a store but could stroll past goods now publicly displayed behind glass. The Rue de Colonnes (1793), which combined an Italian arcade street with the commercial concentration of Paris, enabled strolling and shopping to take place in any weather. For the Parisian arcades at the beginning of the nineteenth century, the use of glass and iron was of pivotal importance. The

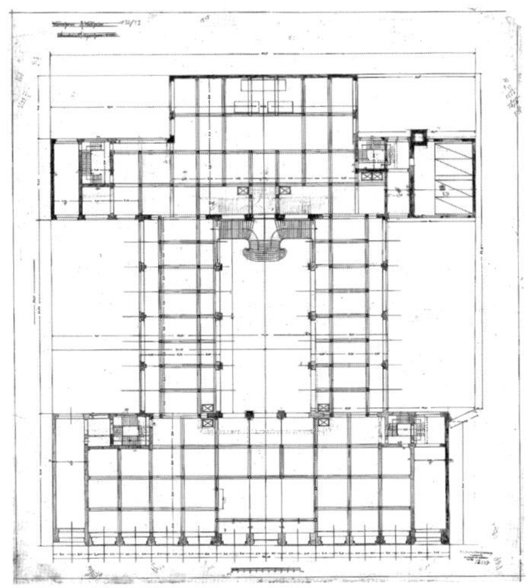

Alfred Messel, Warenhaus Wertheim, Leipziger Straße, Berlin, 1896–1904. Floor plan of the first building stage with a light court (above) and floor plan of the final building stage with expansions of the store along Leipziger Straße and Leipziger Platz, Berlin (below). The configuration of the first building stage from 1896 can still be seen in the lower right-hand corner.

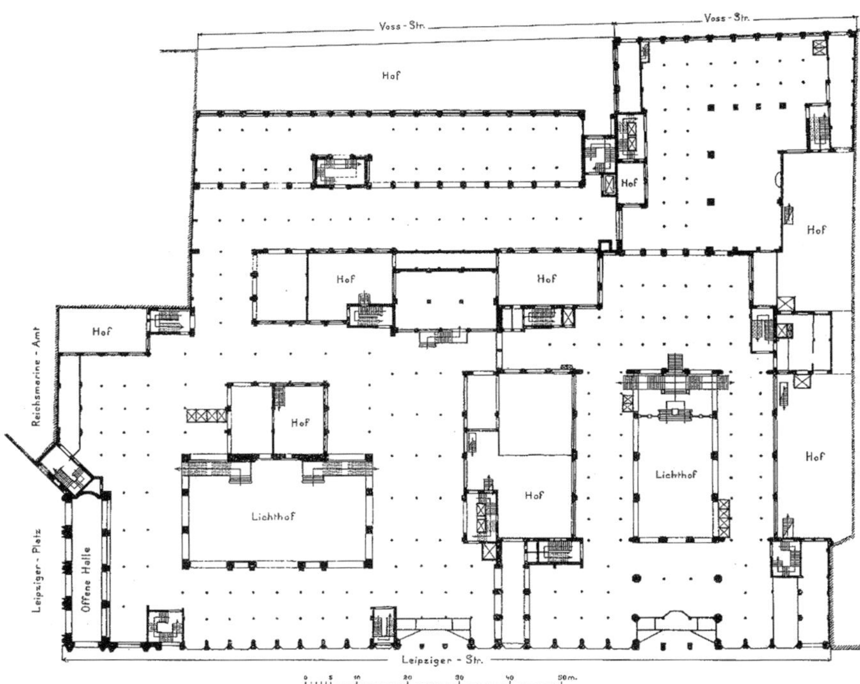

Passage Delorme (1808) emulated and interiorized pedestrian streets, and the 1820s brought the enlargement of these interior spaces into glass-covered courtyards and markets in the centers of the blocks. The new lightness and transparency of such locations as the Bazar de l'Industrie (1827) and the Galeries du Commerce et de l'Industrie (1837) was outdone only by Joseph Paxton's building for London's Great Exhibition of 1851, aptly named "The Crystal Palace."[50]

The spatial development of retail architecture resembles an incremental engulfment: from shops lining the perimeter of the block, to the extension of these spaces into arcades, to the occupation of the entire urban block by the department store. While the interiorization of the city began in the arcades, it was only the department store that captured the entire urban block as a single entity. Over the course of the nineteenth century, the specialized terrain of shopping (designed to handle large crowds demanding mass-produced goods) displaced the diversity of the urban block, which had been composed of housing, retail, and, with less frequency, manufacturing. The expansion of the Wertheim store was a dramatic display of this evolution. Moving to its final location in 1892, the store began by renting four stories of a building at Leipziger Straße 111 for its flagship store; only four years later did its owners ask Messel to design its expansion.[51] The first building stage, which included an unprecedented glass façade as well as a large glass-covered courtyard, was soon superseded as the floor space more than tripled, with retail areas arranged around two large and six small additional courtyards in the final stage.

Messel, however, was not comfortable with his own design, an unease implied in his avoidance of the same openness for later façades. As one of his contemporaries recalled, the architect "was deeply shocked when he saw emerging the naked pillar system of the Wertheim façade."[52] Messel was baffled and maybe even frightened by the scale, transparency, porosity, and complexity of the realization of his store design—a kind of architectural "outcast" that perfected the instrumentalization of technology and the spatialization of commerce. In 1900, Berliners saw Messel's radical façade carried even further when the Tietz department store, designed by Bernhard Sehring, opened its doors; Sehring conceived a seemingly free-hanging prototypical curtain wall that minimized subdivisions—a design explicitly geared toward the demands of shopping. But perhaps it was less the alliance with commerce than the shifting role of architectural design that unsettled Messel. The Wertheim façade likely appeared to him as an artifact of his loss of control over the design and construction process. Involuntarily surrendering that control to the forces of modernity required him to jettison previous aesthetic considerations and adopt a more rational design procedure, in order to address the exigencies of this new building type. Commercial and programmatic pressures had produced an organizational construct that abbreviated artistic gestures so as to amplify the conditions of the department store as an instrument for shopping.

Whereas Messel lamented the pragmatism that the Wertheim store required, Scheffler justified the expediency that the modern metropolis had provoked. Speaking more explicitly to the Wertheim building façade, Scheffler wrote in *Moderne Baukunst*: "The sight of the façade frightened even the most courageous ... but its logic was disarming. Stone and iron were finally accepted as materials for retail buildings, the separation into different floors disappeared, [and] the soaring pillars created a unified whole."[53] For Scheffler, the Wertheim store was the expression of a new architecture that, unlike any other, had embedded itself within the modern city and was equipped to fulfill the demands of the metropolis. Messel was the first to "understand the very being of the metropolis," Scheffler argued. "While his academic colleagues tried to cover it up through stylistic lies, he attacked the metropolitan problem at its core. He gave a new beauty to the new *Notwendigkeit* (necessity) of our time."[54] Opening the entire façade as a glass surface, divided merely by widely spaced piers, not only offered passersby an unapologetic view of the interior, but also exposed the city's speed to those who looked out from the vantage of the shopping floors. The pillar system that vertically joined all stories (which had shocked Messel and "frightened ... the most courageous")[55] opened a large window into both worlds, the city and the store—exposing the building's function and the city's turmoil.

Alfred Messel, Warenhaus Wertheim, Leipziger Straße, Berlin, c. 1898. Detail of the exterior façade from the first building stage, allowing views into the interior shopping floors.

On opening day, the first shoppers witnessed from the inside what local newspapers described as a massive traffic jam on Leipziger Straße, created by a crowd of amazed eyewitnesses whose gazes were drawn into the shop's interior. In a contem-

Alfred Messel, Warenhaus Wertheim, Leipziger Straße, Berlin, c. 1900. Postcard of the interior view from the second building stage with a light court.

porary description of the glass façade, theologist Paul Göhre, later a politician and ally of Friedrich Naumann, observed in 1907: "The entire interior with its masses of goods, masses of shoppers, and flocks of sales personnel is fully revealed to the passerby."[56] Göhre was struck by the reciprocity between inside and outside, which went far beyond a conventional visual exchange. It affected the spatiality of both realms: the city was subjected to the spectacles of the shopping interior, and the interior captured the dynamics of the city. Writers of widely circulating popular textbooks on architecture went so far as to describe the store through analogies with urban flow: "[It] should accommodate large pedestrian traffic without congesting the building or endangering its users."[57] Here, the traditional boundary between city and interior acquires a new reading in which the store's interior essentially belongs to the city. The ether of the metropolis has fully penetrated the interior of the urban block, letting a new kind of urbanism emerge—an urbanism of the interior.

By designing multiple routes through the space in order to facilitate "easy access" and "avoid congestion," Messel spatially linked the different departments with bridges that crossed the courtyards at multiple levels. The complexity was heightened by installing adjacent bridges at different scales, making use of a perspective trickery that suggested a depth exceeding the spatial possibilities of the

Alfred Messel, Warenhaus Wertheim, Leipziger Straße, Berlin, c. 1900. Photographs of the roof terrace, the tearoom, the specialty department, and the winter garden.

building. Posener has already compared this spatial impossibility with Giovanni Battista Piranesi's *Carceri*, where subterranean vaults, stairs, bridges, and machinery inhabit a realm of layered complexity.[58] What Posener called a "spatial exaggeration," the Wertheim store delivered with similar elements, but drawn from the modern city. The delirium of the metropolis, brought about by the acceleration occurring in all areas of urban life, here formed associations with the experience of shopping, making it part of the "everyday" within what Simmel called the "fragmentation" of modernity.[59]

The store was the backdrop against which other programs were projected. It offered a roof garden for relaxation, a library, an art gallery, a tourist information center, a photo studio, a theater ticket agency, and several restaurants—catering to different types of metropolitan individuals in addition to shoppers. The flâneur, the tourist, the intellectual, the detective, and the collector would all feel at home.[60] The Wertheim Emporium thus earned its position as the first Berlin address listed in the *Baedeker Travel Guide*, which notes that the store "well repays a visit [and] no one needs to make any purchase."[61] Another guidebook, *Berlin für Kenner* (Berlin for connoisseurs), puts it even more bluntly: upon arriving in Berlin, all visitors should go to the Wertheim store, where one would "get one's first taste of the tremendous whirl of city life."[62] One might have expected that formal examples of historical or cultural monuments such as the Brandenburg Gate would be the recommended initial stops for tourists; instead guidebooks endorsed the Wertheim store as the starting point for visitors to the metropolis. The department store by some measure had surpassed the metropolis in its capacity to fascinate. The interior city of the store was more "Berlin" than any actual street, traffic intersection, monument, or plaza could ever be. It became the perfect extension of the oversaturated city, where traffic jams could be simulated, light and sound effects tested, engineering works realized, trends instigated, dreams stimulated, and desires satisfied.

For some critics, however, the framing of the Wertheim store's interior pandemonium was less than ideal. Scheffler criticized the excessive use of different materials and complicated details, and argued instead for stripped down interiors in which "the hustle and bustle (*Treiben und Wogen*) around the shopping counters would become the ornament" of the department store interior.[63] Noting that shoppers and sales personnel would roam among the displays of goods at different speeds, clustering in some areas and dispersing in others, Scheffler believed that these movement patterns alone were sufficient to embellish the space. For him, the transitory effects commonly associated with life in the modern city would facilitate the imagining of an architecture for the metropolis. Movement (slow or fast) was no longer limited to the crowded streets, but had entered the department store through the streams of consumers exploring the different floors. In fact, police reports show that the shopping public frequently congested certain locations to such an extent that the municipality fined the Wertheim store for overcrowding.[64] It was this fluid ornament of pedestrian flow—not the coordinated "mass ornament"—that animated the spaces. The "restless movement" of Robert Musil's protagonist in his unfinished novel *Mann ohne Eigenschaften* (*Man Without Qualities*, 1930–1942) was the embodiment of Wertheim shoppers, whereas the silent film by Walter Ruttmann, *Berlin – Die Sinfonie der Großstadt* (*Berlin: Symphony of a Great City*, 1927), supplied the visual score.

While Scheffler's fantasy of an interior that would celebrate the movement of shoppers was never fully satisfied (the lush detailing and cacophony of forms associated with the representation of goods continued to obscure the readability of pedestrian flow patterns), he had to acknowledge that the store's interior had become part of the city. In fact, popular sources were quick to give voice to the new city-architecture relationship that architects and planners had overlooked. In 1912,

Film stills of Walter Ruttmann, *Berlin – Die Sinfonie der Großstadt,* 1927. The film documents a day in the life of the metropolis of Berlin, and the camera frequently shows store windows and scenes of department stores, including the Warenhaus Wertheim. The film culminates in scenes of evening traffic going past glass façades.

Berlin für Kenner notes that visitors ought to return to the scene in the evening. Standing on the upper deck of omnibus number five as it passed the store, riders would "experience the incredible vision offered of a mass of people in motion, of lights and speeding vehicles."[65] Here, the distinction between the city and the store collapses into a mixture of forms and effects, merging the movements and lights of the interior with those of the traffic outside. Not only did the store reproduce the metropolis in the interior, but it also spilled back into the city through its material effects. The store's transparent and reflective glass façade, the illuminated interior, the regular spacing of the pillars, and the movement of shoppers was tonic to the city in motion. It was this blend of speed, spatial complexity, and play of materials and light that Scheffler believed a "metropolitan architecture" would need to engage. The Wertheim's emergent forms resonated with the multiplicities of urban chaos, giving a new expression to the fractured and formless modern city. Here, metropolitan architecture became understood as a product of modern urbanization—as a city of its own, able to cultivate new forms of urbanity that could leak back into the surrounding milieu.

New building types—associated with the new scale, program, and urban character that was emerging from within the metropolis—provided a consolidated form in the midst of an otherwise formless and disorganized city. Metropolitan typologies such as department stores, warehouses, and apartment buildings were particularly visible as they contrasted with the finer grain of the older city. The impersonal and typical, which Scheffler had already detected in the unfinished and unadorned apartment blocks, came to characterize an architectural form that was defined by its large scale, homogeneous surface treatment, and urban continuity. This was most explicit in the Wertheim store expansion.[66] In only one decade, the department store grew from Leipziger Straße into Leipziger Platz, adding and as-

Karl Friedrich Schinkel, Altes Museum, Berlin, 1822–1830. Perspective view with replanted Lustgarten.

Karl Friedrich Schinkel, Altes Museum, Berlin, 1822–1830. Perspective engraving of the upper vestibule with view across the Lustgarten toward the Royal Palace and the city from the main landing.

sembling a collage of spaces and courtyards behind a regular façade that wrapped its perimeter. Scheffler saw its uniformity as a means for architecture to withstand the formlessness of the modern city, applauding the way in which the façade had become a continuous element and created a unified building block able to accommodate the speed of the metropolis.[67]

In this light, Messel's department store joins the trajectory of an urban architecture that Friedrich Gilly and Karl Friedrich Schinkel had anticipated. The latter devoted much of his work as the city architect of Berlin during the first half of the nineteenth century to the reorganization of the Prussian capital through the positioning of architectural monuments and institutions. Unique to Schinkel's approach was the use of architecture, rather than planning techniques, to facilitate the image and workings of the city: the Altes Museum (1823–1830), the Friedrichswerder Church (1824–1830), and the Bauakademie (1832–1835, now demolished) were all autonomous urban blocks and, simultaneously, calibrations of the urban terrain around them. Most famously, the Altes Museum paralleled the façade of the Royal Palace across the Lustgarten and, by doing so, formed an urban tableau from which to view Berlin. One of the most intriguing representations of the museum shows how the stairs to the upper floor turn the visitors' attention back to the city. But instead of portraying ideal views of urban symmetry and order, the building affords viewers dynamic glimpses past a modern stoa.[68] A more elevated but not more organized view of the city was available to nineteenth-century visitors from the tower of the Friedrichswerder Church, which Schinkel demanded to be open to the public. Eduard Gärtner's panorama painted from this very location shows the roofscape of Berlin punctured by individual monuments such as the Altes Museum and the Bauakademie. The massiveness and clarity of these buildings set them apart from the rest of the city, a juxtaposition that Schinkel clearly anticipated. The existing city was a given, not to be organized by ideal urban configurations of streets and plazas, but to be expressed through an urban architecture that positioned itself squarely within the formless city—a tension that highlighted both the emerging metropolis and architectural form.

By the beginning of the twentieth century, some architects were recognizing that Schinkel's plans resulted "not from spatial concepts, but from physical vol-

Next page: Eduard Gärtner, *Panorama of Berlin I* (above) and *Panorama of Berlin II* (below), 1834. Panoramic views from the roof of the Friedrichswerder Church. The first panorama looks south, showing Schinkel's Bauakademie under construction to the left and the Gendarmenmarkt with Schinkel's Schauspielhaus in the distance to the right. The second panorama looks north and shows the Lustgarten with Schinkel's Altes Museum to the right.

Schloss
Bauakademie

Königl. Bibliothek
Opernhaus
Neue Wache

Kreuzberg
Schauspielhaus

Zeughaus
Sophien kirche
Museum
Garnison kirche
Dom
Marien Kirche
Schloss

umes."[69] Although this insightful observation by Friedrich Ostendorf hints at Schinkel's unique architectural urbanism of massive building volumes, it was paradoxically interpreted as proof that Schinkel's work "had nothing to offer to modern urbanism."[70] At a time when architecture struggled intensely with its lack of control over the city, ideal impositions of city planning and regulation seemed more promising than any architectural form. Scheffler was one of the few to see that Schinkel's urbanism of "physical volumes" in the space of the city pointed toward a different kind of city-architecture and, in turn, a *Stadtbaustil* (city-building style). Furthermore, he argued that Schinkel was responsible for crafting "Berlin as an architectural organism."[71] The utilitarianism, typicality, aloofness, and even dreariness that Scheffler associated with Schinkel's work had created a city of urban architecture in which "the emptiness of this style is not without monumentality."[72]

Contemporaries of Schinkel, such as Franz Kugler, had already detected a new form of urban building in the "clear orderliness" of the Bauakademie.[73] This observation speaks to the uniformity and typicality that the Bauakademie expressed through a continuous building façade wrapping the entire volume. The building, which Gärtner's painting shows to be still under construction, was Schinkel's clearest manifestation of a self-contained architecture, one that gave expression to a new urban culture yet was also able to reorganize the city around it. It lacked the frontality that was customary for contemporary institutions and instead invited commercial enterprises into its confines by treating every façade as equally important and by adding shops to the ground floor. While the Bauakademie owes its position in the prehistory of modernism to its early Prussian use of the frame and infill construction, the lack of a clear front was truly unprecedented for a public building.[74] Without a main façade positioned in the direction of a particular street, monument, or plaza, the building operated as volume within urban space. In the emerging metropolis of Berlin, which from 1825 to 1841 more than doubled its footprint and slowly recovered from the Napoleonic occupation, unified architectural volumes stood as strong figures within an expanding and uneven city.

The notion of the continuous façade, anticipated by these early experiments of Schinkel and later developed in buildings such as the Wertheim store, attracted theorists like Scheffler and critics such as Walter Curt Behrendt. Behrendt, who in 1927 would famously declare modernism's triumph in his book *Der Sieg des neuen Baustils* (*The Victory of the New Building Style*), had in 1911 already completed a dissertation that he dedicated to Scheffler.[75] Entitled *Die einheitliche Blockfront als Raumelement im Stadtbau* (The street wall as unified spatial element in city building), it announces the emergence of an urban architecture of large uninterrupted surfaces that encompassed multiple individual buildings and promoted the city

Karl Friedrich Schinkel, Bauakademie, Berlin, 1831–1836. Perspective engraving from Schloßbrücke, showing the Bauakademie to the left and the Friedrichswerder Church to the right.

block as the new unit for metropolitan space. Individual buildings were to be absorbed into the block so that large urban units emerged, only limited by the four surrounding streets. Clearly, this kind of annexing of multiple buildings or sites within the city and their unification into one mega-block architecture required massive investments of capital, dramatically changing the form and makeup of the city as well as the commercial structures within and beyond it—commerce that was increasingly monopolized and steered by large corporations.

Alan Colquhoun called these large segments of urban real estate "superblocks"—a terminology that stresses the sheer size of this new economic and formal unity within the modern city. For Colquhoun the urban limits of a superblock might take the form of a single building, inscribed by the street pattern, or of multiple structures that leaped over to adjacent blocks to form even larger units. Yet they all shared the driving force of capital, which controlled large urban territories. "It is not simply a new type to be added to the repertoire of the city," he concluded, "but a type of types, whose presence is rapidly destroying the traditional city."[76] The modern economy and the superblock radically altered the existing city, a development in which the Wertheim department store participated. Yet this generation of superblocks also reveals that such alterations do not automatically generate an architectural impasse, but can foster a particular engagement with contemporary conditions that results in architectural innovation. Colquhoun had already hinted at this by citing the multiplicity of programs in Chicago's Auditorium Building by Adler and Sullivan (1887–1889), which created "a new kind of mixed-use building—a sort of microcosm of the city as a whole."[77] More recently, Sarah Whiting productively revised the concept of a superblock urbanism: by looking at Chicago's Near South Side of the 1940s, she noted that even postwar urban developments in the US began to reveal spatial and organizational innovations as well as a "new form of public inter-subjectivity."[78]

In light of this research, the mega-block of the Wertheim store, Scheffler's notion of a unified building block, and Behrendt's call for a continuous façade all construct the parameters of an early definition of the superblock and foreshadow the potentials of a new kind of architectural urbanism.[79] The proto-superblock that was formed in this period would become highly influential. In the decade that followed the completion of the Wertheim store, numerous architects developed this project further. In 1910, Bruno Taut submitted his plans for an expansion of the department store that sought to continue the façade while heightening its verticality.[80] The following year, Hans Poelzig built a fluid architectural façade for the *Geschäftshaus* (retail house) on the Junkernstraße in Breslau that continuously wrapped urban space. Echoing this fascination in his speech at the legendary Werkbund conference of 1914, Behrens called for architectural forms that responded to the increasing speed of the city, an architecture that would result in uniformity and large surfaces.[81] This message was passed on to architects such as Erich Mendelsohn and Hans and Wassili Luckhardt, whose smooth-faced superblocks seem to extend the city infinitely with an architecture that could "appreciate and collaborate with the forces of movement."[82] These uniform and uninterrupted building fronts addressed the dynamism of the metropolis. The seamless urban façades that now surrounded entire urban blocks not only provided enough room for architecture to interiorize the city, but also projected a new metropolis entirely—a city of superblocks.[83]

Erich Mendelsohn, Warenhaus Schocken, Chemnitz, Germany, c. 1930. The Schocken department store replaced the measured vertical structuring that was common to its predecessors with a horizontal striation of the building block, an urban form seemingly smoothed by the speed of passing traffic.

Ludwig Hilberseimer, Hochhausstadt project, east–west street view, 1924. Perspectival drawing that highlights the division of urban circulation while visualizing how architectural volumes penetrate and connect the different layers of transportation.

As keen observers of this development, Scheffler and Behrendt imagined that a new kind of city would form if these trends were pursued. A new metropolis would see individual shops consolidated into department stores and housing units amalgamated into single urban blocks. Both saw the urban unity of buildings such as Messel's Wertheim store and Paul Mebes's apartment blocks in Berlin-Charlottenburg as key examples of a metropolitan architecture that as a collective formed a new architectural urbanism. The coming generation would carry forward what these buildings had set in motion. And indeed, it would need a new kind of architect to fully intuit and engage the forces of the modern city. Scheffler even outlined the nature of this new visionary figure by noting that Messel was still too much an academic to solve the mission of a metropolitan architecture, for its most valuable characteristics were the impersonal and typical.[84]

Ludwig Hilberseimer's *Großstadtarchitektur*

The project of a metropolitan architecture of superblocks found increasingly radical expression in the designs and writings of architects and urbanists in the 1920s and 1930s. Ludwig Hilberseimer took Scheffler's call for an impersonal and typical architecture of the metropolis particularly seriously. Shortly after the arrival of Scheffler's book *Die Architektur der Großstadt* (The architecture of the metropolis) in 1913, Hilberseimer began to meticulously study and expand on the potentials of a metropolitan architecture and the concept of the superblock. In 1914, he outlined an article that was modeled on Scheffler's book (in its argument and structure), to which he gave the identical title "The Architecture of the Metropolis." In this draft, he attacked the chaos of the capitalist city as well as the answers with which architects and engineers sought to combat it.[85] His notes confirm a detailed knowledge of the ideas of Scheffler and Behrendt, whom Hilberseimer mentioned by name as well as citing his book *Die einheitliche Blockfront als Raumelement im Stadtbau*. As they had done, Hilberseimer critiqued the "lack of form and rhythm" in the metropolis, but also identified new forms of architecture expressed in new programs and materials. "The only possibility to emerge from this chaos," he noted, was "the most extreme economy of form ... [and the intent] to work toward the essential."[86] It is, therefore, no surprise that Messel's Wertheim department store, the AEG factory buildings by Behrens, and housing blocks under construction reappear in Hilberseimer's drafted essay. This research would set the direction of his work for the following fifteen years. His analysis of the metropolis and explorations of urban conditions—eventually published in 1927 under the title *Großstadtarchitektur* (Metropolitan architecture)—grew from Scheffler's earlier work. While Hilberseimer's austere urban plans for Berlin reveal little of the potentials of the formless city, his writings disclose how even the most severe work of the modern avant-garde was intimately linked to the contemporary city.

What Scheffler imagined as a metropolitan architecture surely looks different from Hilberseimer's projects, but the conceptual parallels are striking. For both, metropolitan architecture was rooted in the actualities of the modern city and depended on the city's size, population density, emerging building programs, and urban cosmopolitanism. Hilberseimer, however, moved beyond an analysis of the conditions of the metropolis and an identification of possible origins for its state of formlessness, and instead set out to develop strategies to engage the new capitalist city. For him, the "*Planlosigkeit*" (lack of plan) and chaos of the metropolis had to be addressed. Whereas Scheffler alluded to architectural potentials within the formless city, Hilberseimer viewed them primarily as problems, but in turn crystallized these conditions into forms of architectural urbanism.

Building on the typologies that Scheffler had already identified within the metropolis (housing blocks, department stores, and suburban villas), Hilberseimer expanded the catalog of types through a list he started compiling in 1914; it eventually included towers, theaters, transportation hubs, and infrastructural and industrial buildings. He regarded each program through its particularities as a metropolitan typology. Devoting the longest of the chapters to housing, Hilberseimer argued for the importance of this typology in the city and that it had been neglected so far. In fact, for him, housing presented "the actual problem of the architecture of the metropolis."[87] The problem was twofold. On the one hand, residential apartment buildings were primarily derived from the single house, which ignored the multiplicity of units and the size of building lots. On the other hand, the focus on the design of the façade rather than the organization of the volume created what Hilberseimer called "the most grotesque deformations."[88] His solution entailed "the planning of residential buildings according to the blocks defined by the street system."[89] Conceiving of an architecture that encompassed entire urban blocks gave Hilberseimer the opportunity not only to imagine a new kind of urbanism, but also to demand a greater role for collectives and trade unions in the "combining of individual parcels of land into a unified urban block."[90] What Scheffler and Behrendt had previously observed as a trend within the metropolis, yet unrecognized by architects, Hilberseimer now articulated as a design approach—one that extrapolates from the metropolis with the ambition to reorient it away from the individual and toward the collective.

Scheffler's call to infer building types from the existing city found its most radical expression in Hilberseimer's Hochhausstadt (high-rise city) of 1924. While the ever-expanding, gridded urban uniformity of the Hochhausstadt goes far beyond Scheffler's wildest dreams—and nightmares—it does imagine a city of urban continuity and anonymous housing blocks. But deviating from the previous agenda to create individual typologies for commerce, urban housing, and suburban developments, Hilberseimer sought to produce a single typology that housed them all in one. He described it as a layering of different cities—the city of slabs above the city of perimeter blocks.[91] Even as early efforts by CIAM and Le Corbusier continued with a zoned urbanism of designated functional quarters, Hilberseimer created a hybrid urbanism of combined typologies, repeated across the city and containing all elements of urban life. In the Hochhausstadt, the lower city is dedicated to commerce, where each block is a mega-office, workshop, and department store, bounded only by its adjacent streets. Each of the four sides appears to be identical and to continue infinitely in each direction, separated only by the street grid. The scheme expands the urban continuity, previously sought for individual blocks, across the city, trumped only by the infrastructural network that runs below.

Of course, a multi-level urbanity that accommodates the different speeds of the modern city had been part of visionary plans for decades, as shown in the captivating representations of existing buildings, such as the circulation spaces of New York's Grand Central Station of the 1910s. This led architects such as Antonio Sant'Elia to celebrate the velocity of the metropolis in his Futurist *Città Nuova*. Hilberseimer was much more reserved in his incorporation of the different means of traffic. Some saw this as an attempt by Hilberseimer to bury the modernity of the city. However, his suppression of infrastructure and movement, and the foregrounding of architectural forms had to do less with a disdain for the metropolis and more with his ambition to resituate architecture as a means for urbanism. After all, he worried about architecture's retreat into what he called façade design and how traffic engineers increasingly dictated the image of the city. In contrast, Hilberseimer saw the role of architecture in its capacity to build the city and so set out to formulate an architecture that was purely driven by the forces of the metropolis. He embraced projects such as Ludwig Mies van der Rohe's reconstruction of Alexanderplatz (1928) because it "attempts to give form to the plaza solely from an architectural viewpoint through individual buildings, and independently of the traffic routes ..."[92] What mattered was not the planning of the city as such, but the forming of architectural typologies that could act as urbanisms of and within the city. The architectural urbanism in the work of Schinkel found in Hilberseimer's Hochhausstadt an updated diagram.

The level of abstraction and the diagrammatics of the scheme become particularly clear in the location of the residential town, siting apartment slabs above the commercial superblocks, so as to conflate the focus on residential buildings during the Weimar Republic with the commercial emphasis of the Wilhelmine period. Hilberseimer imagined the interface between the lower and upper city as a wide sidewalk that extends into a mega-lobby with access to both the commercial and the residential city, in addition to restaurants and small shops. This elevated ground floor, or sky lobby, enables the combination of different types into a hybrid typology, mixing commercial superblocks with residential *Zeilenbau* (straight row system). Indeed, Hilberseimer seems to have had particular cities in mind when placing one on top of the other. The book lists the greatest number of examples from Berlin and Chicago, prominently featuring the Berlin of Messel's department store and the Chicago of Burnham & Root's Monadnock building. Hilberseimer admired the Monadnock slab for its "unmistakable sense of proportion" and the Wertheim store for "caus[ing] innumerable variations."[93] These notes imply that he did not select the buildings for their functional clarity, as the modernist canon might suggest, but for the way in which the buildings acted as architectural forms within the city.

Others had already recognized both buildings as a powerful blend of forces assembled from the modern city. Chicago designers viewed the Monadnock as a

Ludwig Mies van der Rohe, Reconstruction of Alexanderplatz project, Berlin, 1928. Photomontage of urban space created by architectural volumes. This was the only entry that rejected Martin Wagner's competition specification to transfer the form of the roundabout traffic to the architecture.

manifestation of "a direct singleness of purpose," and Berlin's practitioners were "captivated by [the Wertheim store's] clarity and dignity."[94] In Hilberseimer's scheme, the street-bound volume of the Wertheim store reappears in the five-story commercial blocks of the Hochhausstadt, and the proportions of the Monadnock building emerge in the slender fifteen-story slabs above. The un-ornate façade of the Chicago building was a precursor for Hilberseimer's absolute reduction. While Root battled with the idea of a "brick box,"[95] entirely stripped of any ornamentation due to economic demands (not unlike Messel's struggle with his invention), Hilberseimer no longer had any reservations and instead saw the total reduction of the building surface as a necessity. Thirty-three years after Root's hesitant creation of a new building paradigm, produced directly from the laboratory of the metropolis, the building mammoth has multiplied in the perspectives of the Hochhausstadt. The north-south orientation of the narrow Monadnock block proliferates now as *Zeilenbau* in identical direction across an unending field of building canyons. Even the position of the photographer for the 1891 image of the Monadnock building that Hilberseimer used as an illustration in his book is strangely similar to

Burnham & Root, Monadnock building at Jackson Boulevard, Chicago, 1891, in Ludwig Hilberseimer, *Großstadtarchitektur* (1927), 65. The photograph from 1910 also shows the addition to the building toward the south by Holabird & Roche in 1893.

the viewpoint of the north-south street of the Hochhausstadt. Both force the viewer to float in mid-air—"separated from the city," as Whiting wrote in her analysis of Hilberseimer's drawings, "by a gulf of space."[96]

The two schemes are similar in their seeming solidity, weight, and regularity of window openings. Indeed, possibly the most arresting aspects of Hilberseimer's city are its homogeneity, banality, and even bleakness—characteristics that led Hilberseimer himself to declare later on that the project was "more a Necropolis than a Metropolis."[97] Even so, the scheme points at a radicalization of urban living that follows Wagner's and Scheffler's predictions of metropolitan anonymity. Hilberseimer sought as much distance as possible from the image of the single home and instead built on the program of the hotel, forms of modern mobility, and modern work arrangements in slogans such as "suitcase instead of moving van."[98] The course toward metropolitan anonymity within urban culture becomes in Hilberseimer's drawings a display of the most extreme urban architecture. Scheffler's comments on the darkness and gloom of residential buildings under construction appear in hindsight to forecast Hilberseimer's soberness: "Where buildings are still in their raw form and not spoiled by ornamentation, … there appears a kind of monumentality through dry statistical calculation. They are gloomy and sad and yet full of character." Scheffler even described them as "threatening," a characterization easily mistaken for an account of Hilberseimer's Hochhausstadt.[99]

As urban typicality turns truly dark and menacing in Hilberseimer's scheme, it invites the city into the interior. For pedestrians, this invitation begins in the sky lobby, where the ground floor of the narrow Monadnock building is seemingly pulled across the distance between the two slabs. Acting not just as connective tissue between above and below, the interior street that crosses the Monadnock's narrow ground floor over its entire length (therefore doubling the sidewalk and extending the surface of store windows) is in Hilberseimer's lobby multiplied through the vision of an interior city of small shops, restaurants, and services. Knowing the importance that Hilberseimer placed on Messel's Wertheim store, one can imagine how the life of the sky lobby was to continue into the commercial

Ludwig Hilberseimer, Hochhausstadt project, north–south street view, 1924. Each of the linear housing blocks appears to resemble the Monadnock building's proportion and austerity that Hilberseimer admired.

blocks below. Of course, the infusion of the city into architecture, so clearly built into the Wertheim store, has no place in Hilberseimer's drawings and is only suggested in the descriptions of the scheme. What Hilberseimer avoided drawing would be rediscovered several decades later through the super-interiors of Archizoom, the conceptualization of Berlin as nested cities within a city by Oswald Mathias Ungers, and the theorization of New York's delirium by Rem Koolhaas.

But even for Hilberseimer, Messel's continuous and all-encompassing urban volume was more than just a model for the typology of the superblock. In the argument for his City-Center Development of Berlin, Hilberseimer explicitly cited the Wertheim store as an architectural strategy within modern urbanization. In this less utopian but equally radical scheme, he speculated about the rational reorganization of the city center, moving from individual buildings to architecture that encompassed entire urban blocks. What the Wertheim store had initiated by "successively annex(ing) components ..., which today cover an entire street block," Hilberseimer would develop further in his commercial center with offices, stores, and parking below.[100] The Wertheim store had become an example of what the metropolis had produced and from which architecture had to learn. In *Großstadtarchitektur*, Hilberseimer had repeated Scheffler's argument that "Messel sensed rather than acknowl-

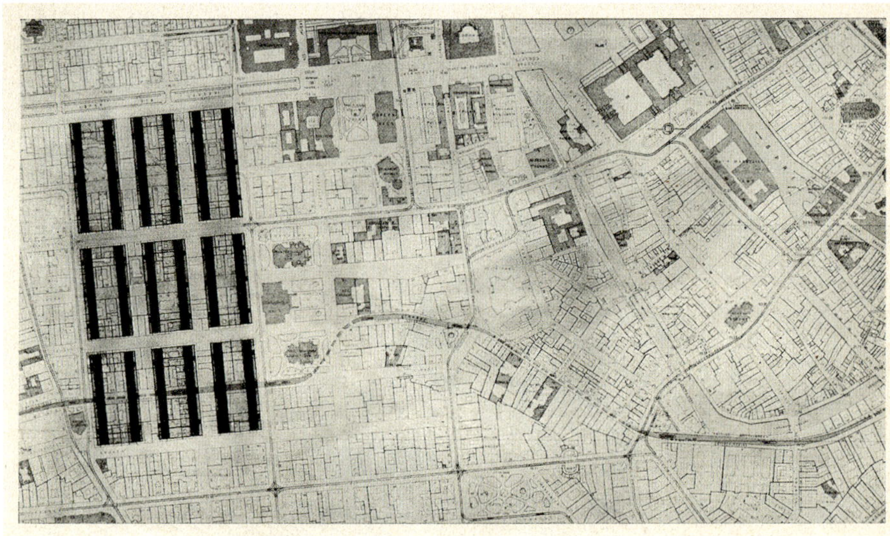

Ludwig Hilberseimer, City-Center Development project, Berlin, 1928–1930. City plan with Hilberseimer's proposal to the left and existing large building structures in dark grey.

Ludwig Hilberseimer, City-Center Development project, Berlin, 1928–1930. Photomontage of aerial view with Hilberseimer's proposal next to the Gendarmenmarkt with Schinkel's Schauspielhaus.

edged the architectural consequences of the constructive principles" of a metropolitan architecture.[101] Hilberseimer now reframed the intuitive design of the Wertheim store as a conscious formulation of an urban architecture. This is an early example of what Albert Pope would recognize in later projects of Hilberseimer as a form of realism and an "attempt to render the salient qualities and characteristics of the emergent urban production."[102]

The aerial photomontage for the Berlin project shows how the nine superblocks are positioned in the midst of the city's center: to the north directly adjacent to the boulevard Unter den Linden, and to the east right next to the Gendarmenmarkt, one of Berlin's most renowned plazas with its French and the German cathedral as well as Schinkel's Schauspielhaus. Many have rightly commented on the shocking juxtaposition between the old city and the superblock architecture, the latter set apart through the scale of its individual components, its expanse in the city, the repetitiveness of its parts, and its materiality or the lack thereof. And, surely, Hilberseimer anticipated the shock value of the scheme. This was not unlike Le Corbusier's staging of the Plan Voisin at the Pavillon de l'Esprit Nouveau at the Paris Exposition of Decorative Art three years prior. But whereas Le Corbusier selected individual monuments to remain as objects amidst the isotropic space of cruciform towers surrounded by highways and parks, Hilberseimer in his design of the City-Center left no space for prior buildings on the site. Instead, the scheme positions the entire area of the new superblocks in relation to the urban monuments of the city neighboring it. Hilberseimer's montage that superimposes the scheme onto an aerial photograph suggests a correlation between the existing city and the proposed urban block dimensions.

Ludwig Hilberseimer, Commercial-Center Development project, Berlin, c. 1925. Drawing of Hilberseimer's design for a commercial building in juxtaposition with a historic structure, connected across the street by a pedestrian overpass.

Hilberseimer had previously conceived of designs that simultaneously juxtapose and link the old parts of the city with the new. Drawings for a commercial center from the mid-1920s dwell on exactly this intersection. Half of the image shows the design for a uniform office block, and the other half displays the dark façade of a historic building. Similar to the photomontages by Mies for the Friedrichstraße Skyscraper and Glass Skyscraper projects, the contrast between the two environments is deliberate and even exaggerated. But Hilberseimer also seems to have been interested in linking the two via a comparable scale and a pedestrian bridge that crosses the street between the two large structures. The size of both buildings is implied through a cropping of the picture frame to evoke how both buildings would continue beyond it. Not only does the montage imply that both structures encompass an entire urban block, but their spatial equality in the city is striking. Reading these studies as possible intersections between the old and the new sheds light on the dramatic juxtaposition in the aerial view of Hilberseimer's Berlin project. It suggests that he read the Gendarmenmarkt as a superblock in its own right, similar to Schinkel's Bauakademie, which is easily identifiable on the right side of the site plan for the project. By drawing attention to existing autonomous building blocks in the vicinity of the proposal, Hilberseimer's City-Center joins a historical lineage that constitutes a new urbanism long in the making.

In the manuscript of 1914, Hilberseimer had already articulated a direct affiliation between the new design and Schinkel's earlier structures. The manuscript views Schinkel as "modern" and in contrast to the nineteenth-century search for style, since he "never forgot to conceive the object outside of convention." The phrase "better from Schinkel to Schinkel" takes on a deeper meaning when viewed in relation to Hilberseimer's Berlin scheme.[103] It suggests that Hilberseimer viewed his project as a direct continuation of Schinkel's urban landscape of freestanding forms. Leaping over the "deviations of the nineteenth century," Hilberseimer's project links back to Schinkel by adding superblocks to Berlin's archipelago of large urban buildings. Hilberseimer's scheme does not rally against the metropolis, but instead selectively reads the history of the city and extrapolates from its tendencies. For Hilberseimer, however, extrapolation would always be an act of radicalization, which made for proposals that could easily be misunderstood as hostile toward the metropolis.

His radical projects during the years of high modernism clearly altered the concept of a *Großstadtarchitektur* as formulated in the 1900s and 1910s, but this iteration also paved the way for more dramatic extrapolations of the city. While the notion of a metropolitan architecture was defunct during the immediate postwar era, the 1960s would see a surge of ideas relating architecture to particular urban conditions. The ideas of Hilberseimer resonated particularly in the Italian circle, where Aldo Rossi sought to articulate an architecture of the city, Giorgio Grassi set out to find principles for the rational construction of types that avoid stylistic expressions, and Tafuri sifted through the history of modern architecture to find projects through which one could understand the processes of architecture rather than the production of objects. "Hilberseimer's work is significant," Rossi wrote in the preface to the second edition of *L'architettura della città* (*The Architecture of the City*) because the study of urban conditions was here dependent on the articulation of a rational architecture and vice versa.[104] For Rossi, Hilberseimer's investment in the city was a precursor to his own definition of architecture, merging the research on urban artifacts with that on form. More recently, Pier Vittorio Aureli emphasized the lineage between Hilberseimer's invention of combined typologies and Grassi's fascination with combinatorial rules leading to new types.[105] Yet the most direct translation of Hilberseimer's mentality toward the city came from the radical collectives that sought alternatives to the historical models of urban architecture promoted at the time. For the Italian Archizoom Associati and their project No-Stop City (1969–1972), Hilberseimer's articulations of an extrapolated urban environment would become the most important point of reference.

Together with the group Superstudio, the collectives would become known as *Architettura Radicale* through two joint exhibitions in Pistoia and Modena, Italy, between 1966 and 1967. The title of the exhibition, "Superarchitecture," communicated the movement's interest in intensifying, even exacerbating, current conditions. Rather than resisting contemporary forces, Superarchitecture embraced them as an "architecture of superproduction, of superconsumption, of superinducement to consumption, of the supermarket, of Superman, of super-high-test gasoline." Even more shocking, Superarchitecture "accepts the logic of production and consumption and makes an effort to demystify it."[106] Exposure of contemporary conditions in the projects of *Architettura Radicale*, however, went further than acts of rendering or critique. In particular Archizoom's No-Stop City—a project with its drawings intended initially for an exhibition in Rotterdam but later published in *Casabella* in 1970 and in *Domus* in 1971—displays an uncanny engagement with reality and a profound relationship to modernists like Hilberseimer. In many ways, Archizoom out-radicalized Hilberseimer. At a moment when design had ruled out modernist concepts, Archizoom achieved escape velocity from entrenched mentalities by intensifying aspects of the modern project. "There was a chance, as a result of the crisis of rationalist modernity," Andrea Branzi, the spokesperson of Archizoom, noted in retrospect, "to go beyond the boundaries of modernity."[107]

He defined No-Stop City as "a mental project, a sort of theoretical diagram of an amoral city, a city 'without qualities,' as Hilberseimer would have described it." And later on he added: "The nihilistic logic of the maximum quantity was the only logic of the system in which we were living; instead of denying this logic, we decided to make use of its inner workings to archive a demystification of all its ideals of quality and ... to carry out scientific research into the real nature of the metrop-

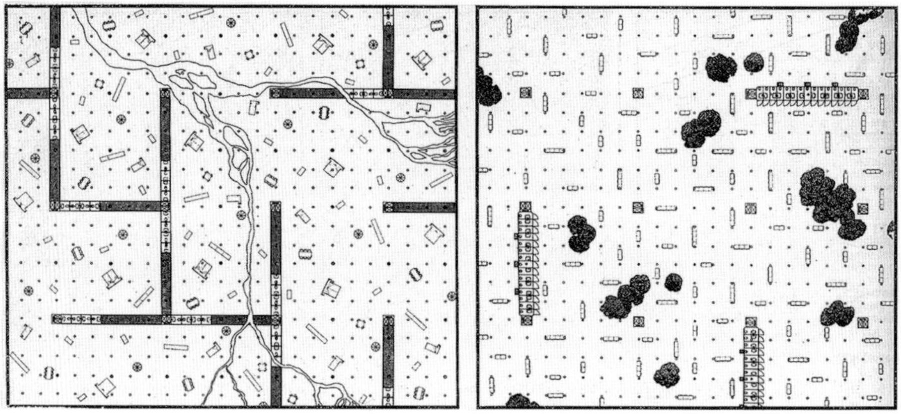

Archizoom Associati, No-Stop City, 1968–1972. Plan configuration of endless interiors.

olis."[108] What Michael Hays identified in the work of Hilberseimer, namely an intensified subject-object dialectic through the reduction of architectural form into serial urban patterns,[109] was for Archizoom already reason enough to define Hilberseimer's city as "amoral." Outlining a city that existed beyond quality was a reference as much to Musil's *Mann ohne Eigenschaften* as to Hilberseimer's organizational urban constructs. The two projects intersected in 1930, when Hilberseimer completed his City-Center proposal and Musil began his magnum opus. Archizoom's project took clues from both, inferring the existing conditions of the capitalist city in order to first lay it bare and then extrapolate from it. While Tafuri's reading of the early work of Hilberseimer was important for Archizoom's rediscovery of these projects, they disagreed on the ways to continue past it. Tafuri saw Archizoom's work pessimistically as "nothing but a provocation for the elite,"[110] whereas Branzi believed the head-on engagement of the contemporary city was the only way to push beyond its current state. The strategy was not to resist any of the existing conditions, but to extrapolate from them until a level of urban surplus brought about a new kind of city entirely. Through Hilberseimer, Archizoom found an alternative (if not a counter-position) to resistance.

Both expand infinitely in all directions by deploying a grid-like organization, where the repetition of the superblock achieves a relentlessness that is so far unmatched. In fact, what makes both schemes possible is the typology of the superblock with its functional hybridity—by holding all aspects of contemporary life, each is identical in appearance in the city. But Archizoom made two important contributions: the group no longer relied on the street-building relationship, and

Archizoom Associati, No-Stop City, 1968–1972. Mock-ups of interiors.

it revealed the interior of locations like the supermarket and the big box store as the new frontier. The exterior is no longer working toward an urban continuity, but rather aims for an entirely undifferentiated sameness. By contrast, the interior is a horizontally layered catalog of differentiated climates that alternate from floor to floor. The perfection of artificial lighting and ventilation makes the city a continuous residential structure (or "a well-equipped parking lot," as Branzi liked to call it), where elevators carry the urban nomads from floors with campgrounds, to laundromats, to dance clubs, and to office landscapes. The interiors have the appearance of big box stores just minutes before opening hour, ready to be inhabited by the contemporary individual who no longer differentiates these interiors from the outside. The plans of No-Stop City, then, effectively call for new forms of inhabiting the city.[111] Similar to the way Scheffler had imagined the hustle in a sea of shopping counters as a new form of inhabitation and an alternative to architectural ornamentation, one that was now spatialized and in motion, so was Archizoom's vision an extrapolation of what exists that is only waiting to be inhabited.

OMA's Hyper-Realism

Hilberseimer's hybrid blocks and the delirium of Archizoom's urban interior landscapes would become essential points of reference in the next iteration of a metropolitan architecture. It is no coincidence that the term reappeared in 1975 in the name of the Office for Metropolitan Architecture (OMA), founded by Rem Koolhaas, Madelon Vriesendorp, Elia Zenghelis, and Zoe Zenghelis. Just as it had for the previous explorations of metropolitan architecture, Berlin would be the primary site of projects during the formative beginnings of OMA. "The Berlin Wall as Architecture" (1971), "Exodus, or the Voluntary Prisoners of Architecture" (1972), and "The City of the Captive Globe" (1972) are all reflections on Berlin even if they prefigure other locations. "Exodus," for example, shows a photocollage where a hallucination of Manhattan appears behind the severity of the Berlin Wall. And even the later analysis of the skyscraper in *Delirious New York* has been credited to OMA's fixations with Berlin.[112]

With Berlin in sight, OMA not only returned to the unique sentiments of a productive metropolis that this chapter identifies in the early development of a metropolitan architecture, but also coupled this mentality with the design inventions of subsequent renditions. In its early work, OMA explicitly positioned itself within this historical trajectory, not so much to give its own project validity, as to direct attention to alternatives within the architectural discourse on the city. This becomes especially clear in the competition entry that OMA submitted to the Internationale Bauausstellung in Berlin (International Building Exhibition, IBA Berlin) in 1980. A key drawing for the housing project on Kochstraße and Friedrichstraße shows the OMA design alongside visionary works, some of them existing and some unbuilt, in an attempt to contextualize OMA's position. The drawing provides a commentary on Berlin's unique history by visualizing a "phantom Berlin" that does not depict reality so much as visualize the power of architectural imagination. It selectively situates OMA's project amidst Hilberseimer's proposal, the Gendarmenmarkt with Schinkel's Schauspielhaus, the glass skyscraper on Friedrichstraße by Mies, Mendelsohn's Headquarters for the German Metallurgic Federation, and the Berlin Wall. While all of these projects resonate in the work of OMA, Hilberseimer's early explorations of metropolitan architecture take on particular meaning.

Seemingly quoting from Hilberseimer, OMA's description for the scheme noted: "A project for Kochstraße/Friedrichstraße should impose a conceptual framework, beyond the literalness of the street plan, that relates the existing buildings."[113] Just as Hilberseimer had called for an urbanism that gave form to the city via architecture rather than infrastructure, so was OMA determined to find an architectural "framework" that could do more in the city than simply align itself with the street. This quotation was literalized in one area of the design along Friedrichstraße (Block #7), where OMA imported the parallel slabs of Hilberseimer's City-Center proposal and let them collide with existing buildings. The appropriation of this earlier work was an attempt to diverge from the respected ideal formalism of the historic city as well as from the social utopias of modernism. At stake was an architectural urbanism that both Hilberseimer and OMA found in the notion of a metropolitan architecture; for Koolhaas it presented one final opening for architecture to reclaim a constructive role within the city. Not only was the modernist project worth revisiting—and its lessons on urbanism appealing—but even the characteristics of the metropolis held values that were productive for the contemporary city. At the time, this could not have been more in opposition to the widely held skepticism toward modernist ideas, driven by modernism's problematic relationship with technology, its unfulfilled dreams of social change, and the reevaluation of urban life that had been substantially affected by the modernization of postwar reconstruction and urbanization.

The entry for Kochstraße/Friedrichstraße vividly documents the opposition between OMA's deployment of modernist strategies and the urban language that the IBA envisioned under the rubric of "*Stadtreparatur*" (city repair). For Hans Stimmann, the senator in charge of Berlin's construction efforts, "repairing the city" was an effort to reconstruct the original layout of Berlin's Baroque expansions.[114]

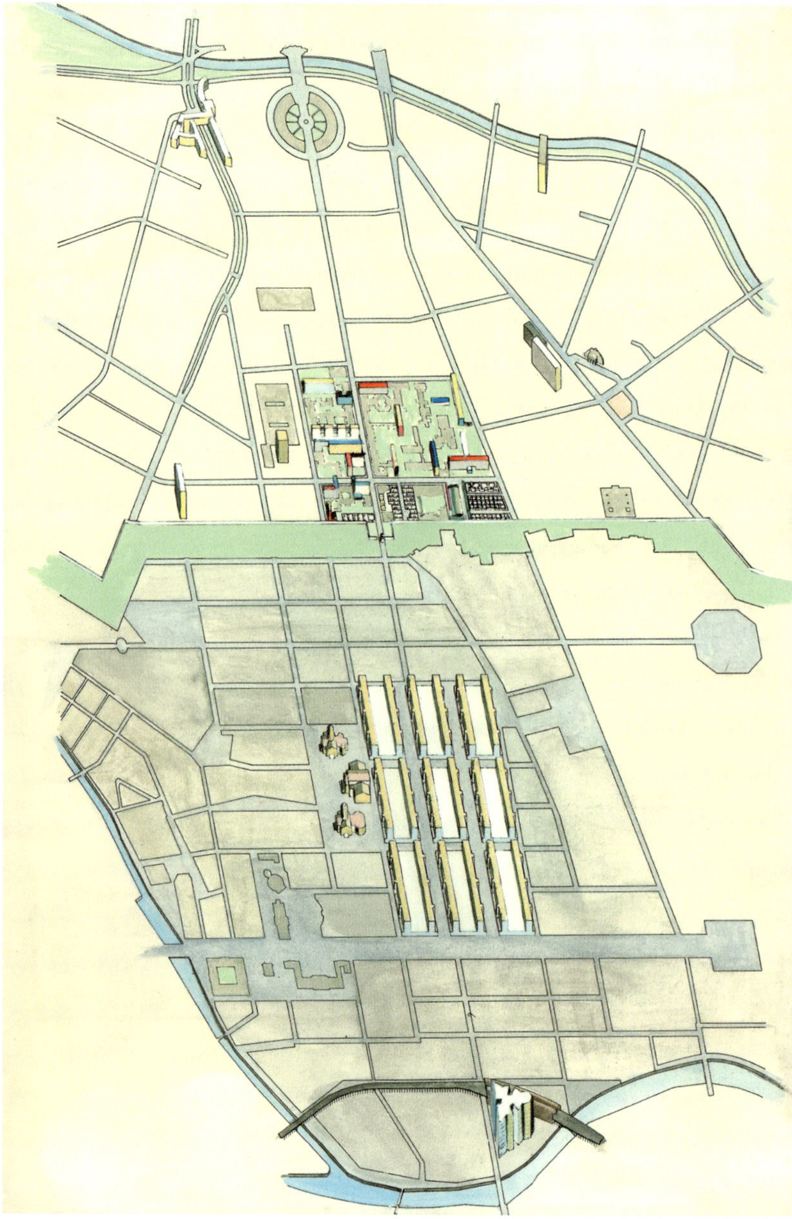

OMA, Kochstraße/Friedrichstraße project, Berlin, 1980. The drawing for the competition entry shows OMA's scheme in the center, the Berlin Wall running from left to right, Mies's glass skyscraper on Friedrichstraße on the lower edge, Hilberseimer's City-Center Development scheme next to the Gendarmenmarkt, and Mendelsohn's Headquarters for the German Metallurgic Federation on the upper left.

The aim was to give the city its urban continuity back by closing the many vacant lots and urban blocks that remained after the destruction of World War II and the reconstruction of the 1950s and 1960s. As such, the IBA also sought to counter modernist planning strategies of freestanding towers or loose agglomerations by regulating building heights (twenty meters to the cornice and thirty meters to the roofline) and requiring perimeter block reconstruction to achieve a new coherence. OMA—in a scheme that expanded over four blocks—instead incorporated existing postwar buildings, densified some areas with Hilberseimer-like slabs, and experimented in other portions of the plan with low courtyard typologies, thereby explicitly learning from Mies. Where the IBA aimed to reconstruct an earlier image of the city without the formal and functional diversity of these earlier organizations, OMA utilized modernist tropes in an attempt to evade the turn to historicist urbanism and in the hope that they might rejuvenate urban ambitions for architecture.

It was this kind of cultural practice that Jürgen Habermas had in mind when he wrote on the unfinished project of modernity. Habermas perceived "modernity" through Charles Baudelaire via Theodor Adorno and, therefore, understood modernism as its cultural response, with architecture being one form of engagement. The timing of Habermas's call for a repositioning of modernity was striking, arriving in the same year that OMA submitted the proposal for Kochstraße/Friedrichstraße. During his acceptance speech for the Adorno Prize, Habermas said: "I believe that we should learn from the aberrations which have accompanied the project of modernity and from the mistakes of those extravagant proposals of sublation, rather than abandoning modernity and its project."[115] Hilberseimer's Berlin proposal was such an aberration linked to the modernist project, from which one should learn. Koolhaas listened most attentively to this call and seemingly replied by asking: "Who does not long for the histrionic branch of the profession that leapt like clowns—pathetic yet courageous—off one cliff after another, hoping to fly, flapping with inadequate wings, but enjoying at least the free-fall of pure speculation?"[116] Both saw the project of modernity as unfinished and as a potent antidote to historicist postmodernism. But whereas Habermas viewed the extravagant proposals of the modern avant-garde as cautionary tales, Koolhaas admired the naïveté of those unfulfilled dreams.

In its search for alternative approaches toward the contemporary city, OMA's early work detours frequently through modernist projects in the hope of rehabilitating their visionary potential—the idea was never to return to these projects but rather to extrapolate from conditions within that work. The modernist superblock, for example, is here updated/"modernized" through the elaboration of a porous

OMA, Kochstraße/Friedrichstraße project, Berlin, 1980. Drawing by Stefano de Martino with Madelon Vriesendorp that shows the housing units for Block 4 in relation to the street while sequentially revealing the building interiors.

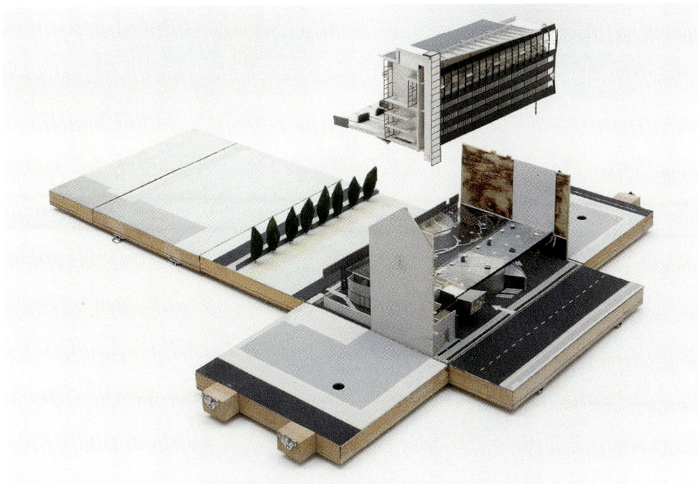

OMA, Model for Checkpoint Charlie Apartments, c. 1985. The unfolded container of the model doubles as streets and blank walls, providing a commentary on the influence of urban conditions on the building.

interior that emulates the city in a manner not unlike the interior campgrounds of Archizoom's No-Stop City.[117] The drawing for Kochstraße/Friedrichstraße by Stefano de Martino—an early associate of OMA from 1979 to 1983—reveals a new interior landscape that belongs to the city or, at the very least, lets the city reign more freely. No longer is the superblock an autonomous construct aiming to tame the tumultuous conditions of contemporary urbanization through its utter difference (as was Hilberseimer's objective), but it now invites urbanization into architectural form, letting it contribute in the search for a new architecture of the city. This collaboration between the two realms predicts an investment in urbanization on the part of architecture that the Checkpoint Charlie Apartments formalized in 1987.

The project, primarily designed by Elia Zenghelis, was the only building that OMA was able to construct in Berlin at the time. The IBA organizers offered the site along Friedrichstraße to OMA after Koolhaas refused to redesign the winning entry with denser and taller urban blocks that would keep with the ambition of reconstructing the block perimeter. The Checkpoint Charlie Apartments (built as required to the fullest height) accommodate not only apartments but also what was then the last checkpoint for non-residents before entering the East Bloc. The site thus presented the opportunity to reroute the traffic of the city through the build-

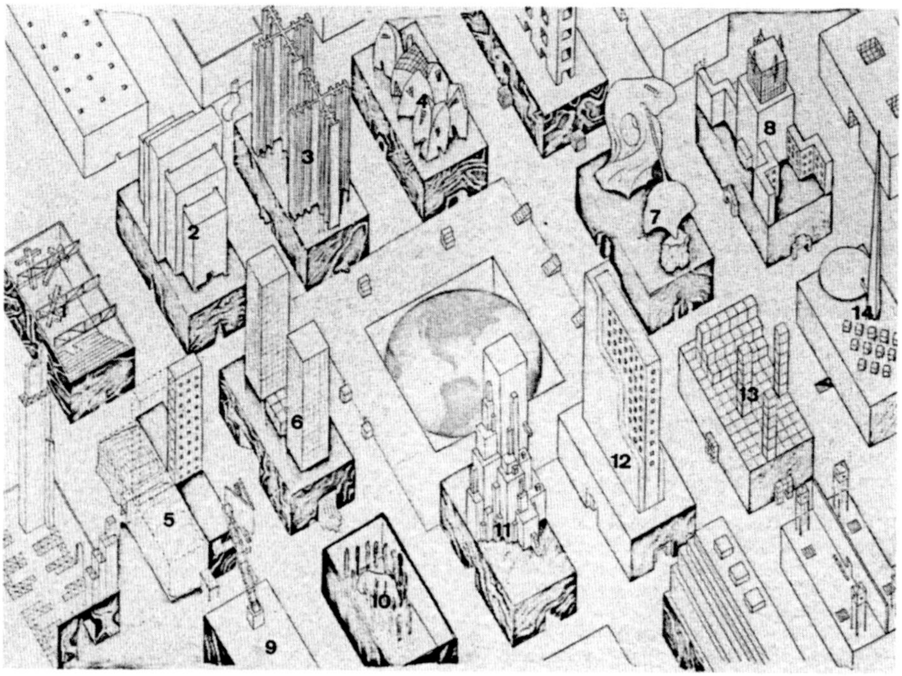

Rem Koolhaas and Zoe Zenghelis, City of the Captive Globe Key, 1972. The different architectural fantasies are described as follows: "Religion in ruins (1)"; "Architecture in the process of reproducing itself (2) ... a subconscious portrait of O. M. Ungers"; "Le Corbusier's Plan Voisin (3)"; "The Cabinet of Dr. Caligari (4)"; "The Waldorf-Astoria Hotel (5)"; "Homage to Mies (6)"; "Dalí's '*Architectural Angelus*,' 1933 (7)"; "Ivan Leonidov's Ministry of Heavy Industry (8)"; "El Lissitzky's orator's stand (9)"; "Outdoor indoor (10)"; "Architecton of Malevitch (11)"; "RCA building Rockefeller Center, 1933 (12)"; "Homage to Superstudio (13)"; "Trylon and Perisphere (14)"; and on the lower right corner is what appears to be a diagram of a mirrored Berlin Wall.

ing before releasing it back onto Friedrichstraße en route to East Berlin. While the ingenuity of the superblock lies in its incorporation of all activities, from production to living and consumption, into one singular architectural form, Checkpoint Charlie manages to expand the catalog of involved programs by including road traffic. As a result, not only does the objecthood of architecture here approximate the complexity of urbanity, but the blurred boundaries and interactive relationship produce a new kind of architecture of the city and, in turn, a form of architectural urbanism. The rigidly polarized relationship between city and architecture shifts to a playful binary affiliation.

Of course, by 1978 Koolhaas had already examined alternative city-architecture tropes in *Delirious New York*. The lessons that he crafted as a retroactive manifesto of Manhattan OMA aimed back at the city through projects such as Checkpoint Charlie. The "Manhattanism" that Koolhaas identified as New York's commitment to technology, its relentless implementation of the grid, its enforcement of a zoning law that encouraged territorial conquests, and the ever-increasing urban density of population and architectural forms ("the culture of congestion") had unintentionally created an urban architecture of the metropolis that in its "exuberance" and "shamelessness" produced unexpected spatial inventions and climatic effects. In his selective reading of episodes of history in Manhattan and Coney Island between 1890 and 1940, Koolhaas viewed them as generators of architectural experiments that remained unnoticed, waiting to be theorized. He presented the now famous example of Starrett & Van Vleck's Downtown Athletic Club (1931) with its layered environments of metropolitan spectacle, from swimming pool via oyster bar to golf course, as a by-product of collective urban forces (grid, elevator, and climate control) coupled with the desires for metropolitan life, culminating in a "techno-psychic apparatus" that choreographed an inventory of stories.

The Downtown Athletic Club expressed most vividly how within Manhattan's grid "[e]ach Science or Mania has its own plot," as Koolhaas wrote for "The City of the Captive Globe" project.[118] The story—included in the appendix of *Delirious New York* and credited to Koolhaas and Zoe Zenghelis—was produced six years prior to the book's publication. It intuits the productivities of the grid, resulting in unexpected legibilities of architectural expression. The project perceives the city as a world in miniature and each building as a city on its own. The solid podiums, however, seem less the fallout of the grid than its formative element. In other words, the repetitive implementation of the building blocks positions them as uniform islands in a sea of urbanization. The streets lack sidewalks, seemingly reserved for the fast-paced circulation of motorized transit, while the life of the block is internalized and only finds expression within and atop the granite perimeter base. As such, the drawing bears a striking resemblance to Hilberseimer's Hochhausstadt, proving to be less a direct display of New York's grid than an exaggeration of the modernist interpretations of the city that Koolhaas found in Manhattan. But unlike the formal repetitiveness of Hilberseimer's scheme, the drawing of the Captive Globe renders each block as a subjective architectural fantasy, which as a collective urban image accumulates into a snapshot of OMA's repertoire. Instead of the linear building slabs of the Hochhausstadt, one sees El Lissitzky's Lenin Tribune, Superstudio's gridded monument, Kazimir Malevich's Architecton, Wallace Harrison's Perisphere and J. Andre Fouilhoux's Trylon from the World's Fair of 1939, Le

Corbusier's Plan Voisin towers, and Salvador Dalí's *Architectonic Angelus of Millet* (1933).

The last was of particular importance for Koolhaas, who utilized surrealist mentalities, specifically Dalí's "Paranoiac-Critical Activity" (or paranoid-critical method, as Koolhaas called it), in crafting a new modernist trajectory; not a historicist postmodernism but a surreal hyper-modernity that he detected in situations of the existing city. The productivities of Dalí's method are clear: in their biased perception of the world, the paranoid individual cannot help but make each event, however trivial or substantial, become part of their own particular thought process. Simulating paranoid tendencies enabled Dalí to fabricate and install unverifiable speculations among proven facts. As he explained, "it tangibly makes the very world of delirium pass to the level of reality."[119] This speaks directly to Koolhaas's self-imposed mission to ghostwrite into existence the episodic delirium of New York. The appendix, the projective conclusion of the book through architectural fictions, serves as the moment of transition from the city's "unconscious architectural production" to OMA's conscious speculation. Or, to quote from the story of the Captive Globe, it is the moment when "A lie has become a truth. A dream from which there is no waking up."[120] Koolhaas engaged the realities of the unfinished project of modernity through the surrealism of Dalí—a connection that history had deemed incommensurable but one that for Koolhaas became particularly productive in his rethinking of the city. While the modernists of the 1920s and 1930s saw the existing city primarily as a traumatized location that needed reformation, the surrealists reveled in the traumas of the formless city and were willing to sample from it.[121] This enthusiasm for the "real" would become in the hands of OMA a similarly intentional and "systematic overestimation of what exists."[122] Here, the existing city becomes a stimulant for the speculative project of architecture. In its deliberate and selective intensification of found conditions, OMA's project is no longer reformative or revolutionary in the modernist tradition, but no less radical in its attitude toward the metropolis.

With an unwavering belief in what urbanization has to offer, OMA renegotiated architecture's place within it—facilitating a process of discovery where even the most commercial architecture of the capitalist city could hold spatial, material, and organizational intelligences, secretly avant-garde yet blatantly non-utopian. With this, Koolhaas was able to conflate the seemingly contradictory realms of the Constructivist social condenser and the commercial skyscrapers of Manhattan, converting even the most devastating conditions into accelerations of metropolitan forces filled with potential. The architectural mutations that the city provoked and that Koolhaas excavated were later reassembled through a kind of constructive

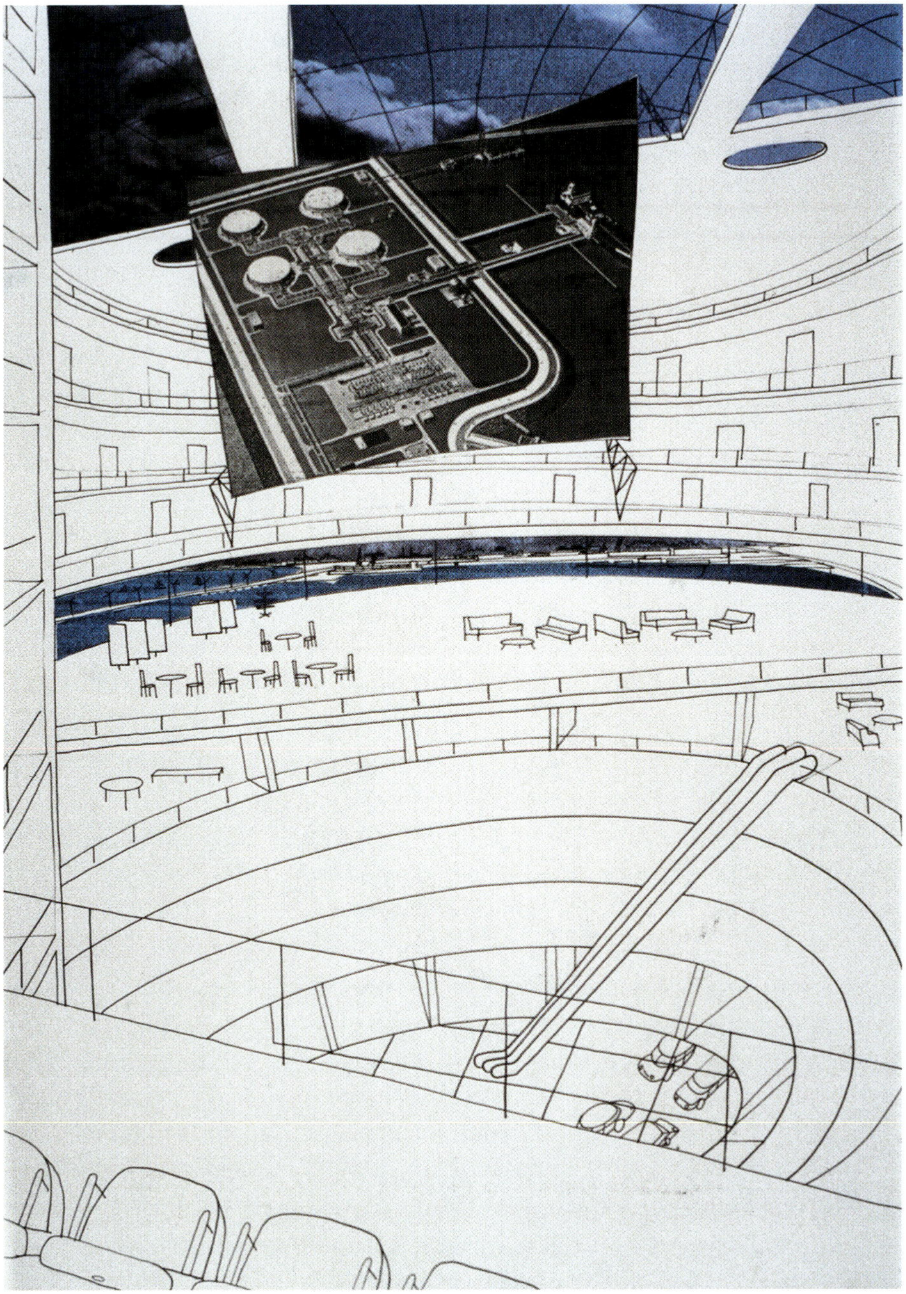

OMA, Sea Terminal project, Zeebrugge, Belgium, 1989. The sketch and photomontage for the competition entry shows the view through the atrium toward the horizon, the restaurant, and into the parking levels below.

OMA, Sea Terminal project, Zeebrugge, Belgium, 1989. Photograph of model, demonstrating the building's formal singularity and its infrastructural connectivity.

surgery in the laboratories of OMA. In contrast to reconstructive surgery that seeks to restore the form and function of a body (or of architectural form), OMA practices a form of constructive or even plastic surgery that shapes and models new relationships between form, program, and city. What began as an "exquisite corpse" in true surrealist fashion developed into a specialized/heightened architecture of and for the metropolis, by internalizing its delirium. Fredric Jameson has described this as a kind of "replication" of the existing city, which in the early works of OMA results in a new "microcosm" or "totality."[123] With that in mind, projects such as the Sea Terminal of Zeebrugge, and its interior in particular, come into sharp focus. The terminal's atrium simulates the city by combining some of the urban landscape's multiple parts. From the swimming pool at the very top, one can look down past the casino, past the hotel and its lobby, past the parking spiral, through to the traffic in the garage below. Here, the city informs architecture, not through a mimicking of images, but through an inhalation of the city's pulsations and effects.

While for Jameson and his analysis of postmodernism this strategy stays in contrast to modern architecture's "radical act of separation and disjunction from that diseased city fabric,"[124] this chapter has also sought to show that the formless metropolis with its *Mietskasernen*, courtyards, and alleys was as much part of the modern discourse as were its schemes that rose on *pilotis* above the existing metropolis. In fact, *Delirious New York* and the reprise of metropolitan architecture were timely in their tactical response to postmodernism and its fascinations with other conditions of urbanity, such as the historical city of Rossi's *Architecture of the City* (1966), the traditional city of Rob Krier's *Stadtraum* (1975), and the popular city of Robert Venturi and Scott Brown's *Learning from Las Vegas* (1972).[125] While all these architects shared a fascination with distinct urban environments, Koolhaas's attraction to modernity was unique at a time of innate skepticism toward the modern project. Not only did he view modernization as an architectural stimulant (he later called it the "most potent drug" for the practice of urbanization), but *Delirious New York* finds a new kind of architecture in the ultimate modern realm of expansion—the grid.[126] Characteristic of urbanization, each block is viewed in the book as simultaneously limiting and accelerating: it confines the building(s) and offers a focused test bed for the elaboration of particularities, not simply as a location but as a site that invites in all forms of urban life, one where a whole world is taken captive. "The grid," Koolhaas wrote, "describes an archipelago of 'Cities within Cities.'"[127] This terminology channels earlier tropes—from Benjamin's observations of the arcades as a world in miniature, to the department store as an address for urban tourists, to the superblocks of Hilberseimer's city—but most explicitly borrows from a project that Ungers had called *Die Stadt in der Stadt* (*The City in the City*).[128]

Launched by Ungers in collaboration with Koolhaas, Peter Riemann, Hans Kollhoff, and Arthur Ovaska, the project examines West Berlin's postwar plight and speculates on its urban and architectural impact. The city—itself an urban island that provided inspiration for early projects by Koolhaas such as "Exodus"—faced a crisis in stark contrast to its metropolitan past of the 1910s and 1920s. After the destruction of World War II and the subsequent division of the city, large sections of Berlin remained empty, a condition only heightened by its economic difficulties and a declining population. Proposals for rebuilding Berlin's large perimeter blocks to remedy the condition were turned on their head when Ungers proposed to not resist trends of de-urbanization—for architects a counterintuitive response—but instead to experiment with its potential as a way forward.[129] For Koolhaas, this was of course an extremely productive challenge to conventional urbanism. And his initial typescript for the project, under the title "Berlin: A Green Archipelago," duly notes that the "inevitable process of retrenchment could be seen as a negative experience ..., but it could also be an experimental project to intensify the experiences of Berlin as an architectural ensemble."[130] The project envisions an accelerated urban shrinkage, which in turn produces a city of individual urban islands drifting in an enlarged post-urban landscape.

In this context, OMA's courtyard typologies for the competition entry for Kochstraße/Friedrichstraße also addressed Berlin's shrinking population. In fact, it is no coincidence that OMA submitted an entry to the IBA competition with a similar ambition to that outlined in the "Green Archipelago"—the scheme that Koolhaas had worked on and that Ungers had prepared to influence the IBA's course of action. Both dreams were crushed: Koolhaas was not able to construct a neighborhood in Berlin, and Ungers lost the dispute over the strategy for Berlin to Josef Paul Kleihues's more overtly popular project of "critical reconstruction." Yet, Ungers's publication from 1977 offers one of the most resonating provocations toward architecture in that it imagines the unbuilding of the city as an urban project. Ungers foresaw that only the strongest architectural ensembles would remain once the rest of the city was demolished and slowly replaced by forest, gardens, and

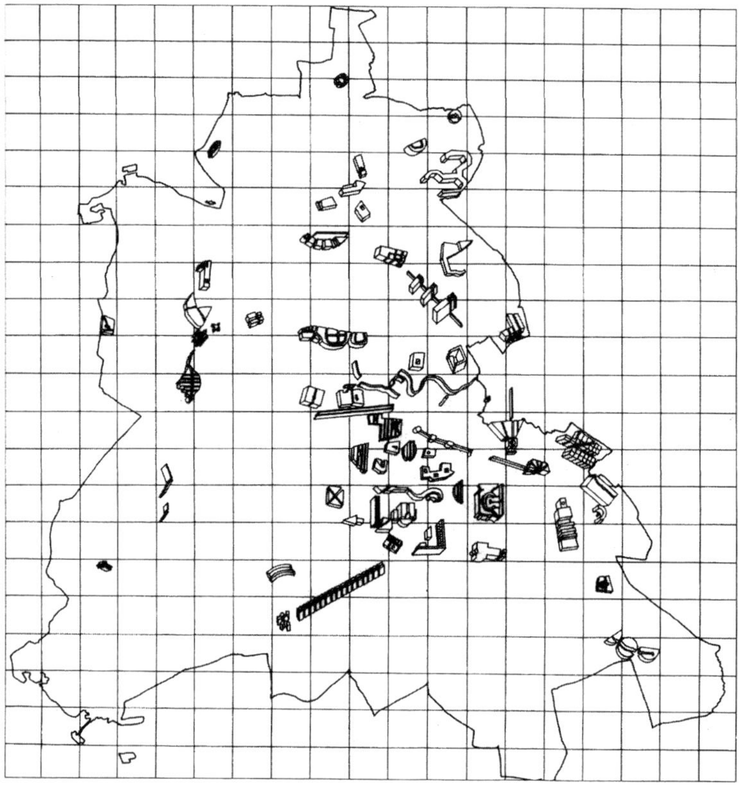

Oswald Mathias Ungers with Rem Koolhaas, Peter Riemann, Hans Kollhoff, and Arthur Ovaska, *Die Stadt in der Stadt: Berlin das grüne Stadtarchipel* (1977), 16. This drawing for thesis #5 shows the identified building formations as individual urban islands across West Berlin.

wildlife. The different shades of nature would directly contrast with the urban forms and heighten their clarity or, as he put it, "intensify the metropolitan experience"—an observation that sounds familiar.[131]

What Ungers in 1966 described as "*Großform*" (large form) for their scale, as well as their historic, programmatic, and formal capacity, he now reconsidered as cities within the city. They, in turn, acted as a precursor to Koolhaas's 1994 concept of "bigness." Each island became a formally distinct and functionally autonomous miniature city, not contributing to a coherent ideal whole, but carrying an urbanism of its own. As such, these "unique" and "antithetical islands" formed part of Michel Foucault's discussion on "Heterotopias," which he defined in 1967 as "real and effective spaces ... [that] constitute a sort of counterarrangement, of effectively realized utopias."[132] The "otherness" of these locations that Foucault identified as "heterotopias" was not formulated as a utopian "nowhere" but instead constituted an utterly real site, defined by the very difference it posed to its surroundings.[133] Ten years after Foucault, the authors of *The City in the City* noted: "There is no need for new utopias, rather to create a better reality."[134] And, indeed, the realities of the city were paramount for the envisioning of a new urbanity. Ultimately, the notion of the city as laboratory found a new meaning: no longer was it simply the territory for architectural tests, but instead it became the very driver of urban invention. Here, urbanization propelled urbanism. Neither utopian speculation nor superimposed planning guided the scheme; instead, the development of the city was extrapolated from its conditions to selectively guide a new architectural urbanism.

In their shared search for a metropolitan architecture and mutual notion of an extrapolated city, Koolhaas, Hilberseimer, and Scheffler can be seen as a collective. Even as they worked decades apart and engaged very different kinds of cities, their common project shares a deep investment in reconfiguring architecture as an urban practice. While an intensification of urbanization saw architecture retreat from the discourse on the city and surrender its position to new disciplines such as planning, metropolitan architecture put the city front and center once again. In contrast to previous and even current attempts to formulate an architectural project of the city, these iterations of a metropolitan architecture no longer view contemporary urban formlessness as the prime target in architecture's struggle with the city. Instead, urbanity is now channeled and deployed through architecture. Its greatest contribution lies in its ability to not only find potentials within urbanization but also develop strategies to extrapolate from conditions that architects commonly hold at bay. As a design strategy, architecture's radicalization is no longer its counter-positioning toward what is there but, paradoxically, its speculative exaggeration of conditions that hover between conventional value judgments. The conscious overestimation of the given urban environment through what can be called a radical contexualism has the potential to upset stereotypes. What generally is understood as problematic, even threatening, to architecture becomes here the discipline's stronghold. Scheffler, Hilberseimer, and OMA deploy the very hostility of adverse urban conditions to divert architecture from its beaten path. This shared history productively complicates the storyline of each endeavor (within early, high, and late modernity) as much as it highlights the trajectory of a still incomplete project.

"*The Megacity (Millionenstadt) with its thousandfold of possibilities.* **Werner Hegemann, *Der Städtebau*, 1910**

[The city] is full of things to charm a storyteller—not only in its medieval nooks, secluded streets, and somber houses, but also in its working inhabitants of every social rank and from all corners of the city—which can only be teased out by dint of observation. **Walter Benjamin, "Das dämonische Berlin," broadcast on Berlin Radio, February 25, 1930**

... the subject is always the urban effect: there is no architecture without the city, no city without architecture. **Bernard Tschumi, *Event-Cities*, 1994**

3 Narration

City Exhibition and the Broadcasting of a "Détourned" Urbanism

In May of 1910, the largest exhibition on urbanization and urbanism to date opened its doors in Berlin to visitors from around the world. With an unprecedented amount of information on urban developments and city plans, the international *Allgemeine Städtebau-Ausstellung* (General City-Building Exhibition) sought to reposition architecture in relationship to the city. With the emergence of the metropolis, the city-architecture relationship had become strained. A deeper understanding of the existing city was increasingly viewed as essential for identifying new ways to engage and reform the metropolis. The exhibition provided an opportunity to excavate information on the city in order to structure alternative narratives on urbanity. While unsuccessful in its attempt to fully comprehend the formless city through an obsessive documentation of all its layers, the exhibition, ultimately, composed and displayed an intricate image of the metropolis—an account that reverberated through the decades to come. The exhibition's narratives about the existing city reshaped conventions and preconceptions and provided a basis for rethinking architecture's place within it. While all the narratives cited in this chapter take the existing city as a starting point, reporting from the trenches of urbanization, they ultimately result in the formulation of a new urban architecture. From Walter Benjamin's didactic urban broadcasts to the subversive remapping of Paris by the Situationists and the cinematic transcriptions of events by Bernard Tschumi, urban accounts would become a way to expose architecture's reality to that of the city. As these cultural agents pursued their analyses, the role of architecture and its relationships to the larger forces of urbanization were repositioned and, eventually, questioned. Over time, Tschumi's initial statement that there can be "no architecture without the city, no city without architecture," evolved into an understanding that the city as an entity "could potentially exist without architecture," yet architecture could never subsist without the city.[1] While not always intentional, this revelation is reiterated throughout the different urban narratives that this chapter interrogates. As we proceed from city exhibition, to urban design competition, to radio broadcasts, "détourned" maps, and urban transcriptions (a sample of urban narratives), the idea of the city is reworked and results in a different kind of architecture in each. This will not only expose the productivities of these particular narratives but, more importantly, foreground the dependency of architecture on the city.

Werner Hegemann's Exhibition of Urban Complexity

From the mid-nineteenth century, the city was increasingly on display, studied as an artifact, and treated as a project to be designed—a development driven by the continuous growth of the metropolis, a new urban and regional connectivity, and the emergence of *Städtebau* as a discipline. The urban population saw an unprecedented number of city exhibitions, urban planning competitions, expansion plans for towns, and public discussions on urbanization and urbanism. During the first decade of the twentieth century alone, one of the earliest urban design and town planning exhibitions took place in Dresden (1903), the journal *Der Städtebau* was founded (1904), the first recognized academic seminar on *Städtebau* was offered in Berlin (1907), the competition for a Greater Berlin was issued (1908), Burnham and Bennett published the *Plan of Chicago* (1909), New York hosted the *Congestion Show* (1909), *Boston 1915* called for plans for the future city (1909), and the *Allgemeine Städtebau-Ausstellung* in Berlin became one of the largest and most influential exhibitions on the city to that point (1910).[2] These milestone events all approached the modern city in Europe and the United States as a dramatically transformed environment requiring analysis. The exhibitions played a critical role in urban research.

Already in 1892, the urban theorist and author Patrick Geddes mounted an exhibition in Edinburgh, Scotland, to inform the public on the city's history, development, and prospects. The short-lived and never fully completed Outlook Tower—containing a viewing platform, a *camera obscura*, and galleries for research documentation—was conceived as a vehicle to display large-scale urban developments. Geddes called for "a science of Cities [in which] our cities should be individually surveyed, scientifically compared; as their architecture long has been."[3] This search toward a systematic study of the city paralleled an interest in the so-called "social museums" that sought to give a comprehensive survey of modern life in the metropolis.[4] Geddes considered the exhibition a laboratory for better understanding and testing the city—mandated to expand awareness about urban problems and possible solutions for a better modern urban environment.[5]

This belief in urban research would also become a major force in the initiation of Berlin's *Allgemeine Städtebau-Ausstellung* in the years leading up to its opening in 1910. The exhibition as well as its sequel, the *Internationale Städtebau-Ausstellung* (International City-Building Exhibition) in Düsseldorf, aimed to offer a detailed "scientific" investigation of the so-far incomprehensible turmoil of the metropolis, laying the groundwork for regulation of its formlessness through urban design. When the exhibition opened in May 1910, at the Königlich Technische

Display of comparative traffic diagrams of major cities at the *Allgemeine Städtebau-Ausstellung*, Berlin, 1910. The display title reads: "Images of high-speed city traffic."

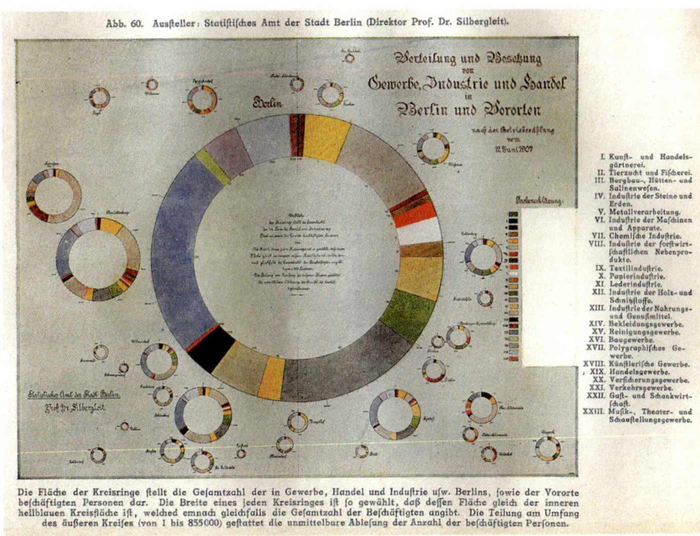

Berlin Department of Statistics, diagram documenting the distribution of business, industry, and trade in comparison between Berlin and its suburbs, 1907, displayed at the *Allgemeine Städtebau-Ausstellung*, 1910. Statistical analyses and logistical diagrams made up large parts of the *Allgemeine Städtebau-Ausstellung* on display at Berlin's Königlich Technische Hochschule.

Hochschule in Berlin-Charlottenburg, a large number of visitors (40,000 in the first twenty days) encountered an equally unparalleled number of records on urban developments. The exhibition collected data and borrowed documents from a host of cities in Europe and the US that were equally invested in the question of the metropolis. Through a variety of media (including photographs, models, descriptions, and statistics) the exhibition communicated information on aspects of urban experience: from urban growth and health-related matters, to studies on traffic and transportation, to workers' housing and settlements, and open public space and gardens.

In Germany, departments for statistics (*Statistische Landes- und Stadtämter*), common since the late nineteenth century, collected information about all aspects of life at the city, county, and state level, making the documentation of the city through numbers effortless. Berlin's fragmented culture made governmental departments especially receptive to the idea of large data collections. The records of the state apparatus were omnipresent, "so one does not think that one can otherwise do or let something be done which escapes statistical registration."[6] Clearly part of an effort to maintain state control and order, this data provided an outline of the fragmented modern urban culture through which it could be understood anew. The de-mystified, abstract, and rational "mass ornament" that Siegfried Kracauer would later describe as regulating fragments of society that simultaneously gave shape to a new culture, can be brought into connection with these exercises in statistics of the German state—a connection that reveals the problems as well as the uses of these new forms of organization.[7] Later, Benjamin established direct links between modern technologies of reproduction and new aspects of information display—a relationship that "manifest[s] in the field of perception what in the theoretical sphere is noticeable in the increasing importance of statistics."[8] Following this logic, statistics become yet another expression of the modern notion of the "universal equality of things,"[9] and a means through which the amorphous and fluid condition of the modern city was to be given form.

The use of numbers, graphs, and diagrams enabled a documentation of urban life that otherwise remained illegible. Seeking to establish a context for urban design and documenting the city in all its complexity, each display in the exhibition gave a clear image of a particular aspect. Yet, the accumulation of all this material did not give more clarity. On the contrary, it created an equally fluid, dense, and impenetrable image of the city, just as overwhelming to the visitor as was the city to the pedestrian outdoors. Diagrams and statistics, initially meant to give form to the diversity of data, flooded the halls of the exhibition and became the ultimate display of the modern city's complex multiplicity and instability.[10]

The urban theorist Werner Hegemann held responsibility for exhibiting this surplus of information. He had studied economics and political science, and was trained to view the city through an analytical lens that captured it quantitatively.[11] Through collecting, illustrating, and relating information about the urban condition, Hegemann aimed to establish a record that would shed light on the development of the metropolis.[12] His notebooks show countless pages of tables and comparisons between city scales, population charts, migration patterns, and building types. His early training would remain visible during his autodidactic studies in architecture and urbanism, his first publications in journals such as *Der Städtebau*, and at the exhibition in 1910. While Hegemann was only twenty-nine years old when he was named the secretary-general of the exhibition, he had already traveled across Europe, visited parts of Africa, and taken multiple trans-Atlantic journeys to the US.[13] Connections made during these trips eventually aided the exchange of information and lending of material from institutions across the world. His uncle, the influential Berlin government architect Otto March, facilitated his appointment, not only by connecting Hegemann early on to the Berlin architectural scene but by introducing him to international figures such as Hermann Muthesius. In fact, Muthesius's call for architects "to face [their] own conditions squarely and ... honestly,"[14] was echoed in Hegemann's ambition to obtain an all-encompassing knowledge of the current urban condition.

His obsessive collection of facts and evidence promised the ammunition to combat metropolitan formlessness. In that respect, Hegemann's work approximates Max Weber's characterization of the scientist as a person with a heightened desire to understand the world. For Weber, however, modernity's increased intellectualization and rational actions were also responsible for "the disenchantment of the world."[15] While for Hegemann full comprehension of the metropolis meant the possibility of its eventual control, for Weber comprehension would lead to an increasingly disillusioned and demystified world. What was clearly a problem for Weber, Hegemann saw as the only way to combat the city's disorder. Yet, as it played out, Hegemann's work proved both Weber's and his own theories wrong. In generating the most complex image of the city through data, Hegemann ended up demonstrating the inadequacy of its description. The exhibition only added to the city's complexity by recounting the metropolis in so much detail that it depicted a city of delirious enchantment. The unintentional result of Hegemann's inclusive view of the city was the most intricate image of the metropolis—an image whose formlessness suggested that the city was not to be disenchanted any time soon.

While Hegemann failed in regard to his self-imposed curatorial mandate, the impact of the exhibition reverberated throughout the urban and architectural dis-

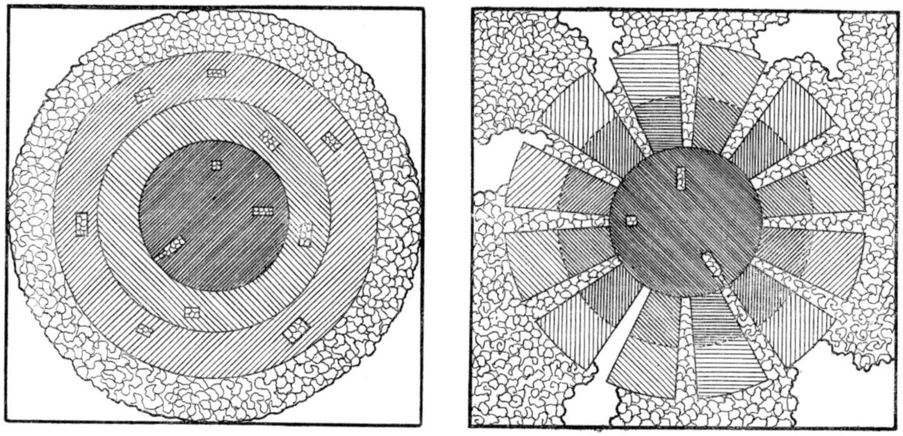

Bruno Möhring, Rudolf Eberstadt, and Richard Petersen, diagrams from "Et in terra pax," entry for the Greater Berlin competition, 1910. Drawing juxtaposing the concentric (left) versus the radial city expansion model (right) and its incorporation of green space.

course for decades—yet not as Hegemann had anticipated. The information-saturated exhibition surely perplexed the general public, but even architects and planners commented on the pandemonium of information that was to completely capture the depth of urban content. Charles-Edouard Jeanneret, who had not yet taken on the persona of Le Corbusier, visited the exhibition during his field studies of the decorative arts in Germany and wondered what visitors might see in these "mysterious graphics."[16] The data bewildered even Jeanneret. Deeply skeptical of the abstruse knowledge that was seemingly conveyed through the displays, he felt equally intrigued by their mystery. Entries in his sketchbook (which during his stay in Berlin in the summer of 1910 were primarily devoted to visits of the exhibition) reveal a shift in perspective on urbanism as an architectural project. Previously, Jeanneret's sketches echoed Camillo Sitte's ideal urban enclosures of the traditional town. Immersed in the study and exposed to the complexities of the modern city, however, the urbanism of Le Corbusier began to formulate, swerving from a Sittesque view of the metropolis as a negative outcome of modernity to a vision of the modern city as a complex product of collective engagements that architects could shape toward modern ends.[17]

During his last visit to the exhibition, Jeanneret viewed only urban schemes, sketched the radial city diagram by Möhring, Eberstadt, and Petersen, and then speculated on applying its rules to the specifics of Berlin's Parkstraße, which encircled the city. In the decades following, Le Corbusier repeated this strategy of pro-

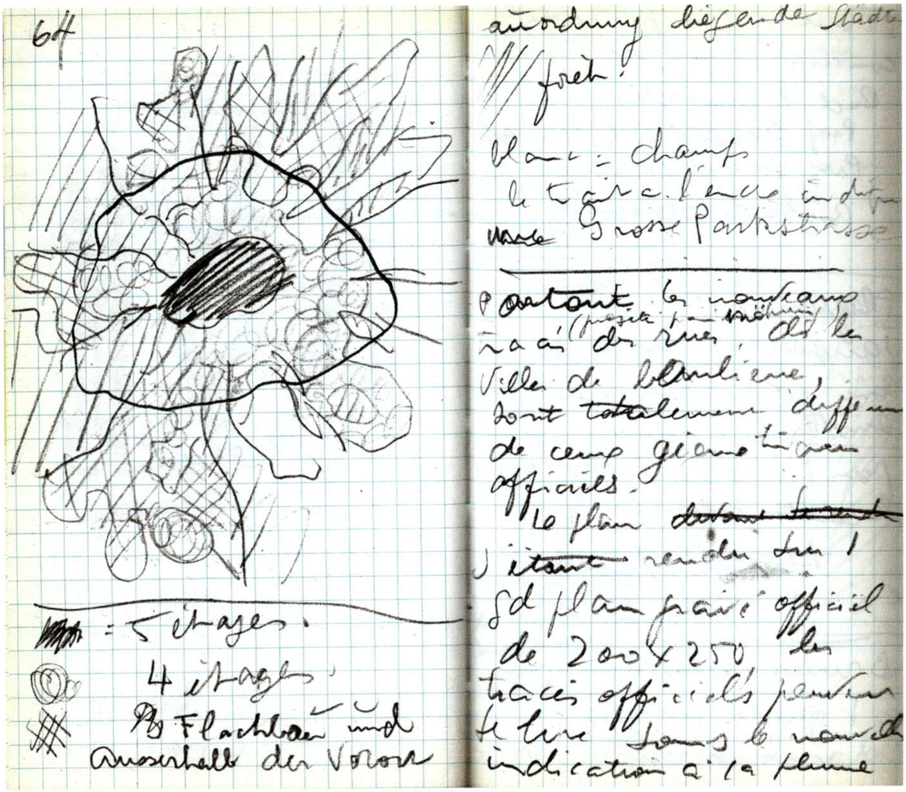

Charles-Edouard Jeanneret, sketch of Berlin with increased green space. Spread from Notebook, June 1910, in *Les Voyages d'Allemagne, Carnets I*, 64–65. Jeanneret (aka Le Corbusier) speculated here on the implementation of Möhring, Eberstadt, and Petersen's diagrams along Berlin's Parkstraße, which can be seen as a dark line encircling the city center.

posing a modern urbanism for the site of his visit wherever he traveled—from the Soviet Union to Latin America. Hegemann's obsessive compulsion to collect data on every aspect of the modern city, though never fully achievable, and Le Corbusier's early design exercise that capitalized on that kind of data, outlines the tension between the city's condition of constant flux and architecture's work toward stability.[18] Even as the exhibition proved the impossibility of comprehending the metropolis, the architect's wish to master the city remained intact and was even encouraged. For the exhibition made equally clear that every architectural maneuver did intervene in and affect the web of relationships that govern the city. This insight allowed Le Corbusier to imagine his own design speculations played back onto the walls of the exhibition and into the field of urban information. The cacophony of urban data in the exhibition, and Le Corbusier's response to it, together display both the intricate qualities of the shapeless metropolis and the growing wish of architects to organize it.

The tension between the city's formlessness and architecture's will to form became most obvious in the publication that followed the exhibition. While intended to provide a record of the different contributions on display, the two-volume document Hegemann delivered might best be described as a stream-of-consciousness urban history. The first volume of *Der Städtebau nach den Ergebnissen der Allgemeinen Städtebau-Ausstellung in Berlin* (City building according to the results of the General City-Building Exhibition in Berlin) focused primarily on the history of urbanization of Berlin, whereas the later volume documented the international discourse on the modern city.[19] The first consisted of only two very long chapters: "Rückblick" (Retrospective) and "Die Berliner Pläne" (The Berlin plans). It was written as continuous text without subdivisions and only occasionally interrupted by illustrations, statistics, diagrams, and quotations. Though the organizer intended that the publication would provide a narrative lacking in the exhibition, Hegemann produced a text so saturated with detailed information, interlacing histories, and urban codes that readers could detect neither a structure nor any central argument. Werner Oechslin, for example, commented that "[Hegemann's] arguments are so multiple and diverse that it is not possible to bring them into conclusion ..."[20] While the two volumes clearly lack a linear narrative and forego any attempt at closure, they unintentionally produce one of the most unique documents on, or better, of the modern city. Their open-ended episodic narration of points of reference, just as in the exhibition, comes close to reproducing the complexities of the city that both aimed to help their audiences to understand.

Looking at Berlin, Hegemann not only found the most vivid expression of modernization but a city situated "at the center of a storm," struggling with entirely new forms of urbanity.[21] He sensed that for Berlin and for modernity more generally, this condition had to be negotiated through design, in order to circumnavigate not just tensions between tradition and new trends, but, first and foremost, between the forces of order and chaos. The whirlwind he saw encircling Berlin was not the Rousseauian *"tourbillon social"* of Enlightenment thought, but the overwhelming metropolitan/industrial landscape continuously propelled toward progress.[22] In this urban climate, he recognized a city that was simultaneously "form-shattering" and "form-thirsty"—imagery encapsulating both the crushing of traditional urban forms and the desire for new ones.[23]

Juxtaposing the formal classical city with the formless industrial metropolis, Hegemann observed that: "Potsdamer Platz, which Schinkel had envisioned as a

Karl Friedrich Schinkel, Potsdamer Tor, Berlin, 1823, displayed at the *Allgemeine Städtebau-Ausstellung*, 1910 (above) and Potsdamer Platz, Berlin, c. 1890 (below). Initially located at the edge of the city, Potsdamer Platz became the epicenter of traffic in only seventy years. In the photograph from 1890, Schinkel's gatehouses can be seen on both sides of the intersection while Messel's Wertheim department store can be deciphered in the far distance.

silent clearing at the edge of the Tiergarten's jungle, has developed into a pandemonium of traffic."[24] Here, Karl Friedrich Schinkel's famous drawing of the Leipziger Platz and its gatehouses is contrasted to the irregular and tumultuous Potsdamer Platz of Hegemann's day, to display the rapid urban developments, constantly expanding city boundaries, and the shift from the previously known urban stability to traffic nodes. While clearly admiring Schinkel's classical tectonic syntax and damning the new environments of metropolitan speed, the writing never clearly indicates how to overcome the historical divide that Hegemann located there. In multiple instances, he even deploys the velocity of the metropolis to take the reader on a rapid journey across the city. "From the Lustgarten toward the forums of the opera and further to the powerful and reviving intersection of the Friedrichstraße (the main artery of the city), from there, the flows of the Street Unter den Linden brings you to the Pariser Platz with the triumphal Brandenburg Gate. At this moment, the 'ordered pomp' of the city is lowered and flows into the ocean of trees in the Tiergarten."[25] The text, so it seems, not only depicts but inhabits the city and its continuously unfolding urbanity. It articulates metropolitan space via a language that speaks through it. Hegemann's run-on sentences that loop from historical events to specific urban locations and back to events appear here as a kind of urban magma that refuses to be contained.[26]

While his arguments, hazy with information, are often hard to pin down, the frequent references to the dire living conditions of tenements are clear in their critique, and would influence the modernist discussion on 1920s housing as well as the urban projects of figures such as Walter Benjamin. But, as Nicholas Bullock and James Read have shown in their work on the reform movement, urban housing conditions in Germany began to be discussed as early as 1840, leading to first debates about housing reform in the 1860s.[27] With an expanding industry and an unparalleled migration of workers, many cities faced a housing deficit, sanitation problems, and growing speculation. In Berlin, many households took in temporary lodgers to offset high rents and relatively low and insecure wages. By 1900, 43 percent of households lived in dwellings that consisted of one room, creating unprecedented urban density, with an all-time high of 29,750 individuals per square kilometer.[28] While an average of twenty people inhabited the building lots of Paris around 1900 and the lots of London had only eight inhabitants, the average in Berlin rose above sixty. Hegemann and others called the dense apartment complexes of Berlin "rental barracks," for their echo of the monotony and unaccommodating conditions of military quarters.

Hegemann sourced these conditions to land speculation in a laissez-faire economy, concerned with quantity rather than quality and generating, what he

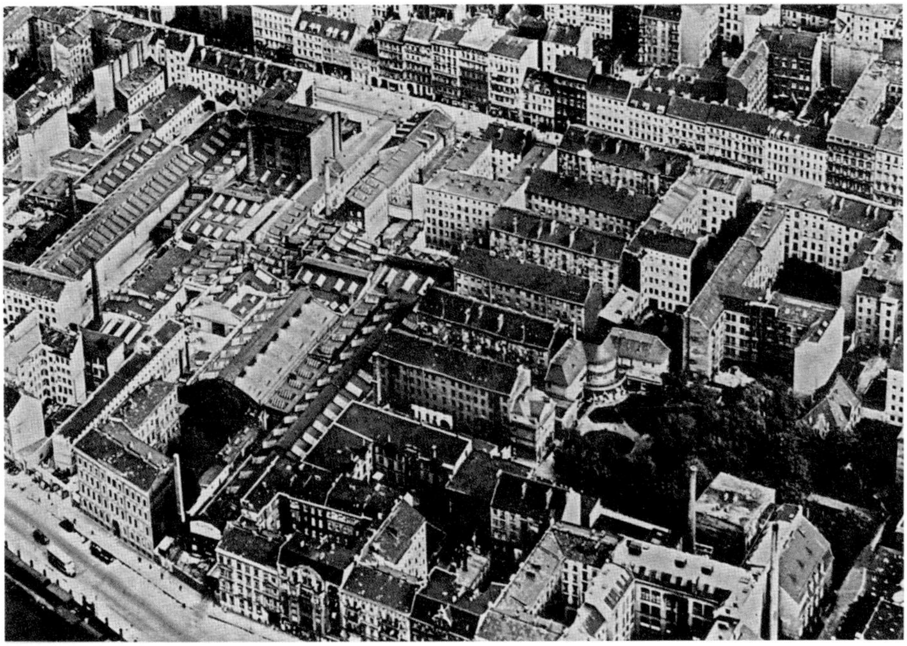

Aerial view of Meyer's Hof, Berlin, c. 1930. Meyer's Hof and its six courtyards, notorious for its density, can be seen in the center of the photograph, with the main entrance on Ackerstraße at the upper part of the photo.

would later call, "the largest rental-barrack city in the world."[29] He spoke of urgencies to illustrate, address, and attack the dense living conditions of the urban population. Thus, his research from the 1910s not only supplied arguments and provided visuals to the later CIAM debates around issues of housing but also anticipated Le Corbusier's famous dictum "architecture or revolution."[30] Hegemann argued in 1911 that "[n]owhere is the danger [of a revolution] greater [than] in the milieu created by Berlin's living conditions."[31] The "rental barracks" became the political terrain of an unfolding housing debate. The ample evidence that *Der Städtebau* presents against the poor lighting, sanitation, and ventilation of urban housing would reverberate in the coming two decades. Le Corbusier's diagrammatic rhetoric against the congestion-ridden centers of capitals (1925), the construction of urban models such as Weissenhof that visualized an urban antithesis to the metropolis (1927), and much of the CIAM debate until the late 1930s would effectively build on and respond to Hegemann's early work. The modern avant-gardes of the 1920s took much of their historical and factual ammunition from his exhibition and publication one decade earlier. Hegemann's *Der Städtebau* became an

José Luis Sert and CIAM, *Can Our Cities Survive? An ABC of Urban Problems, Their Analysis, Their Solutions*, cover (1942). For Sert, the book had to "contain a general line of action to make it interesting and useful" and Herbert Bayer designed its cover with a striking collage that foregrounds the argumentative tone of the book.

important reference not only for Le Corbusier but for a whole generation of architects.

Wolfgang Sonne illustrated how Hegemann's work, in the tradition of Theodor Goecke (a Berlin architect, planner, and editor of *Der Städtebau*), steered the housing debate with a clear preference for urban blocks, while Christiane Crasemann Collins highlighted Hegemann's intellectual framework as a source of ideas for the modern movement, in particular his lively interactions with Erich Mendelsohn and Hans and Wassili Luckhardt.[32] By the 1920s, however, the argument for better housing gained a clarity that enabled its proponents to steer toward design solutions. Whereas Hegemann's investigative urban archeology aimed at revealing the reasons behind the conditions of the metropolis (a cycle he could never escape), the next generation avoided the maelstrom of urban information and parallel histories that swamped Hegemann. Their writings did not detail causes but rather focused on design solutions for existing problems. Giedion's *Space, Time and Architecture*, for example, reads the Renaissance and Baroque city as proto-modernist experiments, where Sixtus V's urban transformations of Rome (1585–1590) ultimately point, via projects such as the Royal Crescent in Bath (1769), toward Le Corbusier's urbanism, in projects such as Plan Obus for Algiers (1931).

Eric Mumford already hinted at this lack of evidence by articulating that "CIAM's universal revulsion of the city of streets and interwoven activities seems based on something deeper. Yet that 'something' is never disclosed in the denunciations of Le Corbusier, and the need to abolish the street is assumed to be self-evident."[33] While Hegemann's earlier work is purely evidential with few design directives, the later work by CIAM seems to forego a clear reasoning and jumps to conclusions. And, indeed, many statements of CIAM become only fully accessible if read against the backdrop of evidence given more than a decade earlier. Now, Herbert Bayer's collage for the book cover of *Can Our Cities Survive?*, which shows a crowd of people packed into a can above Robert Moses's highway intersections, reveals itself not solely as the origin of an avant-garde statement. Instead, it becomes part of a much larger historical and rhetorical trajectory—a train of thought for which exhibitions and publications such as Hegemann's presented an avalanche of evidence that later proponents perhaps took as self-evident. In other words, the surplus of information in the early narratives on the city made more direct and efficient design scenarios possible for the later avant-gardes.

Map detail, northeast Berlin, 1862. New districts according to James Hobrecht's plan, with the newly inserted neighborhoods labeled with roman numerals and distinguishable by the larger block size.

The housing debate that ensued in the 1920s was long in the making and deeply influenced by Hegemann's historical excavations. One of the many villains he singled out in his analysis of the housing situation in Berlin was James Hobrecht, the mastermind behind the city's plan and building code of 1862.[34] Hobrecht outlined two streets that encircled Berlin and Charlottenburg and designated open areas that were subdivided by a wide urban grid, resulting in a new pattern for the extension of the city demanded by the housing shortage. While these rules would set the parameters for the tenement housing that took shape as thick continuous layers of buildings on large urban blocks, only occasionally pierced by the minimum requirements for courtyards, Hobrecht's initial vision was much more optimistic, if shortsighted.[35] He imagined that by providing enough space for all classes to coexist, these large complexes would offer a new social mix. Each block would constitute an urban microclimate of its own, thereby countering the strict zoning of the city and enriching the social coloration of the mega-block. The reality, however, looked very different and by the end of the nineteenth century many perceived the unprecedented density of housing for the working class as the core problem of the metropolis.

Therefore, housing would be at the center of attention for entries to the Greater Berlin competition. Combining the pragmatism of future demand and the semantic preferences of *Städtebau*, the urban design competition was launched on October 15, 1908, asking for proposals that anticipated a population of five million and a territory for the so-called "Greater Berlin."[36] Learning from previous city

Hermann Jansen, "In den Grenzen der Möglichkeit" project, Berlin, 1910. Jansen's entry for the Greater Berlin competition analyzes a residential district at Tempelhofer Feld and proposes to transform the conventional Berlin courtyard into a new urban space.

competitions involving expansion efforts such as Vienna's Ringstraße (1858) or the plans for Barcelona (1859), the Berlin competition became one of the most comprehensive urban design exercises of its time.[37] The winning entries were displayed in Hegemann's 1910 city exhibition, placed alongside research on urbanism from around the world. By correlating the housing situation of Berlin to the deep perimeter blocks that make up large parts of the city, many proposals re-thought the typical building volume and experimented with new ways to open the interiors to more light. The intense congestion of the city was the realm in which architects and city planners saw their calling and city officials were determined to assert their power. For them, the housing problem was only part of a much larger "beautification" effort concerning the city.

The entries had to rethink existing housing schemes, while at the same time "finding a unified large-scale solution" for representing Berlin as a *Weltstadt* (world city).[38] With this in mind, Hermann Jansen's winning scheme "In den Grenzen der Möglichkeit" ("Within the limits of possibility") proposed a widening of courtyards, the configuration of terraced houses around green spaces, and the development of building blocks that meandered across the city and enclosed large semi-private spaces. His proposal is of particular interest since it opens the interior of the building block to the street, making the block-interior part of the urban landscape, and vice versa. The center of the block is neither a public plaza nor a private courtyard but a new kind of urban interior at the threshold between public and private. Keeping fast traffic out but inviting the pedestrians and moderate traffic in, each block was envisioned as an urban oasis that presented the metropolis from within. Jansen's architectural dream suggests a parallel city with its own urban climate, generated through an architectural form that adjusts the speed, sound, and accessibility of the metropolis.

While Jansen took the existing block dimensions of Berlin and made their interior more permeable, other schemes increased the dimensions of the perime-

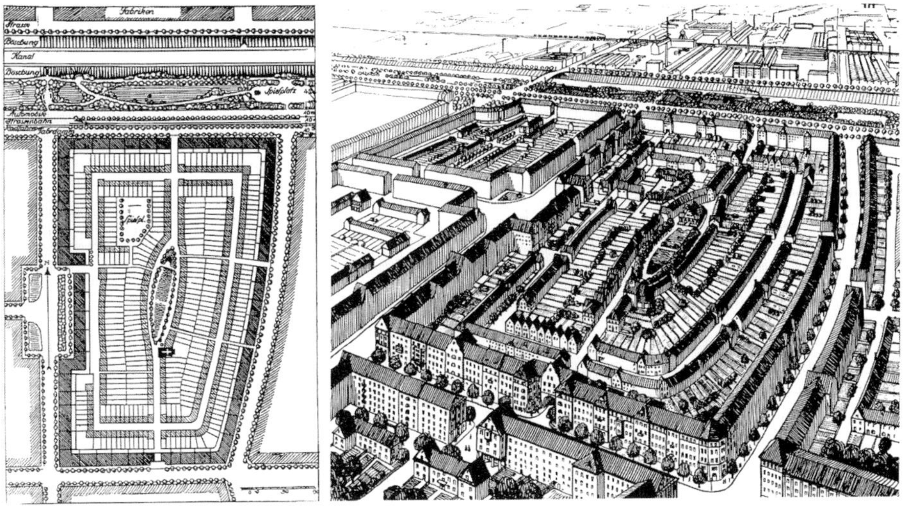

Bruno Möhring, Rudolf Eberstadt, and Richard Petersen, "Et in terra pax" project, Berlin, 1910. The plan and aerial view of this entry for the Greater Berlin competition shows an oversized perimeter block that provides space for a new neighborhood in its interior.

ter. General wisdom thought of the large dimensions of the Berlin block as the culprit behind the dense, light-deprived housing, but others, paradoxically, amplified the urban block in order to rethink its interior. "Et in terra pax," the entry by Bruno Möhring, Rudolf Eberstadt, and Richard Petersen (winners of the third prize), framed large urban blocks with tall perimeter buildings and inserted smaller houses into the center. The interior of the mega-block became a protected site, where rows of country homes, all with their private garden, were laid out according to garden city principles. Here, the country found itself in the center of the metro-polis. Framed by the homogeneity of a mega-courtyard block, the idyllic interior seems drastically removed from the chaos of the metropolis. With a blend of rural and urban dimensions, this project envisioned a new kind of city, where the uniformity and rigidity of the mega-block would meet the reciprocal patterns of the village.

From Jansen's meandering interior-urbanism to the village-urbanism of Möhring, Eberstadt, and Petersen, housing became the prime generator of urban form, in the tradition of Ildefons Cerdà's Barcelona extension. Whereas the practices of *Städtebau* were generally understood as an investigation into abstract formal, organizational, and representational levels of the city in the tradition of Vienna's Ringstraße, the Berlin proposals emphasized housing as the driving forces for urbanism. While clearly influenced by Camillo Sitte's principles and longing for an earlier, more picturesque image of the city, both schemes rethought the relationship between metropolis and architecture. One proposal invites the city into the urban block but manipulates its forces, while the other expands the block yet transplants the countryside into its interior. These proposals gave form to the otherwise shapeless climates of the city. In other words, their architectural form made the multiplicity of possible zones within the metropolis readable. The tall perimeter blocks, for example, visually differentiate a qualitative change from one side of the building wall to the other. With that, the scheme anticipated the discussion of the continuous façade and the mega-block, which would unfold in the coming decade and result in projects such as Hilberseimer's *Großstadt*. Yet Jansen's meandering block aims not at a unified urban form to reduce the complexities of the built city. Instead, it seems to intentionally complicate the architectural form in order to zone areas of different degrees of sound, speed, and vehicular and pedestrian flows. The project no longer aims at countering or clarifying the formless conditions of the city via a simplified and reduced architectural language, but substitutes the existing blocks with a more complex model that winds through the city, adapts to different urban configurations, and cultivates various climates.

The focus in these projects, as in many of the other submitted entries, was the moment of tension between the housing as building mass and the courtyard as void—between the constraints of the metropolis and the alternative environments of the urban interior. The relationship and ratio between building figure and urban ground was contested throughout the first decades of the twentieth century: from the planning entries in 1909, through Hegemann's exhibition and publication, to the confident declarations of the late 1920s. And, while it is difficult to recognize the formal language of these early housing typologies in the modernist schemes of the following decade, it is clear where the ambitions of the later projects originate. Hegemann's 1930 publication, *Das steinerne Berlin* (The Berlin of stone), would, therefore, show images of *Mietskasernen* (tenements) juxtaposed with contemporary housing projects, making their utter difference blatantly clear. Likewise Bruno Taut's GEHAG settlement in Britz (1927) and the GEHAG housing project in Zehlendorf (1928) are placed adjacent to images of rental barracks from the same districts. Buildings of the period by Luckhardt and Mendelsohn are analyzed and praised for their functional innovation and responsiveness to contemporary notions of speed, and Taut's horseshoe-shaped design is depicted as an innovative urbanism that documents a stark contrast to the *Mietskasernen* environment. While Hegemann admired the developments of the modern housing districts that took advantage of the openness that still existed far from the center of the city, in his view they merely displayed what "Berlin could have become."[39]

Hegemann's pessimistic narrative of an urban development of missed opportunities and late innovation was sharply countered in the overtly optimistic readings by the most committed modernists. Adolf Behne studied housing and declared a new type of living in his *Neues Wohnen–Neues Bauen* (New living–new building); Walter Curt Behrendt famously announced the *Victory of the New Building Style* (*Sieg des neuen Baustiles*) with a cover showing the newly opened Weissenhof housing settlement; Walter Gropius saw a new international architecture emerging, linked to a new lifestyle (*Internationale Architektur*); and Ludwig Hilberseimer related this architecture to new forms of urban life through what he called "metropolitan architecture" (*Großstadtarchitektur*). For these writers, the struggle toward a modern architecture was intimately linked to modern housing. Interestingly and not by coincidence, all of these publications appeared in 1927, the year in which Weissenhof opened and just before CIAM would gather modernist architects for the first time.

Aerial views of Prager Platz in Schöneberg, Berlin, 1910 (above) and GEHAG settlement in Britz, Berlin, 1927 (below), in Werner Hegemann, *Das Steinerne Berlin* (1930), 309. By juxtaposing historical quarters with Bruno Taut and Martin Wagner's urban forms, Hegemann sought to highlight the inadequacies of the older housing.

The two narratives—Hegemann's history of the rental barracks that could not be overcome, and the modernist evolution toward open housing settlements to which the rest of the world had to catch up—produced two different kinds of cities. Hegemann's pessimism saw no real option to overcome the chaos of *Mietskasernen* housing whereas Behne, Behrendt, Gropius, Hilberseimer, and Mies saw only opportunities in the new modernist developments. While both sides originated from the dealings with the modern metropolis, its repercussions in society, and its transformations through design, they would eventually end up on different ends of the spectrum. The enthusiasm and passion for modernity was countered by criticality and negativity. The climate of change that one side wholeheartedly embraced as it appeared to hold potentials for transformation, the other side saw as hopeless sorties in an already long-lost battle for a better city. Where one side expressed a city that "might be," the other described the city that "could have been."

There were just as many enthusiasts, toying with the productivities of modernity, as pessimists, who no longer saw any escape from (nor means to steer) the all-encompassing onslaught of transformation. Speaking for the latter, Weber had already illustrated the "cosmos of modern economic order ... as iron cage."[40] In his view the straitjacket of modernization had produced only specialists, caught up in the idea of "attain[ing] a level of civilization never before achieved."[41] In retrospect, this attack on rational thought, specialization, and hopeful visions reads like a preemptive critique of the modernist thinking that would unfold two decades later. Perhaps predictably, since Hegemann's research in 1910 was partially responsible for the urban world's disenchantment, by the 1920s he had joined in with Weber's skepticism.

The gulf between the two conceptual frameworks—commitment to modernity on the one hand versus deep-seated distrust of it on the other—was what Marshall Berman detected in the rigid polarities of the totalizing conceptions of the early twentieth century. In contrast to the ability of nineteenth-century thinkers to be simultaneously enthused about and opposed to modernity, their twentieth-century successors "either embraced [it] with a blind and uncritical enthusiasm, or else condemned [it] with a neo-Olympian remoteness and contempt."[42] From these perspectives, the city was either viewed in its hopeless formlessness or filled with terrains to reform. Between those polarizing urban narratives, however, lay the existing city. This was not the nineteenth-century city of the past that had created the metropolis, nor the modernist city of the future that was to combat urban formlessness through new housing typologies. Instead, it was the city where modern housing projects stood alongside the disordered monumentality of *Mietskasernen*. This would become the terrain that some of the most effective urban narratives straddled in their simultaneous criticism of and admiration for the existing city. Therefore, Berman is not entirely correct when suggesting that mentalities of "either/or" completely suppressed mindsets of "both/and." The latter continued to exist and, in fact, most narratives that sustained both realms preserved a level of simultaneity through a close reading of the two polarities.

Walter Benjamin's "Radioactive" City

When Walter Benjamin took to the airwaves with his first radio broadcasts in the late 1920s, he reported from within the city of the present by occupying the spectrum between the metropolis of *Mietskasernen* and that of modern housing experiments. Most of his programs between 1927 and 1933 aired from the Südwestdeutscher Rundfunk in Frankfurt and the Funkstunde in Berlin, and centered on topics that related to the metropolis, revisiting disputed urban areas and exploring the city as the origin of storytelling.[43] For those explorations, Benjamin relied heavily on architectural publications, including the urban research of Hegemann's *Das steinerne Berlin*,[44] Behne's modernist propaganda *Neues Wohnen–Neues Bauen*, as well as literary works by figures such as E.T.A. Hoffmann. He added the "fictional" spaces of stories to the "historical" perspectives of the city and the "prospective" experiments of designs. Reflecting on particular urban conditions, describing architectural works, and, most interestingly, calling on the listener to visit specific sites within the city, Benjamin's radio talks encouraged an active engagement with the city and its architecture. The new medium of the radio became in Benjamin's hands a vehicle to expose the everyday of the metropolis by making the listeners active participants in the material and spatial discoveries of the city they inhabited.

While during its early years radio was predominantly used for either the dissemination of bourgeois culture or the broadcasting of amusement, Benjamin offered a different model that explored urban culture through local observations, a fictional re-reading of urban environments, and, ultimately, the construction and setting up of a different, a parallel city, saturated with potential. Elaborating on the productivities of the medium, Benjamin wrote: "In comparison to the theater, radio represents not only a more advanced technical stage, but also one in which technology is more evident [and] the masses it grips are much larger."[45] Indeed, after the radio exhibition of 1926, which inaugurated Berlin's Radio Tower that Moholy-Nagy would soon photograph, Berlin had become the city with the greatest number of radio owners worldwide. With one out of three households tuning in, radio was now one of the most effective media outlets. Of course, its very capacity to reach large segments of the public by the early thirties simultaneously made it the centerpiece of the German propaganda machinery. But, whereas most of his colleagues came to view the radio as a mere propaganda outlet and distanced themselves from it, Benjamin refused to abandon this new public realm to the conservative movements and instead developed programs that were able to talk back as well as propose alternatives.

The broadcast of "Das dämonische Berlin" (The demonic Berlin), for example, explored possibilities of an altered reading of the city. By citing one of Hoffmann's stories, Benjamin explained that "Berlin is full of things to charm a storyteller ... which can only be teased out by dint of observation."[46] The mysterious figures, artifacts, and environments that Hoffmann detected became here captivating evocations of a city so far unseen—creating an analogous world that emerged from observations of everyday Berlin. Hoffmann as well as Benjamin were looking for urban situations that held the possibility of multiple interpretations. These locations were of particular interest since they offered the possibility to become sites for scenarios that could engage and, potentially, rework the present. Through the broadcasts, these ideas found their way into the consciousness of the city—reintroducing the concept of the saturated urban environment filled with things to discover, but this time with an operational twist. While Hoffmann based his stories in real urban locations in order to bring the narratives to life, Benjamin reversed this approach and viewed the story as a means to give access to an increasingly perplexing city. His readings of the metropolis became calls for its re-imagination and, occasionally, even calls for action.

In his broadcast on the *Mietskasernen*, Benjamin encouraged the listener to visit particular sites in the city.[47] The Meyer's Hof, one of the largest rental barracks and home to over one thousand people, was such a concrete location. "Go and see for yourselves," he urged the listeners and made the address known: Ackerstraße 132. In the next sentence, Benjamin recalled the scenery and with that placed the listener in front of the building: "If you look from the street down the row of courtyards, it's as if you were looking into a tunnel."[48] The radio was utilized to connect the living room with the street—appropriating the medium for an urban broadcast that was specific and collective, local and universal, domestic and urban at the same time. Entering the listener's everyday life, the radio had the potential to render the city from within. It addressed the audience on their own ground—meeting listeners more than halfway, in the relaxed settings of their homes, and inviting them to discover the city anew.

Techniques that Benjamin had previously observed in Bertolt Brecht's epic theater—like the portrayal of specific situations and the interruption of established plots through montage—became instrumental for his broadcasts.[49] Not only would the readings superimpose different scenes, locations, and histories onto each other and with that disrupt conventional structures of narration, the spatial setting of the radio would also collage conditions of the city into the domestic spaces of the home. The outcome was a double montage, once in the structure of the story and again through the very nature of radio. The domestication of the medium resulted in a diminished authority of the author and the increased responsibility of the audience—a Brechtian aspiration that aimed at turning consumers into producers. In the essay "The Author as Producer," Benjamin articulated his larger ambitions as follows: "first to induce other producers to produce, and second to put an improved apparatus at their disposal."[50] He detected this apparatus in Brecht's theater, in film, and in photography, and deployed it through radio. What was essential for the effectiveness of these apparati is that they do not reproduce situations but discover them and "thereby compel the listener to adopt an attitude vis-à-vis the process."[51] From that directive, the *Mietskasernen* broadcast became a vehicle to discover the city anew and to call upon the listener to take a position vis-à-vis the particular urban context. Most important, for the purposes of this chapter, is to recognize Benjamin's broadcasts for their capacity (or, at the very least, for their ambition) to detour and upset established narratives and to cultivate new attitudes toward the city.

Meyer's Hof, view from Ackerstraße 132/133, Berlin, c.1920. From the main entry along Ackerstraße, a clear view across all six courtyards opens up as each building volume doubles as a gate into the next courtyard.

This was even the objective for such universally ridiculed places as the *Mietskaserne*. While both sides of the spectrum had honed in on the *Mietskasernen* negativities, Benjamin viewed the courtyards of these housing blocks as voids within the thick layers of buildings and as places for stories to unfold. Inhabited by the ghosts of E.T.A. Hoffmann and the wanderers of Franz Hessel, the courtyards countered the pace and sound of the metropolis through an introverted yet publicly accessible urban space—changing the perspective on the world around. The analysis of the inhumanely dense housing and the modernist insistence on the need for transformation were here augmented. After he adopted *Das steinerne Berlin* as guide through the city, he addressed this position in a review of the book by noting: "These *Mietskasernen*, slum housing though they are, have created streets whose windows reflect not merely suffering and crime ..." After all, Benjamin continued, "the city child has always extracted potentials from the stairwell and the street ..."[52] For Benjamin, to identify with the life of the metropolis was a prerequisite to an effective argument—for "what you want to annihilate, you must not merely know; to complete the job, you must also have felt it."[53]

Benjamin supplied the housing debate with a strategic mechanism that on the one hand offers to find potential where it is most deformed while, on the oth-

Film stills of László Moholy-Nagy, *Berliner Stilleben*, 1931. At midpoint in the two-minute film, the camera enters Meyer's Hof from Ackerstraße and documents the activities in the different courtyards by focusing on childhood play.

er, keeps the target of productive transformation in sight. The tenor of negativity, associated with contemporary urbanity, is reworked through a dialectic in which the recognition of metropolitan productivities is just as imperative as the critique of built forms, with their origins in capitalist speculation. Against outright negation, Benjamin offered a theory capable of detecting and intervening when "one extreme turns into another one, where the positive coincides with the negative and the negative with the positive."[54] He did not disagree with the critique of the *Mietskasernen* but differed on which techniques to deploy to overcome the housing conditions. Benjamin positioned his "constructive principle" of the historical materialist against the universal, additive approach to history, which lacked a theoretical armature but "muster[ed] a mass of data."[55] Benjamin's dialectics capitalized on forms of montaged, urban narration, and an insistence on finding moments where the negative and positive intersect.

To demonstrate a possible rethinking of the city, Benjamin solicited a childlike imagination, where the dark courtyards of the *Mietskasernen*, for example, are recalled as the sites of childhood dreams. Through the eyes of a child, the courtyards (the gaps within the city) created a labyrinthine metropolis where a new world opened up—a world animated by the reflections of the surrounding windows and shadows of passersby. Illustrations of this imaginary world based on the real and grim conditions of urban living arrived shortly after the broadcast. László Moholy-Nagy followed Benjamin's invitation to visit the infamous *Mietskaserne* at Ackerstraße 132 and captured these intricate environments with his camera. He aimed at documenting the everyday life of the metropolis through a collage of scenes, and in 1931 his work was released as a short film, entitled *Berliner Stilleben* (Berlin still life). Interestingly, many of Moholy-Nagy's shots and particularly the scenes at the *Mietskaserne* zoom in on children's experiences and their playful engagements with the world of the courtyard.

As if he had seen Moholy-Nagy's footage, Benjamin would in the following year further elaborate on the unique spatial conditions of the courtyards and describe them as "one of the places where the city opened itself to the child."[56] His *Berliner Chronik* (*Berlin Chronicle*, 1932) and *Berliner Kindheit um neunzehnhundert* (*Berlin Childhood around 1900*, 1938) would both recall urban locations from childhood memory. For Benjamin, children possessed a heightened receptiveness and unique capacity to imagine alternative worlds or, as he had already explained in *Einbahnstraße* (*On-Way Street*, 1928), an interest in "produc[ing] their own small world of things within the greater one."[57] This makes it perhaps less surprising that his radio appearances were all programs for youth that became productive settings for the testing of ideas.[58] The child's imagination proved to be the most prolific source for a re-thinking of the city, since "the world is full of the most unrivaled objects for childish attention and use."[59] Just as a child is able to collage an imaginary scene onto the existing city that productively transforms it into another world, so Benjamin tried to juxtapose images of his childhood with perceptions from the present, while Moholy-Nagy montaged scenes of child play with images of fast-paced urban life. In the case of the latter, scenes of pedestrian flow and reflective surfaces over entries of department stores jump cut directly to the mysterious environments of rental barracks. While these scenes could not be more estranged, when montaged they articulate a metropolis of contrast and difference.

Such contrasts also suggested for Benjamin an alternative reading of architecture within the metropolis. The juxtaposition that Moholy-Nagy's movie camera captured on the ground, Benjamin spotted from the air, where "you see how grim, severe, gloomy, and military the rental barracks look in comparison to the peaceful houses of the garden plots, which are so amicably juxtaposed with one another."[60] While Benjamin found potential in the life of the metropolis and especially in the density of the *Mietskasernen*, he left no doubt of his support for modern architecture's experiments in housing. By expanding the urban imagery to aerial views of past and present conditions, Benjamin described two drastically different cities—the thick urban layers of tenements placed against the regular patterns and widely spaced rows of modern housing. He referred here to the same two photographs that were published in *Das steinerne Berlin* just months before.[61] Yet, Benjamin's selective reading of the book communicated to the listener a perspective of a city largely unknown; a perspective from the air that highlighted the openness and regularity of new master plans by architects and planners such as Fritz Bräuning, Martin Wagner, and Bruno Taut.

In addition to the two photographs, Benjamin was inspired by the writings of Behne and Giedion, whose books *Neues Wohnen–Neues Bauen* and *Befreites Wohnen* (Liberated living) reflect on new forms of living. Both developed a vocabulary that would become instrumental for Benjamin's interpretations of these new urban environments for living. Where the two publications contrast the historical fortress to a new architecture of lightness and transparency, so would Benjamin describe how "stone is replaced by a narrow frame of concrete and steel, the compact and impenetrable façades by giant glass plates."[62] Benjamin saw this as a dramatic departure from previous forms of dwelling. The transparency of glass, the lightness of structure, the flexibility of interior organization, and the openness of the urban plan, all contributed to an instability that uprooted the notion of the home as a permanent and stable condition. No longer was the home a retreat from the city around it, nor was it anymore a bastion of self-expression. Instead, it foreshadowed a transient and nomadic living of uncompromising flexibility, openness, and simplicity. "Dwelling in the old sense of the world, where security had priority, has had its day. Giedion, Mendelsohn, Corbusier turned the abiding places of man into a transit area for every conceivable kind of energy and for waves of light and air."[63] And, of course, for radio waves as well. The future, Benjamin concluded, "is dominated by the idea of transparency."[64] But transparency involved new kinds of impoverishment as well as radicality. A poverty that for Benjamin involved not just loss but gain.

While Paul Scheerbart's *Glasarchitektur* (1914) heavily influenced Benjamin's reading of glass, the true potentials of the material surfaced for him not in Scheerbartian expressionism but instead in the experiments of Le Corbusier, J.J.P. Oud, and the Bauhaus. Works by those architects presented in Benjamin's view the fullest potential of a glass architecture, capitalizing on a material that is simultaneously clear and reflective, brittle and smooth, austere and elegant, see-through and undocumentable. With these conditions in mind, Benjamin wrote in 1933 about

4

Schlafzelle in einem 1928 erbauten Zuchthaus

Foto „I. A. Z."

Nicht nur Zuchthauszellen sperren wir von Luft und Licht ab. Eisen und Eisenbeton gestatten dem Licht freiesten Einlaß. Aber Behörden und „aesthetische" Paragraphen sorgen dafür, daß unsere Wohnhäuser und öffentlichen Bauten, Kranken- und Schulhäuser, Postgebäude, Banken, zwecks Erhöhung ihrer „Monumentalität" ihre freien Öffnungen durch steinerne Attrappen wieder verhängen. Künstlich umgeben wir uns mit Kerkermauern.

5

R. DÖCKER

Krankenhaus Waiblingen

1926/28

Foto R. Döcker

Ausblick von einem Zimmer auf die Terrassen und die Landschaft (vgl. Abb. 57, 58). Der Skelettbau gestattet, die Wand in Glas aufzulösen. Nur die Konstruktion bleibt stehen. Die Landschaft strömt herein. Der Kranke fühlt sich nicht mehr von der Welt isoliert. Der Kranke braucht Licht und psychische Erheiterung ebenso notwendig wie Antisepsis. Wir aber bauen im allgemeinen unsere Krankenhäuser wie Zuchthäuser und Kasernen.

Sigfried Giedion, *Befreites Wohnen: Licht, Luft, Öffnung* (1929), 4–5. Comparing a jail cell (left) to a room in a modern hospital (right), Giedion wrote below the hospital image: "The skeletal frame allows the wall to be dissolved through glass ... [currently, however] hospitals are built like jails and barracks."

the "Experience and Poverty" of glass, which he perceived as an instrument toward a new subjectivity.[65] In its transparency, glass is understood as the enemy of secrecy just as much as it is the enemy of property, in that everything is available for all to view. In addition, its smoothness makes it nearly impossible to fasten anything on it or to leave any traces. This makes glass not only the counter-material to the bourgeois home of souvenirs and knick-knacks but it also becomes the material of the fugitive and of resistance. To further extrapolate, a glassed-in environment might be the ideal condition of the revolutionary, hiding in plain sight in a space that accumulates no traces, with one's exact location distorted and fractured through reflectivity.

With that in mind, Benjamin's phrase: "to live in a glass house is a revolutionary virtue par excellence," gains a more direct meaning.[66] The multiple dimensions of glass gave Benjamin an opportunity to speak of the growing dangers of nationalism, surveillance, and state control.[67] Radicalizing the material to the level of impoverishment was, therefore, an act of passing through the optimism of modern architecture and deploying its most productive material as apparatus to fight the rise of Fascism. Detlef Mertins has already shown how Benjamin's readings of glass relate to a technological unfolding that brought about a new "kind of barbarism whose destructiveness had a positive moment" in that it "takes us to a milieu in which the tracelessness of the fugitive becomes an image for a groundless ground on which collective dreams pass into reality."[68] And, Hilde Heynen, concluded that glass for Benjamin "should be regarded as a material that literally expresses the transparency of the new society that would be founded on revolutionary lines."[69] However, with the potentials of glass, came also the limitations of construction and the impossibility to rework entire cities—an impossibility so vividly displayed in the utopian expressionism of Bruno Taut's *Alpine Architecture*. In other words, living in modern homes, surrounded by large surfaces of glass, was only granted to a few individuals, while the majority of urban residents lived in tenements from the nineteenth century.

Benjamin's radio broadcasts reached and engaged much larger groups of the public via properties similar to those of glass. Just as transparency can disclose parts of the interior, so do radio waves penetrate walls and leap through and into the sheltered homes of the everyday city. But radio waves, as a type of electromagnetic radiation that travels at the speed of light, do not simply pass through objects, walls, and buildings; they are slowed down by architecture. As such, they penetrate the city and simultaneously register its built form. It is, therefore, no coincidence that Benjamin equates the modern homes of Adolf Loos to the "political radioscopy of sexuality and family."[70] Glass can reveal the interior or, to borrow from radioscopy, can allow views into the inner structure of opaque objects. Indeed, the technology of radioscopy paralleled the developments in modern architecture, to the extent that analogies and comparisons between glass façades and X-rays became common in popular culture as well as in the architectural avant-garde. As Beatriz Colomina has pointed out, this enabled a new language of modern architecture in which transparency became intimately linked to the rhetoric of sanitation and health.[71] Radio waves, at the time also called "invisible light,"[72] penetrate the city like X-rays proceed through the body. The difference is that Benjamin's radical radio left instructions behind—instructions that enabled listeners to discover the city anew. X-ray vision turned into sonic experience, saturating the ether of the metropolis with ciphers for the discovering, decoding, and reworking of the city.

When Benjamin circled back to the modern home in his radio broadcasts, he shared Giedion's expectation that the openness and transparency of these architec-

László Moholy-Nagy, *Berliner Funkturm*, 1928. The Radio Tower became understood as a conduit to change the perception of the city. According to Moholy-Nagy, this occurred through the spatial properties of the structure, while Walter Benjamin saw its power in the technology of broadcasting.

tures would generate a different mentality. This enthusiasm was broadcast to the general public in a message that was just as hopeful and remarkably assertive: "The many people that will live in such buildings will gradually be transformed by them ... This future image of the city will inspire people at least as much as airships, automobiles, or ocean liners do today."[73] Of the many references to modern architecture in the work of Benjamin, his radio broadcasts stated his endorsements most plainly—and even more confidently than most of the architects who designed the modern *Siedlungen* (housing settlements). On radio, simultaneously the most public and most private form of dissemination, Benjamin became most outspoken. He changed the narrative on the *Mietskaserne* at a time when the verdict of its negativity was nearly universal, and he supplemented a vision of the modern *Siedlung*, which had yet to be discovered by the general public.

In addition, he also implied a new urban future. For Benjamin, living in the modern housing settlements would promote an awareness of the new capacities of an architecture that revises and eventually defies spatial boundaries, visual restrictions, and structural limitations. Again, Moholy-Nagy's "new optics" would become instrumental for Benjamin. As he recorded in his notes for the *Arcades Project*, his fascination with Moholy-Nagy's photographs of the Pont Transbordeur in Marseilles (1928) originated from the extended spatiality, the machined vision, and the gravity-defying qualities of the structure—a new kind of space that pushed architecture beyond its limits by narrating a new relationship between architecture and city. In this image as well as in Moholy-Nagy's photo series of the Berlin Radio Tower, a technologically mediated vision recalibrated the view. The familiar environment of the city is cropped and abstracted, providing a new, unfamiliar topography saturated with unexpected visual productivities. While views from the Radio Tower offered Moholy-Nagy glimpses of a city so far unseen, Benjamin's radio descriptions transmitted these experiences to the living rooms of tenements. His alternative visions, from the playful stories based in the contentious realm of the tenement courtyards to the properties of transparency in the open *Siedlungen*, aimed at more than just the cultivation of new urban images. At stake was the formulation of a new kind of cultural production to which the medium of the radio was particularly well suited. Listeners, able to evaluate all they heard against their own milieux, would emerge as critics and, ultimately, as effective instigators and producers of alternative narratives.

Benjamin's deployment of the radio to engage and activate the territories of culture and the city might be best and most succinctly described as "radioactive." Theodor Adorno had used the term in 1950 to articulate the transformative power of Benjamin's writings, but it serves particularly insightfully in the context of his broadcasts.[74] Hinting at the potential dangers of the work, its explosiveness, and its lasting impact—contaminating all territories that it reaches—it also implies dispersal across spatial and disciplinary boundaries. One degree removed from associations with radiation, the term combines the means of the radio with that of action, even activism. Undeniably, the radicalized narratives and images of Benjamin's urban broadcasts aimed at disputing preconceptions about existing urbanity; at the very least, they suspended routines and, at best, they entirely transformed established norms and invented new forms of cultural practice. The broadcasts challenged the very idea of the city by operating through an urban dialectic that finds as much potential in the negativities of the *Mietskasernen* as in the coolness of modernist housing. Even as he became one of the most outspoken advocates of the *Siedlungen*, Benjamin viewed both urban conditions as productive spatial and organizational constructs that not only affected the way people live but also the way they see the future. The city was newly engaged through alternative models of urban narration that performed a catalytic role by extrapolating found conditions, "détourning" existing conventions, and inferring new possibilities.

Situationist City *Détournement*

More than two decades later, Benjamin's "radioactive" ideas would find a continuation through a group of young French radicals who emulated his broadcasts and took to the airwaves in an attempt to engage the passivity of what they called the "society of spectacle." This time, however, the transformative capacities of his techniques were aimed at an already modernized city. In the aftermath of World War II, modernist planning principles had become a prominent force in reconstruction efforts, by swiftly shifting accelerated war-time production to a postwar mass-assembly of architecture and urbanism.[75] However, in the context of postwar housing settlements—often only vaguely resembling their modernist precursors—the hopeful visions of modern experimentation encountered a growing skepticism, which questioned architecture's abilities in relationship to social and political ideologies. Narratives of the existing, historical, and everyday city became paramount in the pursuit of alternatives to the homogenizing forces of modern planning principles, the commodification of architecture, and the spectacles of media that soon penetrated all aspects of modern life. For two collectives—the Lettrists and later the Situationist International (SI)—the modernist urban renovation efforts increasingly canceled the complexities of the existing city, resulting in some areas in a vacuous urban uniformity while in others in the "museumization" of the historical city. In addition, home technologies such as radio and television further transformed the city through a retreat from public life into domestic confines.

Deploying the very media they critiqued provided the two groups with means to infiltrate the environment of passive consumption and to use it against itself. René Viénet, one of the SI associates, outlined it thus: "By appropriating the very suggestions of the spectacle, we may at once provide the reasons for present and future rebellions."[76] Le Corbusier's motto "Architecture or Revolution?" became "Architecture *and* Revolution!" And, when Viénet spoke of the subversive qualities of radio, he seemed to have Benjamin's broadcasts in mind, establishing a direct correlation between messages in the airwaves and actions against the status quo via pirate stations. "We know that any radio ham can inexpensively transmit to the neighborhood, and that the small size of the necessary equipment allows for a high level of mobility and thus for evading attempts at tracing the broadcast location."[77] Radio broadcasting was simultaneously understood as a means of propaganda that uses the opponents' tools against them and as a technique to derail existing conditions through diversion and misappropriation.

In his interruption of preconceptions and biases, Benjamin had already reworked established narratives of the city through recontextualization, making his broadcasts a proto-Situationist act of *détournement* (diversion) in which the radio enabled a diversion from existing contexts into new milieus. The proximity between Benjamin's revolutionary use of the radio and the Situationist spatial practice of revolt becomes especially clear when the later experiments with radio are viewed against the backdrop of these earlier broadcasts. In 1954, the Lettrist International announced in their fifteenth *Potlatch* newsletter that they had just completed a series of "radio propaganda" pieces, which they offered to any station that was "willing to take the risk of playing these unusual tapes."[78] Just like the rumblings of *Potlatch*, which today read as if all members are speaking and shouting at the same time to set up new forms of engagement, so were the radio broadcasts giveaways that in return asked for a thorough analysis of what is being read or heard. If *Potlatch* was, as Greil Marcus has convincingly described, "an attempt to start a conversation ... that could only end in the discovery of a new language, with a new subject, which was to say a new idea of social life,"[79] then the radio was, of course, a natural form of broadcast, with abilities that the Situationists eventually came to see also in film.

Guy Debord, a leading member of the Lettrists and the main instigator of the SI, published his scripts for a radio program in consecutive volumes of *Potlatch* in 1955 under the heading "The educational value," a name that again links back to Benjamin's works for youth radio. The scripts outline a fictive dialog among different voices, taken from a multitude of sources that could not be more distinct: ranging from the *Communist Manifesto* to the Biblical books of Jeremiah and Samuel, from the French evening news to a sixth-grade textbook on geography. While each voice on its own is comprehensible, the topics are vastly different and intentionally juxtaposed. The first voice begins with the phrase "Let's talk about the rain ...," which is immediately followed by the second voice reciting the rape of Tamar from the *Book of Samuel*, only to have the third voice theorize the bourgeois family. What is presented as a single radio program is, in fact, the insertion of one into many others. It sounds similar to slow turns on the radio dial that allow listeners to scroll past different stations, fading in and out of a diversity of interviews, readings, and reports, a mock scanning of frequencies in the ether. Yet this broad sampling was no random collection of sources. While its thickness spoke to the saturation of contemporary media, it altered existing conventions by "détourning" religious, political, and popular contexts, through a dramatic recontextualization.

The technique of *détournement* at work here involves a deflection and diversion of sources, a misuse and hijacking of contexts, and a misappropriation and turning of existing milieus onto themselves. The technique that aimed at breaking down all boundaries of common understanding in order to form new associations would become fundamental to the SI's rediscoveries of the city and the formulation of other kinds of urbanism in the trenches of contemporary urban life. From Debord's collages of deflected phrases, to Asger Jorn's attacks on masterpieces with splashes of paint, to the appropriations of streets as a battleground by students in 1968, the aim was not just to alter but to overthrow existing conventions and to create alternative forms of collectivity. Just as Jorn announced in 1959: "Painting is over. You might as well finish it off,"[80] so were the streets of the city dismantled when pavement stones became projectiles against De Gaulle's police force in Paris. This suggests that *détournement* always comes with a certain degree of ferocity, which Marcus described as "a politics of subversive quotation" in which familiar scripts are torn apart.[81] Yet *détournement* does not solely unhinge and obliterate; in fact, the aim was always to infiltrate the medium under attack and to transform its directives. "Long live painting," Jorn's final line of his manifesto on "détourned" painting, is as much a reminder of this ambition as was the discovery of the beach-like sandy ground beneath the streets during the 1968 protests.

Street view after demonstration, Paris, 1968. The dismantled street reveals the sand under the pavement, just as the slogans of '68 promised.

When slogans like "beneath the pavement—the beach" started appearing in the form of graffiti on walls throughout Paris, they were at first a Situationist forecast of another urban life to come. They soon became successful psychogeographic experiments, where sand was indeed found under the cobblestones of city streets. *Détournement* became effective within the city, the ultimate realm of Situationist interpretation, imagination, and intervention (in that order). The discovery of sandy beaches on the "shores" of Parisian streets also suggested that the city still held all kinds of magical conditions that far surpassed conventional routines of capitalist efficiency and commodity spectacle. Taking reference from surrealist techniques and coupling those with the long tradition of detecting emotional attributes in urban conditions, the Situationists came to the conclusion that "cities have psychogeographical contours, with constant currents, fixed points and vortexes that strongly discourage entry into or exit from certain zones."[82] The city is described as an intensely emotional topography—a condition that Debord found illustrated in the seventeenth-century *Map of Tenderness* by François Chauveau.

The map in its first iteration had been inserted into Madeleine de Scudéry's novel *Clélie*, effectively spatializing the treacherous landscapes of love and friendship, and translating the written page into geographic mapping. Anthony Vidler has called this moment a "spatial diversion from the narrative of the novel."[83] When Debord juxtaposed this map with an aerial view of Amsterdam, an altered narrative was indeed constructed between the two illustrations. He seems to suggest that under the city's pavement, in the shadow of its monuments, in the depth of its urban blocks, and along its narrow canals are hidden territories: mountain ranges of emotions, oceans of danger, and lakes of indifference. Amsterdam is here

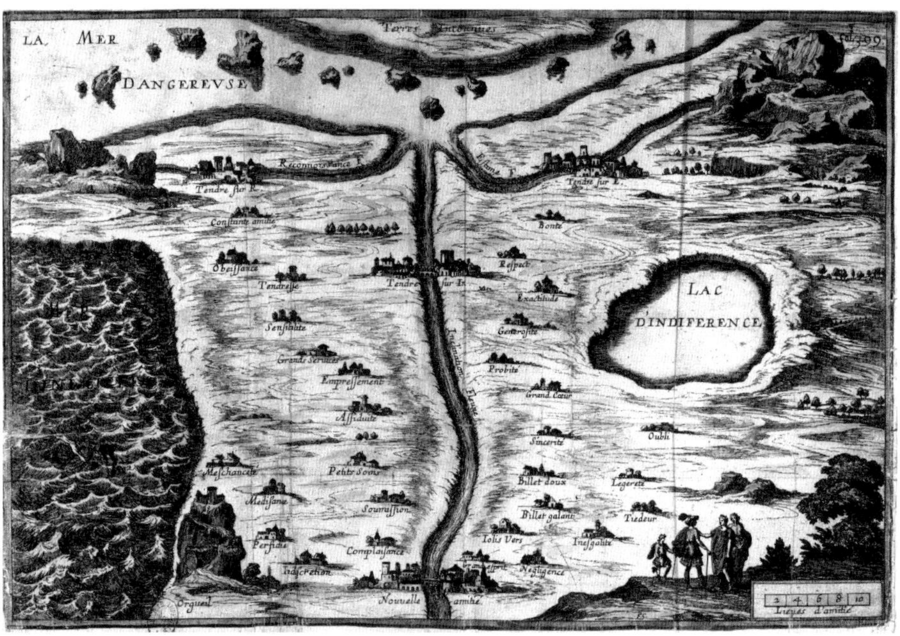

Aerial view of the center of Amsterdam (above) and *Map of Tenderness* by François Chauveau, 1654 (below). By juxtaposing the two terrains in an article in 1959, Guy Debord aimed at conflating both in order to make visible a different kind of city, guided by passions along and below Amsterdam's canals and buildings.

"détourned," approximating states of mind and conditions of events rather than physical locations of sites. The illustration that previously had supplemented a narrative was now utilized to construct an altered urban plot, which the SI aimed to unearth. The psychogeographical detection of these often hidden territories utilized what the Situationists called a *dérive*, a kind of urban sonar in search of layers, vortices, and flows that would give access to a different kind of city, removed from commerce, routines, and conventions.

The *dérive*, or drifting, was defined as "a technique of rapid passage through varied ambiences [that] involve[s] playful-constructive behavior and awareness of psychogeographical effects."[84] The Situationist drifter would surrender to the forces of the city, not in a passive manner that privileges chance, but through a productive exchange in which the urban conditions, signs, and qualities guided the steps. If done right, the *dérive* bypassed the monotonies of urban habits and instead followed the buried contours and narratives of the existing city. To that extent, the *dérive* is the final *détournement*—it diverts the drifter's course through the city, leading to the uncovering of latent urban situations and, eventually, to the setting up of new ones. The Situationists were particularly intrigued by urban conditions that resisted assimilation into the modernizing city; they were fascinated by the immediacy, morbidity, and roughness of certain sites that defied a clear reading of urban space; and captivated by moments in which the fabric of the city breaks open.

Benjamin's earlier psychogeography already described "unequaled fascinating thresholds ... where at countless places in the great city one stands on the edge of the void."[85] The dramatic topographies that Benjamin found in the urban courtyards, peripheries, no-man's-lands, and formal inconsistencies of an earlier city, were systematically occupied, interrogated, and mapped by the Situationists. While they encountered very different cities, the locations that Benjamin and the Situationists embraced were similar, not coincidentally. The former found potential in conditions brought about by the forces of the metropolis that planning sought to apprehend, while the latter group detected locations that were not yet subsumed by the harmonizing techniques of modern urbanism. Both understood these moments of discomfort as conditions set against the homogeneity of the contemporary city and, therefore, as zones prone to experimentation. Returning to the blind spots of the city, the Situationists entered them in an effort to trace their boundaries and decipher their raw urban imagery. The formlessness that in Benjamin's city had seemed overwhelming to most, was three decades later understood as the last vestige of urban imagination left among the increasingly dominating city of commodity spectacle.

View of the shelter at Missions Etrangères square, Paris. Michèle Bernstein not only accepted but also admired the strange shelter in the square as well as the austere, tall, and blank wall that borders it.

Michèle Bernstein, a frequent collaborator with Debord and passionate drifter herself, wrote an article for *Potlatch* in 1955 that drew attention to the Missions Etrangères square in Paris. At first, the location reveals no significance if judged according to conventional urban or architectural analysis. Yet her account discloses a place where different city-forms clash—a location that hovers between the 6th and the 7th Arrondissement, between an empty public square and semi-public gardens, between private courtyards and urban blank walls, and between the utilitarian demands of a bus stop and a small commemorative monument to Chateaubriand. Bernstein described all of this in a rapid, telegraphic prose, which even further exaggerates the already convoluted conditions that result from the fallout of urban construction, rather than design considerations. Parts of the space, she noted, are enclosed by "blackened walls over ten meters high" that are, in fact, "the backs of some large buildings."[86] Bernstein had effectively entered the spatial leftover of the modern city, a forgotten piece of urban density, untouched by the calibrating beautification efforts of modern urbanism.

The area had "no obvious socioeconomic complexion," Simon Sadler noted in his analysis, "other than its unfashionableness. Yet there was something here to haunt the visitor."[87] In the shadows of the representational Parisian boulevards, avenues, and plazas Bernstein spotted a land mass so removed from its surroundings that its otherworldliness even encouraged actions. As Bernstein wrote, "[the square] may be used for receiving visitors, for being stormed by night and for other psychogeographical purposes."[88] Despite its apparent matter-of-factness, Bernstein's few paragraphs on the Missions Etrangères were not simply recollections of an urban space but rather a perception-bending narrative to instruct readers to experience and inhabit the city differently. An urban situation of the most profound incoherence and formlessness became through Bernstein's voice-over a space of utmost quality and an example for a different kind of city and a different kind of life within it. For Bernstein and her co-conspirators, these locations presented opportunities to inhabit the city differently. Because the space lacked urban

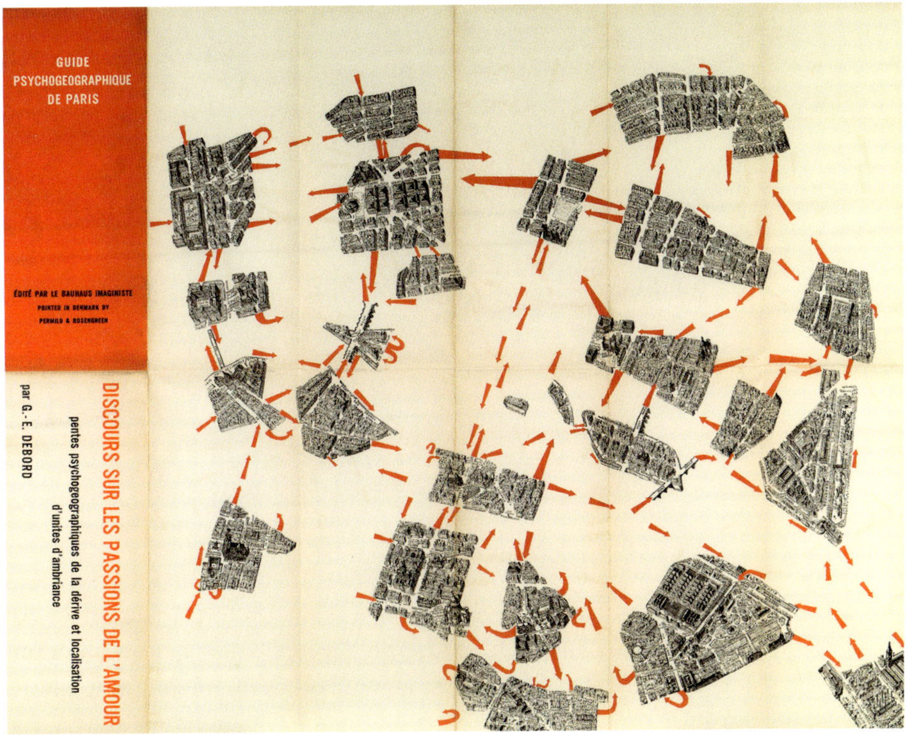

Guy Debord and Asger Jorn, *Guide psychogéographique de Paris: discours sur les passions de l'amour*, 1956. Composed with cut-outs from Georges Peltier's *Plan de Paris à vol d'oiseau*.

structure, or better, was the fallout of multiple conflicting structures, it had remained open to interpretation, inhabitation, and deviation—as Bernstein suggested, it could be besieged at night and steered to other ends.

One year after Bernstein's article, Guy Debord and Asger Jorn isolated situations like these and reassembled the city of Paris by creating a map that described an experience of spaces set into relationships. In the 1956 *Guide psychogéographique* they collaged the activity of their journeys, entering and exiting working-class districts and urban in-between zones that the Situationists deemed worthy of study. Shortly thereafter the information was further abstracted into the *Naked City* (1957). The first urban assemblage is of particular interest since the city fragments are shown in an axonometric view, enabling the onlooker to more readily enter the three-dimensionality of the city. Debord and Jorn deployed the *Plan de Paris à vol d'oiseau* drawn by Georges Peltier—a highly detailed depiction of the city that not only labeled the streets and plazas but also showed the façades of the buildings, the

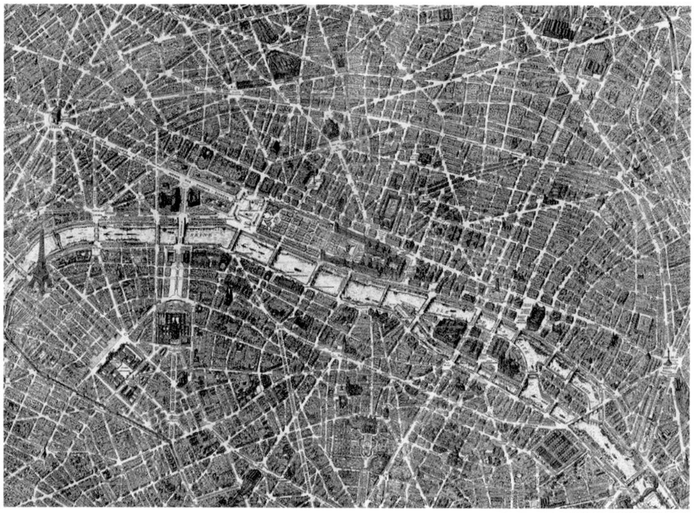

Georges Peltier, *Plan de Paris à vol d'oiseau*, 1951. Peltier modeled his drawing on the celebrated Turgot plan of Paris (1739).

foliage along the streets, and even enabled views into courtyards. While Peltier's drawing aimed at the most detailed depiction of Paris in order to give the city form, coherence, and orientation, the Situationists "détourned" the map by only selecting the most incoherent parts and cutting away the rest. In contrast to Bernstein's earlier narrative about one existing urban situation, the *Guide psychogéographique* assembled multiple urban fragments in order to formulate a new urban terrain, where the viewer was taken on a journey through a radically fragmented city. The parts that evaded modernization and that had so far withstood the homogenizing order of urban renovation were composed into an imaginary city. In the *Guide psychogéographique*, a district such as Les Halles (still existing in 1956 but razed in 1971) drifted from its central position to the upper left corner of the reconfigured map. The *Guide* articulates a city devoid of coherent form, with red arrows narrating the fractured, temporal, and disordered conditions of the formless city. In these moments of urban juxtaposition the Situationists saw the opportunity for an alternative urban life, where one could still detect the range of socio-economic mixture, and where gentrification had not yet advanced.

These were also the territories from which the Situationists fought back—districts simultaneously understood as examples of and seeds for a different kind of city and, therefore, a different kind of social life. With that ambition in mind, the red arrows on the psychogeographical maps might not only stand for the rapid

Christo and Jeanne-Claude, *Iron Curtain*, Paris, 1962. On June 27, 1962, a wall of 89 oil barrels closed off the Rue Visconti.

passage from one neighborhood into another but might also signal a transfer of one urban atmosphere into its neighboring blankness. In this light, the maps serve no longer just as tracings of urban qualities worth preserving but become battle plans for the setting-up of counter-sites. In the final passages of his 1956 "User's Guide to *Détournement*," Debord had already written: "If *détournement* were extended to urbanistic realizations, not many people would remain unaffected by an exact reconstruction in one city of an entire neighborhood of another. Life can never be too disorienting: *détournement* on this level would really spice it up."[89] Here, the importation of one district into another became a prospect through which Debord speculated on urban *détournement* at the scale of the city. This vision was first mapped out through the moving regions in the *Guide psychogéographique* and *Naked City*, was later tested with individual urban installations, and eventually found widespread use when students took to the streets in 1968.

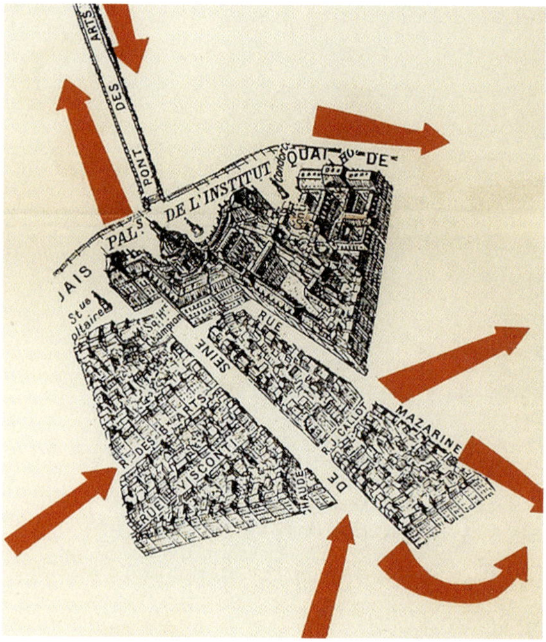

Detail of the *Guide psychogéographique de Paris*. The Rue Visconti, where Christo and Jeanne-Claude staged their *Iron Curtain*, is at the lower left.

By the early 1960s, Debord's aspiration to divert parts of a city and stage its confusion came to pass. An early work by Christo and Jeanne-Claude (who were not part of the SI) piled oil barrels to block a street on the southern banks of the River Seine. With this kind of installation, *détournement* entered the city and challenged existing urbanities—after all, "Life can never be too disorienting." Hal Foster and Tom McDonough have already written about the political dimensions of this work (suggested also by the title of the piece, *Iron Curtain*) and its deployment of a "semi-Situationist strategy."[90] For the purpose of this chapter, it is worth expanding these arguments to include the resemblance of this work to Debord's use of urban importations and to recognize it as a manifestation of a Situationist urban architecture. With that, the work shifts from the detection and passage through existing situations to the setting-up of new conditions. In fact, the *Guide psychogéographique* already included the Rue Visconti, where the *Iron Curtain* was installed, and it highlighted the surrounding neighborhood, which the work would affect. This overlap suggests a possible reading of the map as a planning device rather than exclusively as a guide to the "discourse on the passions of love" in urban ambiances, as the subtitle implies.

More than an act of urban forensics, the map might be understood as the basis for setting up new situations, spatial experiments, and urban pranks. In the case of Christo and Jeanne-Claude's *Iron Curtain*, a massive wall blocked a narrow one-way street between two important arteries, effectively creating two dead-end alleys and, therefore, a rerouting of traffic and pedestrian routines. Constructed overnight and without official permit, this act of urban sabotage occupied the street only for a few hours but for that time returned one street to its pedestrians. It, furthermore, rearranged urban typologies by setting up two facing cul-de-sacs, an antithesis to the modern urbanism of traffic with its smooth connectivities and calibrated flows. Not only did the makeshift urban wall intentionally rupture the existing neighborhood, but it also provoked a different use of the city and rethought modes of urbanism. Nonsensical in the eyes of planners and traffic engineers, the installation was a direct assault on infrastructure and a hostile gift to the capitalist city—a Situationist offering that wanted to be so much more than just an instant. The installation's "principle can be extended to the whole area of an entire city,"[91] the description reads and, with that, adds this strategy to the Situationist catalog of means toward a "unitary urbanism." After all, the SI wanted "at the very least to build cities, the environment suitable to the unlimited deployment of new passions."[92]

The urban obstacle that the *Iron Curtain* erected with oil barrels was multiplied and expanded across the city of Paris in May 1968 by turning burning cars into barricades and declaring universities like the Sorbonne as "autonomous people's institution." In Paris, the events of 1968 began with calls for educational reform and sexual integration of dormitories, and quickly escalated into massive demonstrations, street fighting, and thousands of arrests.[93] Situationist tactics were deployed on the urban battlegrounds of this and other cities, making common practice of the invasion and appropriation of public spaces and buildings and the *détournement* of infrastructures through barricades. The nomadic and deterritorialized practices that the Situationists had previously outlined in their maps, reports, photo-essays, posters, records, films, and radio scripts, were now set into action. Certainly, the impact of the group on the events of 1968 was retroactively inflated by comments such as: "Where there was fire, we carried gasoline." But their proximity to '68 was not just self-inflicted. After all, the Situationists contributed narratives that privileged active engagements with the city. In contrast to common architectural understandings of the city as a built form composed of volumes and open space (of figures and ground), the Situationists began to see the city not purely as an architectural construct but primarily as a terrain of events—a terrain in which actions, procedures, and happenings continuously unfolded and interweaved.

Even the most architectural enterprises by members of the SI always expressed a collective building, experiencing, and rebuilding of spatial configurations for the playful unfolding of life. For example, Constant Nieuwenhuys's New Babylon project, which was named by Debord but had his support only until he and Constant (as he was known) parted ways over their competing definitions of unitary urbanism, was an environment for a continuous and unending *dérive* through sensory stimulation and artistic mediation. Indeed, the plans for New Babylon can be understood as the spatialization of the psychogeographical maps, with zones,

Constant Nieuwenhuys, *Group Sector at New Babylon*, 1962. Constant's drawing offers a vision of an interior that, similar to the city, is impacted by various speeds and the constant alteration of spatial conditions at the hand of its inhabitants.

vectors, passages, and sectors of ambiances that float above the city—a structure that aides the traversing of its interiors at different speeds. What modern urbanism had taken away, namely "disorientation on a daily basis,"[94] was to return to the city through a suspended structure of atmospheres that encouraged the collective perplexion of its inhabitants, for whom art and desires would become lifestyle. While the architect sponsored the framework, the inhabitants of New Babylon were to engage the structure through constant changes, iterations, and alterations. "The more perfectly defined the form," Constant wrote already in 1948, "the less active is the onlooker."[95] While this note challenged conventional architectural practice—which according to Constant was too concerned with forms that limited the unfolding of imaginative inhabitation and events—it also came to haunt Constant's own project.

Just as his work made room for conditions that lacked formal definition in order to convert inhabitants into builders of situations, so did the project inadvertently endorse the existing city as the quintessential formless condition and, therefore, as the ultimate stimulant for the urban drifter. One of Constant's conceptual collages from 1969 even represents the network of zones through maps of different cities. Street maps are cut up and collaged into a new network, where the configuration of one neighborhood moves across or is set against a district from another

Constant Nieuwenhuys, *Symbolic Representation of New Babylon*, 1969. By assembling plans from different cities, Constant imagined the collision of city forms and climates that develop into a new kind of urban interior, where the drifter moves swiftly from one atmosphere into the next.

city. Constant effectively exchanged the arrows of the *Guide psychogéographique* with districts from other cities. He not only literalized Debord's earlier proposal of importing one city into another, but New Babylon inhaled the organizational forms of cities from around the world for an incessant urban unfolding. The selected zones from places such as Venice, Berlin, London, Barcelona, or Bern are already abundantly intricate—a complexity further heightened when juxtaposed against one another. This collaged network suggests a vast interior filled with different urban qualities; a terrain of radical contrast. Rivers threaten to flood street grids, avenues launch into parks, and buildings suddenly turn into alleys. Of course, the technique itself had been used before, extending from the random mumblings of Dadaist poems and the collective iterations of surrealist drawings to William S. Burroughs cut-ups. But with Constant's New Babylon these methods reached a new dimension: deployed at the scale of the city, cut-ups of maps now realigned to form an urban "exquisite-corpse."

The project remained an abstracted representation of existing situations within the city and, therefore, a constant reminder of urban complexities that architecture can always and only approximate. Yet, the polemics of the project also far exceed the realities of building. Its ambitions seem clear: an aggravation of the modernized city and its routines; a work that Mark Wigley called "a provocation rather than a city" and that Constant himself aimed at "stimulat[ing] action."[96] New Babylon turned deliberate Situationist agitations into designed spatial atmospheres and, from there, into a polemic for a different kind of urban life. Through lectures by Constant and exhibitions of New Babylon, the project developed into a directed assault on the modern rational city and a piece of propaganda for a radical collective urbanism. Therefore, images of the scheme in conjunction with Constant's rhetoric became the ultimate carriers of the project. Photographs of the many models that Constant produced became even more central than the original artifacts. They rarely just document the models; instead, they seem to be in pursuit of placing the viewer inside the space, sometimes adding special effects, and eventually superimposing different negatives in order to further exaggerate the spatial complexity.[97] Finally, film was used to capture the movement around and inside the structures, the fluidity of space, and the complexity of these urban interiors. While Constant seems to have always considered the photographs as a cinematic series through which the models can be played, in the end, the image sequencing reworked the project as urban propaganda. In this respect, film was New Babylon's truest and final format—one that not only had the capacity to playfully inhabit staged models but also one through which New Babylon could be conceived as an apparatus that motivated action and, therefore, held the potential to turn passive onlookers into spatial actors, consumers into collaborators, and witnesses into producers.

But whereas Constant continued to believe that a new city had to be built in order for a unitary urbanism to unfold, Debord had lost faith in the possibilities of a Situationist architecture as an explicit form or framework. In 1960, Constant resigned as director of the Situationist "Bureau of Unitary Urbanism" and Debord and his allies at the SI increasingly questioned the role of the architect. Constant had always understood "unitary urbanism" as a spatial art, while Debord rejected aesthetic reflection in favor of collective construction. Of even more importance was a difference in philosophy about the existing city. While New Babylon departs from the context of the city by lifting itself off the ground and essentially establishing an alternative environment to which the drifters could escape, Situationist actions would demand a critique of daily life in the form of a dialectical engagement with the existing city. Even though Constant sampled from other cities, the Situationists began to see New Babylon as a semi-autonomous structure that misrepresented their ideas.[98] Yet the quarrel between the two entities also points toward a larger struggle—one that sought to position a cultural practice in relation to the existing city, a practice that would more evidently unfold in the decades to come.

Notwithstanding the short lifespan of their collaboration, the experiments of both Constant and the SI pushed architectural narrative toward a radical polemic, able to critique most of the existing city while simultaneously celebrating terrains of urban formlessness for their capacity to free fixed patterns of urban life. This polemic sought to form and speak to a new kind of public that would become involved in the building of an architectural city, collectively. Here, architecture would no longer be viewed in its individualized form but conceived instead as a type of urbanism, or better, as a city—collectively built and continuously changing. The inhabitants, now promoted to architects, would become important not only for their shared effort in imagining this city, but their actions would be essential in describing and creating it. After all, Constant's layered photographs were seemingly taken just seconds after a group of drifters had roamed through. Motivated by the actions within and around a given space, this work opened up the possibility of rethinking architecture on the basis of movements, encounters, incidents, and interventions—not reconfiguring the event of architecture but prefiguring the architecture of events.

Bernard Tschumi's Urban Transcriptions

The Situationist experiment would have a lasting impact on architectural discourse. Its influence can be felt in the sampling of city plans in the urban designs of OMA and becomes most palpable in the spatial and atmospheric narratives of Bernard Tschumi. The latter would test boundaries by devising notational systems that enabled architecture (as an idea and as drawing) to describe atmospheres and actions that it housed.[99] The urban complexities that the Situationists emulated and that Constant interiorized, became indispensable in the formulation of Tschumi's architecture of events. As he noted, there was "no architecture without the city."[100] Put differently, the phrase might suggest that it only exists because of the city—a concept that dramatically repositions architecture, understanding it no longer as the sole inventor of form but rather as a form of radical utilization of the city.

Of course, by the 1960s Aldo Rossi had already formulated a theory of architecture as that of city excavation and reassembly, with the aim of recovering the immovable elements from the history of architecture and, thereby, rescuing it from being overrun by the forces of consumerism and short-lived everyday market values. In that regard, Rossi and the Situationists had the same enemy. But whereas Debord and Bernstein performed a subversion of the existing city and eventually also unhinged architecture, Rossi returned to the limits of the discipline through a morphological study of urban artifacts and their development over time—or what Anthony Vidler at the time called the "third typology." According to Vidler, who was embedded in the very movement he theorized, the Italian New Rationalists had found an architectural typology in the history of the city, a typology "born of a desire to stress the continuity of form and history against the fragmentation produced by the elemental, institutional, and mechanic typologies of the recent past."[101] While Vidler links each of the three periods to the city—the Enlightenment typology that ranged from Marc-Antoine Laugier's primitive hut to Bantham's Panopticon found as much expression in Laugier's image of the city as garden as the modernist typology of Le Corbusier and Walter Gropius registered in the rational garden city—the third typology could no longer rely on concepts of abstract nature or social utopias. Only the traditional city could still be identified. The history of architecture as that of the city became the primary site for the identification of artifacts and types, and their combinatorial potentials into new urban forms.

The city became here the imperative point of reference for architecture, an approach that Tschumi would steer toward contemporary urban life. For Rossi, the history of architecture was bound to the city, and, for Tschumi, architecture only existed because of it.[102] Yet, less concerned with urban history, Tschumi interrogated instead the realities of existing urbanity in all its complexity, violence, and desire. While still a student at the ETH (the Swiss Institute of Technology), Tschumi found himself at the center of student protests, and was detained for one night in a Parisian jail in the spring of 1968 for street fighting.[103] Shortly after graduation, the young architect together with his friend Fernando Montes, developed a project that examines one of the massive Parisian housing projects of the 1950s. This had been one of the prime targets of Situationist critique, and it was now engaged as a Do-It-Yourself City—a project that hovers between logistics and activism. The pro-

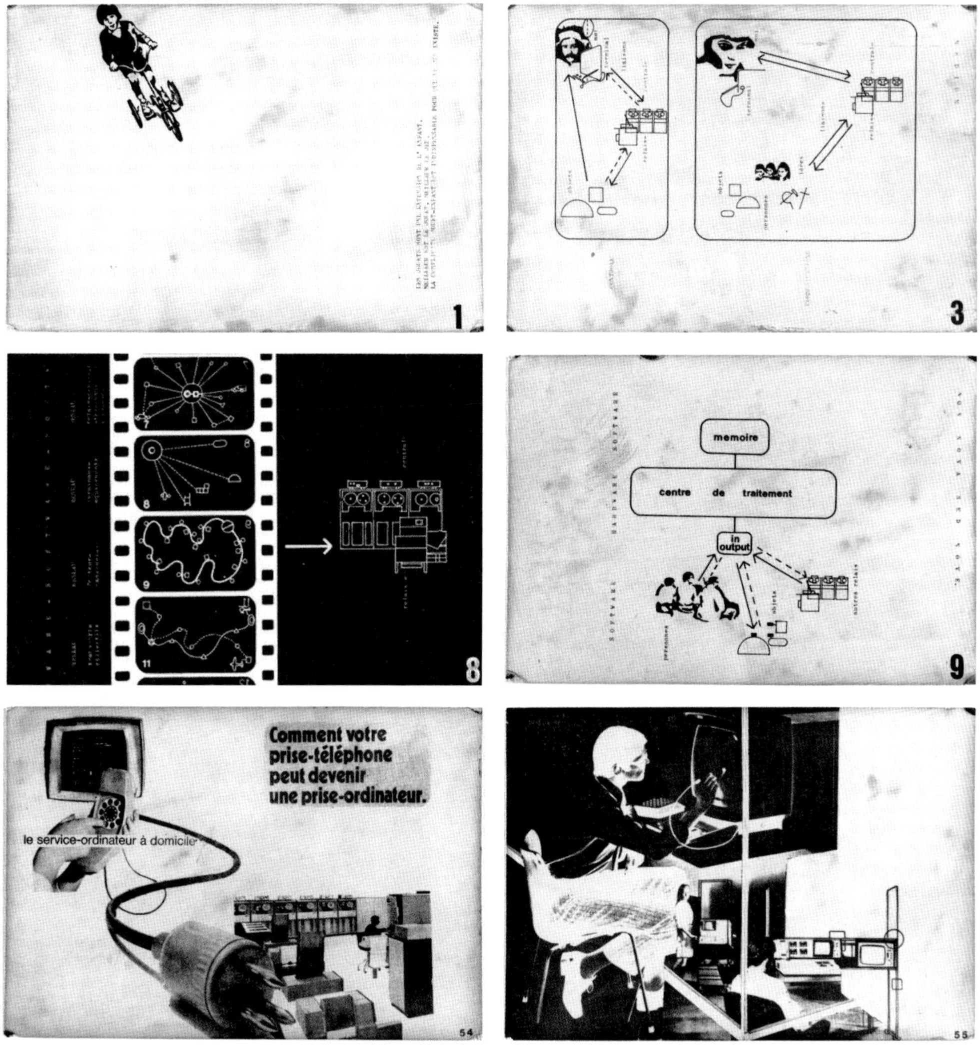

Bernard Tschumi and Fernando Montes, Do-It-Yourself City project, 1970. The team imagined a series of mobile stations that electronically connected different parts of the city with the aim to assist interaction — a proto-social network scenario that nevertheless has physical repercussions in the city.

posal describes how a series of computer stations would be distributed in the city, to facilitate playful, public engagement with situations in the built world. It effectively turns the city into a New Babylon. Ultimately, the project depicts not a designed blueprint but a network of relationships and connections that unfold through scenarios, which, in turn, aim at the dissolution of permanence and the introduction of play. Reminiscent of Cedric Price's Potteries Thinkbelt project for a traveling university that hijacked existing infrastructures, and coupled with a "détourned" use of the computer and of city networks, Do-It-Yourself City stages a different kind of urban design—one devoted to the un-planning of the city.[104]

Just as the Potteries Thinkbelt re-envisions planning as the distribution of movements and the production of education, so is Tschumi's early project an experiment in dissolving architecture into the city. This release of scenarios into the substance of the urban condition should be understood as an attempt to activate the entire neighborhood as a field of forces that collectively address the housing conditions of Paris. The definitive realities of housing blocks are here confronted via the informal forces of the city. In other words, giving design no definitive form but instead letting it play out in actions became one way to cultivate alternatives when facing a system so rationally planned. To discharge a formless swarm of actions became a strategy to reclaim some territory of the city that was otherwise lost to postwar modernist rationalization. The project not simply steps away from architectural form in order to test its boundaries but it steps toward and attempts to reroute the existing networks, movements, procedures, and technologies of the city that are now diverted by the collective forces of social, temporal events. Here, architecture manifests in procedures, events, and actions. As such, the project can be understood as an early transcript of behaviors and actions in the streets in order to release these actions as spatial strategies at the scale of the neighborhood.

Do-It-Yourself City was the first in a series of projects by Tschumi that began formulating an architecture defined by event and, therefore, as he wrote five years later, "disrupts the form that a conservative society expects of it."[105] It set the stage for an exploration that Tschumi defined over the next decade. At first participating in the spatial actions of the Situationists, then influenced by the writings of Henri Lefebvre and Roland Barthes, and later motivated by the *Tel Quel* literary circle, Tschumi would eventually discover the writings of Georges Bataille, whose surreal transgressions enabled a further rethinking of the architectural object in relation to subjective experience. Tschumi read Bataille's juxtaposition of the "pyramid" and the "labyrinth" as essential tendencies within architecture—tendencies in which models of reason and form confronted the perception of space. While the pyramid conveyed the conventions of architecture, the labyrinth evoked an inner experience and emotional response to architectural space. The former, Tschumi saw as a reasoned construct that acts of architecture (such as drawings) could communicate but that could not be experienced as such, whereas the latter was the experience of architectural space that disciplinary conventions could only approximate. Ideal versus real space, concept versus experience, reason versus senses, therein lay the paradox of architecture. The acceptance and intensification of that paradox would for Tschumi come in the form of an exploration of "experienced space," which he eventually articulated as an architecture of events.

Of course, the city had plenty of events and actions that architecture struggled to express, and would, therefore, become a constant reference point. This was the case for both Tschumi and Bataille. Yet the work of Bataille has primarily been read through Denis Hollier's 1974 study *La prise de la Concorde*, later translated as *Against Architecture*, which focused on architecture as ordering device, intimately linked to structures of power, where "monuments are erected like dikes, opposing the logic and majesty of authority against all disturbing elements."[106] And, while architecture is clearly presented here as a means of silencing the multitude, it can never be fully separated from its position in the city. In that regard, another text by Bataille is instructive, as it differentiates two urban conditions, the Inca capital of Cuzco and that of the Aztecs, Tenochtitlán. "Extinct America" depicts both cities as structured through oppressive edifices, yet the hidden sacrificial acts within the bunker-like temples of Cuzco are interpreted as a way to deny the freedom of its inhabitants while the Aztec temples created an open display of humanity's monstrosity and, therefore, preserved a level of agency for its citizens. The essay juxtaposes the closed-off city of Cuzco to the openness of Tenochtitlán, where the "streaming, human slaughterhouse" is next to "a veritable Venice, with canals, footbridges, ornamented temples, and, above all, flower gardens of extreme beauty."[107]

This suggests that the city is the oxymoronic space par excellence, turning toward either an inescapable openness or an oppressive order—Bataille's labyrinth or pyramid, respectively—and often one aspect would emerge in response to the other. For Bataille, this constellation also held lessons for the modern city as discussed in his essay "The Labyrinth," which in 1936 likely took reference from Benjamin's reading of the metropolis as a labyrinthine space.[108] Bataille and Benjamin were in regular contact during the 1930s, when Benjamin frequented the National Library in Paris, where Bataille worked as librarian and eventually was entrusted to hide Benjamin's papers during the Nazi occupation of the city.[109] In 1932, Benjamin had already spoken of neighborhoods that appeared as labyrinth. And while the Berlin of his childhood marked the first encounter with this strangely disorienting territory, it was in Paris where he came to know ways to engage the labyrinth. "Paris taught me the art of straying," Benjamin wrote, "it fulfilled a dream that had shown its first traces in the labyrinths on the blotting pages of my school exercise books."[110] Interestingly, this description not only identified areas within the metropolis as labyrinthine, but the territory was to be engaged through a technique that closely resembles the *dérive*. After all, Benjamin considered it banal and even ignorant to correctly navigate the city, whereas "to lose oneself in [it] ... calls for a quite different schooling."[111]

Some forty years later, the condition of the labyrinth was again associated with the loss of orientation, which in the formulations of Tschumi reminds one of the complexities of the city. In his 1975 essay "The Architectural Paradox," the labyrinth produces a heightened sensation and intensified experience, which is contrasted with the reasoned construction of rationality on the other side of architecture's duality.[112] While the text explicitly interrogates the circumstances of architectural space and only mentions the city in passing, the characteristics of the labyrinth are analogous to that of urban terrains that Tschumi was to investigate in the years following; a territory impossible to grasp, for its totality is never revealed and its thresholds are simultaneously exits and entries. What the essay defines as a chasm within architecture, Tschumi long recognized as the struggle between architecture and the city—between disciplined, rule-bound forms and the nebulous environments of the city, between cultivated singularity and disturbed multiplicity.

A study of the city and the mining of its sensual transgressions became Tschumi's means of introducing these dichotomized conditions into architecture. Between 1976 and 1981, he executed a series of urban excavations, presented in consecutive exhibitions. They eventually formed *The Manhattan Transcripts*—a transformative, graphic, urban analysis that sent seismic shifts through the bedrock of architecture. While the title suggests a mere transcription of urban conditions that traces and takes notes on the makeup of the existing city, Tschumi actually took on the role of detective—not a creator of the new, but one who interrogates, discovers, and reveals in order to unearth hidden meanings, organizations, and events. It is a fitting role, as the scenes in the *Transcripts* encounter destruction and violence. The first episode traces the mystery of a murder in Central Park; the second follows a stalker in his pursuit of his victim along 42nd Street; the third records an inmate's fall through the floors of a prison tower; and the fourth charts a fight for survival in the confines of an urban block. On Tschumi's drawing board, these scenarios become more than just an architect's contrarian position on the status quo of architectural function, they are a forcefield that disrupts conventional dualities, neutralizes established relationships, and constructs a multitude of new spatial readings. With that, the stories of the *Transcripts* perform a *détournement* on the city.

The episode "The Tower (The Fall)," for example, is simultaneously the spatial exploration of an office worker's vertigo, the fall of a prisoner from a tower, and a hotel guest's deadly elevator ride, unstoppably heading toward the ground. Not

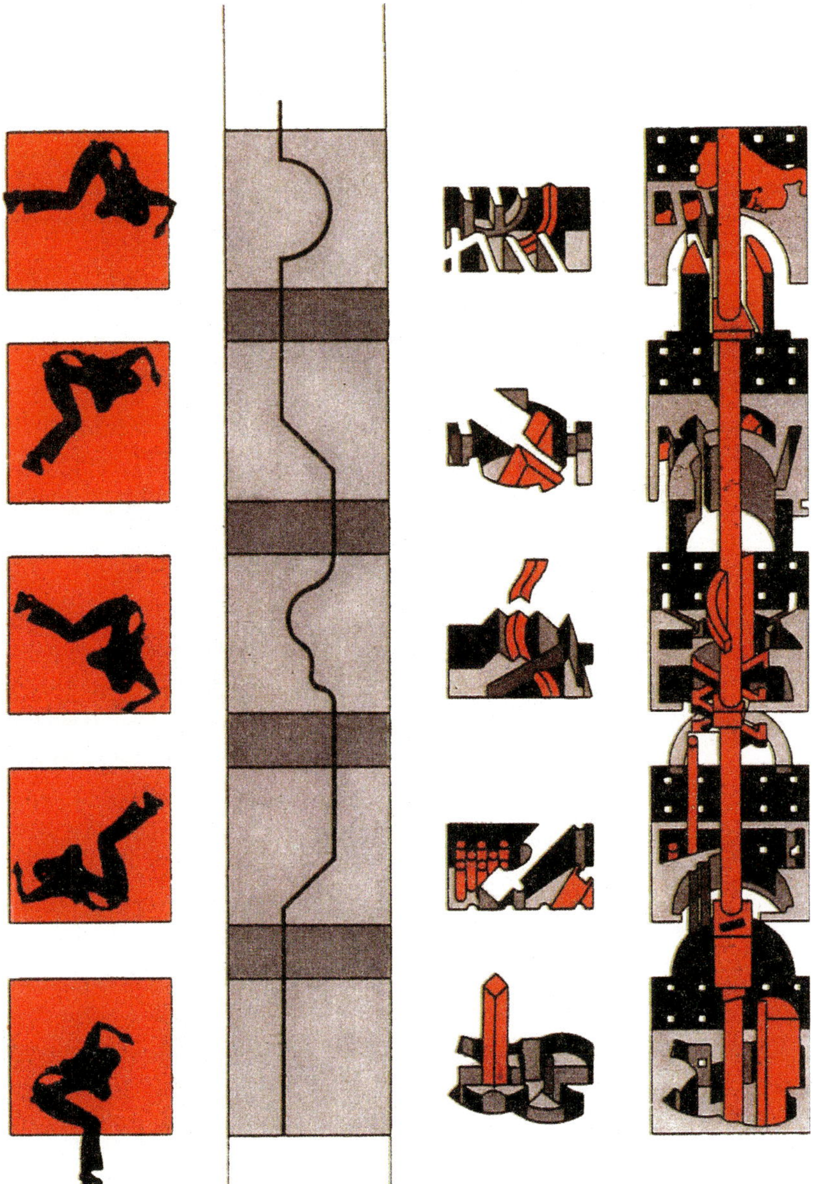

Bernard Tschumi, "The Tower (The Fall)," in *Manhattan Transcripts* (1980). "The Tower"—or the story of an inmate falling—is the third in a series of four graphic explorations of Manhattan that between 1976 and 1981 were created for individual exhibitions. The drawings became architectural interpretations and extrapolations of urban realities.

Bernard Tschumi, *Advertisement for Architecture #8, High Window*, 1979. The series of nine *Advertisements for Architecture* was produced over multiple years, each composed of a slogan, a photograph, and a short paragraph that tested the limits of architectural representation.

only does each possible reading combine a location, a typology, a form, an emotion, a movement, and an event but it also establishes new relationships among these categories. Here, the extreme events of the *Transcripts* (in true Bataillean fashion) become instrumental. By going far beyond conventional programmatic considerations (including murder), the *Transcripts* push beyond the limits of typology and space, and set up a new territory in which architecture first and foremost is witness. To imagine these events in their most extreme form gives legibility to the experiential and sensual reality of architecture, which "The Architectural Paradox" already accounted for and his postcard-size series *Advertisements for Architecture* would vividly express. *Advertisement #8*, a 1979 addition to the series that Bernard Tschumi began three years prior, shows a shadowy figure in mid-fall only a short distance from a woman reaching over a window sill. One might ask: Was this an act of murder or a failed rescue? While the author seems to have made up his mind, the wording, though intentionally cryptic, hints at architecture as the first witness to any action. And indeed, Tschumi's *Advertisements* and *Transcripts* should be understood as a kind of urban forensics that connects the dots between the abstract world of architectural objects and the actualities of movements and events within it.

It is no coincidence that this *Advertisement* was produced concurrently with the *Transcripts*. While for the first graphic experiments of the *Advertisement* series, Tschumi used his own photographs of Le Corbusier's deteriorated Villa Savoye (in order to describe architecture as an act of sensuality and eroticism as much as a calculated outcome of drawing), the later *Advertisement #8* samples an event from the reality of the city in order to confront the realities of architecture. This most essential city-architecture relationship traverses the different works of Tschumi to the extent that the murder in the city, once depicted in the *Advertisements*, is thrown back into architecture by the *Transcripts*. Now, the free fall of the figure continues its descent through the different levels of a tower (1979). The event is not only depicted (in photographs), located (in axonometric drawings), and traced (through notations), but the fall itself is diagrammed and described as a space, carving a central vertical corridor through all stories. What in the *Transcripts* was still viewed as an "elevator ride [that] had turned into a chilling contest with violent death,"[113] was later interpreted as a skydive through the elevator shaft, effectively subverting an existing space through a new form of inhabitation. From the chills and pleasures of a given event emerged a new programmatic constellation, a playful realignment of space and happening that Tschumi subsequently termed "cross-programming." Transcribing the city or, better, narrating its spatio-temporal landscape of events, would provide the grounds for such strategic diversions of space as pole vaulting in the chapel, bicycling in the laundromat, and, of course, skydiving in the elevator shaft.[114] All of these iterations inserted an unfamiliar event into an orthodox space, meanwhile discovering a programmatic realignment through misuse. Of course, the city always provided an infinite directory of misappropriations.[115] The contemporary city was the true inventor of dis-, trans-, and cross-programming; a realization that brings Tschumi's fascination with the city surprisingly close to Rossi's caution toward function.

While Rossi's and Tschumi's positions on program differ, Rossi's idea of the permanence of urban artifacts can be instructive for a better understanding of urban narratives and its relationship to program and event. In fact, the notion of continuity in architectural types provides historical evidence for programmatic iterations within the same architectural form. Citing the Palazzo della Ragione in Padua, Rossi noted, "that the physical form of the past has assumed different functions" across history.[116] On the one hand, for Rossi, this proved that "function alone is insufficient to explain the continuity of urban artifacts... [as it] hardly accounts for the phenomenon of survival."[117] It rather confirmed the strength of typology, which, in turn, called for an investigation of *The Architecture of the City*. For Tschumi, on the other hand, the very same evidence verified that architecture could not only withstand the infection with non-complementary events but also provoke new forms of program.[118] This parallel reading of both theories suggests that programmatic changes over time were as important for Rossi's concept of the urban artifact's permanence as were typological dispositions for Tschumi's idea of an architecture of events. Most importantly, however, the development of an architectural language was for Rossi as for Tschumi intimately linked to a reading of

Aldo Rossi, Elementary school at Fagnano Olona, Varese, Italy, 1976. The stair in the schoolyard that leads to the gymnasium is also the stage for class photographs, linking architectural form to collective memory.

the city, which both articulated as a terrain made evident by human events. Michael Hays, for example, observed how Rossi retrieved objects and events from the city in order "then to return their forms (cognitive structures that mimic the social) to the City's matrix and persist in surroundings utterly alien to them—analogues of a single unfinished architectural narrative, a great collective story whose end, for Rossi, is as impossible to achieve as its process is necessary to perform."[119] Indeed, Rossi's urban archeology identified events and objects in the historical project of the city while Tschumi's spatial cinematics locate them in the representational margins of contemporary urbanity.

And even as both developed very different repertoires, some building elements would consistently appear as platforms for the continuous unfolding of human events. The stairs between the schoolyard and the raised gymnasium of Rossi's elementary school at Fagnano Olona (1976), for example, programmatically resemble Tschumi's stepped seating atop the Grande Bibliothèque project for Paris (1989). Both are meeting grounds, whose programmatic doubling derives from the city and is now injected into architecture. Rossi's stairs are as much the monumental steps of a city-assemblage as they are conceived as photographic backdrops for yearly class gatherings. The steps at the Grande Bibliothèque are similarly urban. They hover between running track and library, at once functioning as reading room and stage seating—a dualism that Tschumi hopes to broaden. For Rossi, this setting relates back to a collective memory, a reading that Tschumi substantially expands through possibilities of chance encounters and erotic tensions that result from the intentional crossing of programs.

In Tschumi's competition entry for the library, the different logistics—from the movement of visitors and administrators to the circulation of books and electronics—are taken as a spatial reference of intersecting circuits and different speeds. The oval shape of the exhibition circuit, for example, is formally mirrored but programmatically sped up with a suspended running track that carves into the reading rooms and book stacks above. Crossing a library with a running track, the

Bernard Tschumi, National Library of France project, Paris, 1989. The close-up photograph of the model reveals how the running track parallels the step seating that doubles as an outdoor reading room—a spatial construct intended to provoke unexpected exchanges, such as may happen in the city.

project effectively combines a space of the Enlightenment with that of modernism—the quest for knowledge with the quest for the fit body. It introduces an exercise of the outdoors into the silent halls of learning and, conversely, brings the reading room into the city. The stage seating on the roof would have overlooked both, the running track and the city of Paris, steps where the scholar reads and the competitor relaxes, where the librarian meets the athlete. The project exudes a certain erotics that we know from the city. It spatializes Bataille's *Eroticism* and enacts Tschumi's principles of pleasure.[120]

On the stairs at Fagnano Olona and the stage seating at the Grande Bibliothèque, architectural space turns back at the city. Each in their own right is not only an element sampled from the city but both also construct a city-moment within architecture. Yet, these works do not capture the city interiorly, as forms of metropolitan architecture would, they rather practice what could be called an unfolding of the city. Rossi turned the elementary school into an analogous city-construct with public plazas, alleys, streets, buildings, and monuments, while Tschumi constructed a city-event by exteriorizing the reading room as a stage seating that overlooks the city of Paris. Here, the very elemental nature of architecture turns into a different kind of urbanism. It proceeds from streets into alleyways to courtyards and from there climbs the stairs in front of Rossi's gymnasium and continues on a running track through Tschumi's book stacks, only to arrive on the roof seating that turns its view toward the city. This new Nolli plan depicts a different kind of city, one where spatial transgressions, typological appropriations, and urban events reconstitute the connection between city and architecture—an urban apparatus that is more game than machine. It acknowledges and embraces architecture's dependency on the city while, at the same time, it is keenly aware of the city's independence from architecture. The latter point is not to suggest that the city is anything other than "a gigantic man-made object,"[121] as Rossi noted, but that there is a limit as to architecture's impact on the overall city—a limit imposed by modernity and metropolitan urbanization.

With the recognition of the impossibility of architecture's existence without the city came the realization that "the city could potentially exist without architecture."[122] Of course, this is the very same city-architecture relationship that Koolhaas called "pathetically one-sided" during the 1996 conference on the American avant-garde. "The city inspires but it does not respond. ... the bottom line is that the avant-garde needs the city but that the city can do very well without the avant-garde."[123] This revelation persists, if not always explicitly, in the urban narratives that this chapter has analyzed. Hegemann fully believed in the power of architecture to rethink the city, yet his exhibition displayed its utter hopelessness when facing formless urbanity; Benjamin was confident in the architectural and social implications of modernist housing but did not see them reform entire cities; and the "détourned" urbanism of the Situationists at first radically questioned architecture and eventually abandoned the project of architecture altogether. All these instances—from metropolitan exhibitions, to urban broadcasts, to "détourned" maps and city transcripts—expose the city's great importance for architecture and simultaneously question, if unintentionally, architecture's role in the city.

These narratives offer no resolution as to the city's unilateral relationship to architecture. Importantly, however, they outline an unfolding of the city through their very format. The city-narrative, in its relentless interrogation and elaborate commentary on urban locations, became instrumental in the re-telling of urban accounts, their subsequent extrapolation, and ultimate adaptation or subversion. This is not to be mistaken for a fictionalization of the city; after all, the city is stranger than fiction. Rather, accounts of the city become the very structure from which architecture is formed and whence it can leap back into, relate to, and inform the city. With that, architecture has now the capacity to move beyond the one-off building form: from the iterative sequencing of housing courtyards in early Berlin, to the modernist housing urbanism on its outskirts; from the connected neighborhoods of Debord's maps, to the endless unfolding of Constant's new city; and from the filming of Manhattan in the *Transcripts,* to the exteriorization of architecture's inner parts in Tschumi's Grande Bibliothèque. These examples describe an architectural urbanism that not only questions the objecthood of architecture but rather functions as a city-extension. Here, architecture makes the city an offer it cannot refuse.

4 Conclusion

The City Is Dead, Long Live the City!

The dictum "The City no longer exists!" has been as often repeated as it has been misunderstood. It is not the city as such, but the city as we knew it that exists no more. As Marshall McLuhan observed early on, and Félix Guattari later reminded us, the city is no longer an entity. It has developed into something with no defined center, no boundary, and no clear differentiation from what lies beyond it.[1] Not only have those conditions multiplied, blurred, and reconfigured but dramatic urbanization and advances in communications and information networks have created an urban haze, resulting in an endless city with no defined form. This city of constant flux never stops absorbing, regularly morphing to take on new roles, and even sacrificing parts of its own terrain without hesitation. It is a condition clearly heightened by an exhilarating global urbanization that according to well-rehearsed predictions will soon be everywhere. Not only does the city still exist, but its distinction from its predecessors lies predominantly in the extent of its development. In other words, the contemporary city is more extensive than ever before and ever-changing, leaving architecture in a precarious position: on the one hand keenly aware that it constitutes the city in essential ways while, at the same time, conscious of its lack of impact on that very urban terrain.

In light of this conundrum, only intensified in our time of extreme urbanization, I have identified an alternative position of architecture toward the city in twentieth-century urban theories of the architectural avant-garde. Here, one can observe a shift in mentality where the city is no longer an opposing force but becomes a territory saturated with potential: from the persistent optimism of August Endell, Reyner Banham, and Robert Venturi and Denise Scott Brown, via the radical contextualism of Karl Scheffler, Oswald Mathias Ungers, and the Office for Metropolitan Architecture (OMA), to the emergent urbanisms of Werner Hegemann, Walter Benjamin, and Bernard Tschumi. The first set of projects cultivated an analytical hunger to find opportunities in the most unlikely places, the second instrumentalized the forms of the here and now, and the third extrapolated existing tendencies to speculate on possible urban futures. Where others had ruled out using the forces of urbanization, in these projects the tables turned and architecture was re-envisioned through an engagement with what the city has to offer.

While Anthony Vidler's influential discussion of a "third typology" bound architecture to the historical city, I have sought to show how the conditions of the metropolis (its forms and the lack thereof) were integral for the development of the modern architectural avant-garde. Building on Vidler's earlier terminology, the metropolis might here be understood as a site of a "fourth typology." Whereas the third typology "is explicitly critical of the Modern Movement ... [and] utilizes the clarity of the eighteenth-century city to rebuke the fragmentation, de-centralization, and formal disintegration introduced into contemporary urban life by the zoning techniques and technological advances of the twenties,"[2] the fourth typology solicits the ambiguity of the contemporary metropolis to engage its formal dissonance. Similar to the trope that Vidler associated with the modern movement, this added typology remains deeply critical of the dense quarters of the industrial city and yet it is capable of identifying isolated potentials within it. It invents its techniques and develops its urban architectures by analyzing, redirecting, or extrapolating the disintegrated forms of the modern city; hence its name, metropolitan architecture.

Throughout the preceding chapters one theme has remained constant, though it appeared under different circumstances and to various effects: the formless metropolis (or what Vidler called the "formal disintegration" of the city) became simultaneously a challenge and a motivation for architecture. A challenge because it stands in utter contrast to the formal ambitions of architecture, and a motivation because it provides a terrain of infinite multiplicities for architecture to sample and test. Early on, the concept of the formless city was invoked as a last resort whenever the multitude of urban forces rendered the city incomprehensible. Of course, with the emergence of the metropolis, this had increasingly become the inescapable reality of cities and, in turn, that of architecture. Yet, the "formless" was never fully defined, only traced as a vague quality that intruded into all corners of the city—associated with the indefinable, ungraspable, and open-ended. Not contours but landscape, not configurations but terrain, not organizations but conditions; these are the constituents of the formless that figures like Endell, Scheffler, and Hegemann uncovered in the 1910s and that penetrated the architectural discourse. As I have sought to demonstrate, the formless metropolis was an imperative force within modern architecture, leaving traces of its doing and undoing just about everywhere.

The concept of the formless (or "*formlos*," as the early generation named it) created openings in the understanding of the metropolis that made accessing it anew possible, enabling the articulation of conditions that previously were intangible. Each project channeled the formless city differently: be it as a source for imagination, as a condition that gave license to extrapolate, or as a vehicle to invent architectural narratives for alternative responses to the city. The architects and urbanists highlighted here shared a fascination with the formless and its repercussions in the city. This points toward the conceptual richness and operational capacities for architecture of this otherwise slippery and elusive term. Scheffler, for example, conceived of the formless city as an environment that created *Spielraum* (a margin or room to play) without which new architectural forms could not be found within modernity. While architecture conventionally associates the formless with conditions of chaos ("without form") or destruction ("form-shattering"), it was here defined as a productive condition and strategic idiom. It gave architecture room to maneuver and to test alternatives.

The formless in the realm of the city approximates what Georges Bataille described in his short text on the *"informe"* (1929). In this pseudo-dictionary entry, Bataille proposed that in a world where form is required for everything, the *informe* [or formless] "is not only an adjective having a given meaning, but a term that serves to bring things down in the world."[3] In other words, Bataille's *informe* performs by reducing the possibility of forming entities; it is a process at work, yet entirely without utility. Bataille's text not only questions the role of the dictionary in its attempt to categorize and articulate and, therefore, frame things in the world; but it also undercuts the role of the thinker/architect, whose desire for things to take shape is undermined by the formless. "All of philosophy has no other goal: it is a matter of giving a frock coat to what is, a mathematical frock coat. On the other hand, affirming that the universe resembles nothing and is only *formless* amounts to saying that the universe is something like a spider or spit."[4] Of course, the formless is a paradox that de-figures what comes in its way—it even undoes itself.

As has been pointed out by others, Bataille's *informe* varies slightly from formlessness as the term is used more generally. The latter is a state that lies outside form yet has a location, while the former operates as an idea and as process that has an effect on concepts and on the world.[5] Although the city locates the formless, it also constitutes a terrain that is simultaneously inescapable and operative. In other words, it gives the formless a locale, yet without limiting its effectiveness. Connecting the formless to the city, at once describes the city through that which is ungraspable and at the same time exemplifies the formless (à la Bataille) through that which cannot be located. With the intimacy (almost equivalence) between the city and the formless in mind, its relationship to architecture becomes even more fundamental; the city's formlessness inevitably acts upon architecture—eating away at its core, undermining its premise, and weakening its status. Looking back at the present study however, the challenge to architecture made by the city brings surprising revelations and carries unexpected promise. Even and especially in its provocations of failure (as in Hegemann's attempt to exhibit the metropolis) the formless city not only denies the representation of its own terrain but also offers itself as the very environment for speculation (as in Le Corbusier's first urban experiments during the Berlin exhibition). On the one hand, the criticality of the formless seems limitless to the point that it destabilizes itself, on the other, its commitment to challenge also clears away the status quo and makes room for things to come.

It is through the formless city that we gained access in this study to the aesthetic and visual theories that influenced much of modern architecture; that we grasped an understanding of metropolitan architecture that lives so prominently in one of the most important practices today; and that we detected in urban accounts possibilities for rethinking the city as a project. Furthermore, acknowledging the formless as native to the city (almost tantamount) enabled us to implicate architects and thinkers that dealt with the city very differently and to detect a productive engagement with urbanization in their work. The hallucinating observations of Endell, the spatial complexity of Moholy-Nagy's photographs, the repetitiveness of Hilberseimer's mega-blocks, the cinematics of Venturi and Scott Brown's signs, and the violence of Tschumi's transcriptions can be understood as operative transformations. These projects hint at the evasion of conventional attitudes toward the formless city—as they no longer resist or embrace the urban condition—and, instead, move within and through its nebulousness. While some of those studied here will surely disagree with the interpretations or affiliations that are drawn, my intention has been to identify a larger collective of works (rather than figures) that together point at architecture's fundamental bond with the city.

While disciplinary rhetoric tells us otherwise, I have sought to expose architecture's ongoing fascination with the formless city, including, in each of the preceding chapters: the relationship of the formless city to perception and imagination, a commitment to the city through extrapolation rather than suppression, and the possibility of constructing alternative city-architecture narratives. The first of these relates to a non-utopian visionary, the second reads metropolitan architecture as the inhalation of urbanity into building interiors, and the third extends architecture via the city and vice versa. From that perspective, the relationship between architecture and the city forms a new constellation that disputes disciplinary habits. As some architects and urban thinkers recognized the city as saturated with potential, they also seemed to sacrifice critical distance in exchange for embedded criticality. This position not only abandons the elevated view of the conventional planner who aims to compose totalities from above, but it also challenges the confidence of the architect in the conditioning of singularities from within. Here, architecture appears to engage the scale and multiplicity of the city, without seeking a new totality. With that ambition in mind, this practice begins to oscillate between urbanism and architecture, between multiplicity and singularity, between entropy and order, between urban formlessness and architectural form. And yet, this is no average median, instead, it directs attention to a third site within the midst of both disciplines, simultaneously part of both worlds, or, better, annexing a territory in the center of the other.

Notes

Introduction

1 Yve-Alain Bois and Rosalind E. Krauss, *Formless: A User's Guide* (New York; Cambridge, MA: Zone Books; MIT Press, 1997), 40. Rosalind Krauss and Yve-Alain Bois have examined works of modern art through the lens of Georges Bataille's concept of the *informe*. Here, the structure of the history of modernism is challenged by displacing the concepts of form and content through "the operational, performative 'force' of the 'formless.'" (9).

2 Lewis Mumford, *The City in History: Its Origins, Its Transformations, and Its Prospects* (1961; San Diego: Harcourt Brace & Co., 1989), 544.

3 Sigfried Giedion, *Space, Time and Architecture* (Cambridge, MA: Harvard University Press, 1941), 100.

4 The metropolis served not only as a social and cultural center, but also as a center from which the country's colonial endeavors were directed—activities that ultimately contributed to its power. As Stuart Hall articulates: "Colonization was never simply external to the societies of the imperial metropolis ... (but) always inscribed deeply within them." See Stuart Hall, "Post-Colonial," in *The Imperialist Imagination: German Colonialism and Its Legacy*, eds. Sara Friedrichsmeyer, Sara Lennox, and Susanne Zantop (Ann Arbor: University of Michigan Press, 1998), 246.

5 By the nineteenth century, these forces would include colonization, industrialization, global trade, credit networks, institutional systems, transportation networks, and emerging communication technologies.

6 Ildefons Cerdà, *Teoría General de Urbanización* (1867; Madrid: Electa, 1996); partially translated in *The Five Bases of the General Theory of Urbanization*, ed. Arturo Soria y Puig, trans. Bernard Miller and Mary Fons I Fleming (Madrid: Electa, 1999). Already Cerdá's expansion plan for Barcelona (1859) included a short description, entitled *A Theory of City Building*.

7 The influence of Piranesi on later developments is evident in discussions on concepts of the formless, the fragment, the negative, and the strange: Koolhaas's essay on urbanism, for example, starts with an illustration of the *Campi Martii antiquae urbis*, and for the Situationists, Piranesi was a psychogeographer. See Rem Koolhaas, *Small, Medium, Large, Extra-Large* (New York: Monacelli Press, 1995), 959; and G.-E. Debord, "Exercice de la psychogéographie," *Potlatch*, no. 2 (June 1954): "Piranesi ... is psychogeography in the staircase." Here quoted from Simon Sadler, *The Situationist City* (Cambridge, MA: MIT Press, 1998), 75.

8 Immanuel Kant, *Kritik der Urteilskraft* (1790; Frankfurt am Main: Suhrkamp Verlag, 1974), 165: "*formlos ... und Unbegrenztheit.*"

9 Ibid., 174–175.

10 Manfredo Tafuri, *Architecture and Utopia: Design and Capitalist Development* (1973; Cambridge, MA: MIT Press, 1976), 16.

11 Heinrich Wölfflin, *Renaissance and Baroque* (1888; Ithaca: Cornell University Press, 1966), 15.

12 Ibid., 33.

13 Ibid., 38, 34.

14 Marc-Antoine Laugier, *An Essay on Architecture*, trans. Wolfgang and Anni Herrmann (1753; Los Angeles: Hennessey and Ingalls, 1977), 129.

15 Friedrich Engels, *Die Lage der arbeitenden Klasse in England* (Leipzig: Otto Wigand, 1845), 48.

16 First in England (1851), and shortly after in France and Germany, official definitions were drawn up that demarcated the urban grounds of the city from the rural, agricultural, and natural landscapes around it. In addition to the separation between landscape and city, one also saw an increasing difference in the appearance of larger versus smaller cities.

17 At the international conference for statistics in 1887, the term "*Großstadt*" was linked to cities with a population above 100,000. While the common translation of "*Großstadt*" is "metropolis," we should also keep in mind that the German term refers to the size of the town whereas "metropolis" reflects a leading political, economic, and cultural role by which the larger society is influenced. Therefore, cities such as Berlin were not only classified as *Großstädte* but also increasingly described as *Metropolen* or *Weltstädte* (world cities).

18 The two departments that Haussmann established and through which his endeavors were coordinated are the Department of Promenades and Parks and the Department for General Planning. As he stated, he wanted to employ "men with clear vision"—so the former department was led by engineers and the latter by surveyors.

19 In the first edition of the *Städtebau* journal, for example, Theodor Goecke and Camillo Sitte (the editors) outlined: "*Städtebau* is the collaboration of all technical and artistic arts in order to form a coherent whole ... *Städtebau* is a science and an art with specific goals for research and with practical objectives." In *Städtebau*, no. 1 (1904), preface.

20 Baumeister uses Engels's theory of city growth to talk about the possible increase in inhabitants in Berlin: from 1820 to 1850 Berlin's population rose from 200,000 to 400,000 (30 years), while from 1850 to 1872 the population rose from 400,000 to 800,000 (in only 22 years); therefore, the projection for the year 1886 was a population of 1.6 million inhabitants. In reality the population in 1886 was 1.3 million. For further reading on Baumeister, see George Collins, *Camillo Sitte and the Birth of Modern City Planning* (New York: Random House, 1965), 26. There, Baumeister is identified as the theorist who "laid the basis for city planning as a scientific field of endeavor."

21 Reinhard Baumeister, *Stadt-Erweiterungen in technischer, baupolizeilicher und wirtschaftlicher Beziehung* (Berlin: Ernst & Korn, 1876), 12: "*Es ist wichtig für anwachsende Städte, den Nachteilen ihres Anwachsens möglichst zuvorzukommen, und*

das Hauptmittel besteht wohl in einer gut geordneten Stadterweiterung." And, 91: *"Die Stadterweiterung besteht [im] wesentlichen in der Feststellung der Grundzüge aller Verkehrsmittel ... [und in der] Gruppierung verschiedenartiger Stadtteile."*

22 Otto Wagner, *Die Großstadt: Eine Studie über diese von Otto Wagner* (Vienna: Anton Schroll, 1911), trans. "The Development of a Great City," *Architectural Record* (May 1912): 500.

23 Andrew Lees, *Cities Perceived: Urban Society in European and American Thought, 1820–1940* (New York: Columbia University Press, 1985), 3. In addition, see Brian Ladd, *Urban Planning and Civic Order in Germany, 1860–1914* (Cambridge, MA: Harvard University Press, 1990), 7–35; and Philipp Oswalt, *Berlin – Stadt ohne Form: Strategien einer anderen Architektur* (Munich: Prestel Verlag, 2000).

24 Ludwig Mies van der Rohe, transcript of interview with John Peter, 1955, 15. Here quoted from Detlef Mertins, "Living in a Jungle," in *Mies in America*, ed. Phyllis Lambert (New York: Harry N. Abrams, Centre Canadien d'Architecture, Whitney Museum of American Art, and Museum of Modern Art New York, 2001), 623.

25 Marshall Berman, *All That Is Solid Melts Into Air: The Experience of Modernity* (New York: Simon and Schuster, 1982), 36.

1 Imagination

1 Denise Scott Brown, "Learning from Pop," *Casabella* (December 1971): 359.

2 Friedrich Nietzsche, *Also sprach Zarathustra* (1883). Here cited from *Thus Spoke Zarathustra: A Book for All and None*, trans. Walter Kaufmann (New York: Random House, 1995), 176. Nietzsche used the term *"große Stadt"* (great city), which by the mid-nineteenth century was frequently employed to indicate the size of a city and amount of its population at the largest possible scale. By the end of the century these characteristics were conveyed by the consolidated term *"Großstadt."*

3 Ibid., 178.

4 Friedrich Nietzsche, *Die fröhliche Wissenschaft* (1882). Here cited from Friedrich Nietzsche, *Gay Science*, trans. Walter Kaufmann (New York: Vintage, 1974), 280.

5 August Endell, *Die Schönheit der großen Stadt* (Stuttgart: Strecker & Schröder, 1908), 21–22. This text as well as the other articles by Endell mentioned in this chapter have never been translated in full into English but have been republished multiple times in German: August Endell, *Vom Sehen: Texte 1896–1925 über Architektur, Formkunst und "Die Schönheit der Großen Stadt"* (Basel, Boston: Birkhäuser, 1995); August Endell, *Zauberland des Sichtbaren* (Berlin: Verlag der Gartenschönheit, 1928); and Endell, *Die Schönheit der großen Stadt – Architextbook Nr. 4* (Berlin: Archibook-Verlag Düttmann, 1984). Recently, Zeynep Çelik Alexander translated parts of this text as "The Beauty of the Metropolis," *Grey Room*, no. 56 (Summer 2014): 116–138. Translations are by the author unless otherwise indicated.

6 August Endell (Breslau, Akademie für Kunst und Kunstgewerbe), *Letter to Gottfried Heinersdorff* (Berlin, Kiefholzstraße 72), 1918 (Berlin: Berlinische Galerie), Endell Hefter, *Architekt Endell*, folder 19.

7 Endell's connections to the work of Nietzsche are numerous. In 1891, Endell began to study philosophy and psychology at the University of Tübingen and transferred one year later to Munich. In Munich, Endell was enrolled until the winter semester 1895/96. According to letters, Endell became acquainted with the work of Nietzsche through his studies in Tübingen and Munich and through his cousin, history professor Kurt Breysig, who was one of the first to lecture on Nietzsche. In 1986, Lou Andreas-Salomé contacted Endell for the first time, and they became lifelong friends. By that time Andreas-Salomé was already known as a Nietzsche scholar. On Endell's book cover design, see Tilmann Buddensieg, "Der Erste Moderne Bucheinband? August Endell und Friedrich Nietzsche," in *Ars Naturam Adiuvans: Festschrift für Matthias Winner zum 11. März 1996*, eds. Matthias Winner, Victoria von Flemming, Sebastian Schütze, and Hans Werner Henze (Mainz am Rhein: P. von Zabern, 1996), 664.

8 August Endell, "Die Straße als künstlerisches Gebilde," in *Jahrbuch des Deutschen Werkbundes: Der Verkehr* (Jena: Eugen Diederichs, 1914), 18–19.

9 Endell, *Die Schönheit der großen Stadt*, 13.

10 Georg Simmel, "Die Großstädte und das Geistesleben" (1903). Here cited from *Simmel on Culture*, trans. Frisby and Featherstone (London: Sage Publications, 1997), 184–185.

11 Endell visited Simmel's lectures at the University of Berlin and the correlation between both texts comes, therefore, as no surprise.

12 Turn-of-the-century literary work seems to have particular affinities with Endell's idea of a "pure seeing" if one considers the work of Karl Heinz Bohrer and his concept of "suddenness" and "instant." Bohrer identified in the works of James Joyce, Virginia Woolf, Marcel Proust, Robert Musil, Franz Kafka, Walter Benjamin, and the French surrealists an instantaneous aesthetic experience that couples "emphasis and an unclear justification for that emphasis." What he also described as "an absent reference" can be seen in relation to Endell's immediate way of experiencing without intellectual association. Karl Heinz Bohrer, "Instants of Diminishing Representation: The Problem of Temporal Modalities," in Heidrun Friese, *The Moment: Time and Rupture in Modern Thought* (Liverpool: Liverpool University Press, 2001), 113–114. In addition, see Karl Heinz Bohrer, *Suddenness: On the Moment of Aesthetic Appearance*, trans. Ruth Crowley (New York: Columbia University Press, 1994). I want to thank Sandy Isenstadt for suggesting Bohrer's work.

13 Lou Andreas-Salomé, *Lebensrückblick, Grundriss einiger Lebernserinnerungen* (Frankfurt a.M.: Insel-Verlag, 1968), 113: Speaking of the time that Lou Andreas-Salomé, Rainer Maria Rilke, August Endell, and Frieda von Bülow spent in Wolfratshausen, Andreas-Salomé states: "Endell and Rilke were now soon connected through friendship (*August Endell ... der sich mit Rainer bald freundschaftlich verband...*)." On the relationship between Endell, Andreas-Salomé, Rilke, and Nietzsche, see my essay "Visual Discoveries of an Urban Wanderer: August Endell's Perception of a Beautiful Metropolis," *Arq: Architectural Research Quarterly* 11, no. 1 (March 2007): 71–80.

14 Rainer Maria Rilke, *The Notebooks of Malte Laurids Brigge*, trans. Stephen Mitchell (1910; New York: Random House, 1982), 5, 19. Rilke's only novel was first published in 1910, only two years after Endell's *Schönheit der großen Stadt*.

15 Theodor Lipps, *Ästhetik, Erster Teil* (Leipzig, Hamburg: Leopold Voss Verlag, 1903), 125.

16 Robert Vischer, *Über das optische Formgefühl; ein Beitrag zur Aesthetik* (Leipzig: H. Credner, 1873); Konrad Fiedler, *Über die Beurteilung von Werken der bildenden Kunst* (Leipzig: S. Hirzel, 1876); and Heinrich Wölfflin, *Prolegomena zu einer Psychologie der Architektur* (Munich: Kgl. Hof- & Universitäts-Buchdruckerei, 1886). For the translation of all texts, see Harry Francis Mallgrave and Eleftherios Ikonomou, *Empathy, Form and Space: Problems in German Aesthetics, 1873–1893* (Santa Monica: Getty Center for the History of Art and the Humanities, 1994).

17 Endell was exposed to the encompassing approach of Lipps during his doctoral studies at the University of Munich, where he even began to write his dissertation under the title "Emotional Contrast" (1896). For other works by Lipps, see *Psychologische Studien* (*Psychological Studies*, 1885), Ästhetische *Faktoren der Raumanschauung* (*Aesthetic Factors of Spatial Experience*, 1891), and *Raumästhetik und geometrisch-optische Täuschungen* (*Space-aesthetics and Geometric-optical Deception*, 1893).

18 August Endell, *Um die Schönheit: Eine Paraphrase über die Münchener Kunstausstellungen* (1896; Munich: Franke & Haushalter, 1986), 11.

19 August Endell "Formenschönheit und dekorative Kunst," *Dekorative Kunst* (November 1897): 92–93.

20 Immanuel Kant, *Kritik der Urteilskraft* (1790). Here cited from *Critique of Judgment*, trans. J. H. Bernard (New York: Hafner, 1951), 66.

21 Arthur Schopenhauer, *Die Welt als Wille und Vorstellung* (1819). Here cited from *The World as Will and Representation, vol. 2*, trans. E. F. J. Payne (New York: Dover Publications, 1966), 367–371. This intellectual trajectory, set in motion by Kant and Schopenhauer, can be followed in the ideas of Hermann von Helmholtz's early scientific models of physiological optics (1856–66), Wilhelm Wundt's cognitive psychology in theories of the senses (1962), Ernst Brück's psychology of colors (1866), Robert Vischer's optical form-feeling (1872), Conrad Fiedler's pure vision (1878), Heinrich Wölfflin's psychology of architectural form (1886), Ernst Mach's studies of optical perception (1886), Adolf Göller's notion of abstract spatiality (1888), August Schmarsow's idea of architecture as spatial construct (1893), and Theodor Lipps's aesthetic empathy (1903).

22 Jonathan Crary, *Techniques of the Observer: On Vision and Modernity in the Nineteenth Century* (Cambridge, MA: MIT Press, 1990), 84.

23 August Endell, "Formschönheit und Dekorative Kunst," part 1, "Die Freude an der Form," *Dekorative Kunst*, no. 1, issue 2 (November 1897): 75–77; and part 2 and 3, "Die gerade Linie" and "Geradlinige Gebilde," *Dekorative Kunst*, no. 2, issue 9 (June 1898): 119–125.

24 Nikolaus Pevsner, *Pioneers of Modern Design, From William Morris to Walter Gropius* (1936; London: Penguin Books, 1964). Pevsner witnessed in Endell's façade study an "astonishing similar[ity] to those of certain German houses after the First World War. The shape of the second-floor windows and the flat roof are again almost 'misdatable'." 194.

25 Endell, *Die Schönheit der großen Stadt*, 23.

26 Ibid.

27 Ibid., 24.

28 Ibid., 48, 52, 56.

29 Ibid., 48: "even in these dreadful heaps of stone, lives beauty."

30 Ibid., 47.

31 Ibid., 57.

32 Ibid., 48–52.

33 A stark contrast between Endell's embedded vision and the preferred perspective of planners and urbanists can be gathered by the passion to reach ever higher vantage points: from the first urban panoramas, and early aerial photographs from the hot-air balloon by Nadar, to Le Corbusier's obsession with the perspective from the cockpit of an airplane.

34 Charles Baudelaire, "The Painter of Modern Life" (1863), in *The Painter of Modern Life, and Other Essays*, trans. Jonathan Mayne (London: Phaidon, 1965), 13.

35 Georg Simmel, "Soziologische Aesthetik," *Die Zukunft*, vol. 17 (1896): 206. Here cited from David Frisby, *Fragments of Modernity: Theories of Modernity in the Work of Simmel, Kracauer, and Benjamin* (Cambridge, MA: MIT Press, 1986), 57.

36 Endell, *Die Schönheit der großen Stadt*, 50.

37 Ibid., 45.

38 Endell not only published articles in magazines such as *Pan* and *Kunst und Künstler*, which had previously introduced impressionism to the German audience, but he was also in contact with the Berlin art scene around the director of the National Gallery Hugo von Tschudi, the painter Max Liebermann, the art dealer Paul Cassirer, the author Julius Meier-Graefe, and patrons such as Harry Count Kessler. Both Tschudi and Liebermann had returned from their legendary visit to Paris in 1896 with impressionist paintings for the National Gallery in Berlin and were, therefore, fundamental for the development of impressionism in Germany and, through their connection with Endell, also influenced architectural thinking.

39 Camillo Sitte, *Der Städtebau nach seinen* künstlerischen Grundsätzen (Vienna: Georg Prachner Verlag, 1889); and Hendrik Petrus Berlage, "Bouwkunst en impressionisme," *Architectura*, no. 2 (1894): 93–95, 98–100, 105–106, 109–110.

40 Sitte, *Der Städtebau nach seinen* künstlerischen Grundsätzen, 53. On the relationship between modern urban space and phobias, see Anthony Vidler, *Warped Space: Art, Architecture, and Anxiety in Modern Culture* (Cambridge, MA: MIT Press, 2000), 25–50.

41 Endell, *Die Schönheit der großen Stadt*, 22.

42 Franz Marc, "Thesen über die 'abstrakte' Kunst und über die 'Grenzen der Kunst'" (1912–1913). Here cited from David Morgan, "The Enchantment of Art: Abstraction and Empathy from German Romanticism to Expressionism," *Journal of the History of Ideas* 57, no. 2 (April, 1996): 327. In relation to the work by Marc, see Wilhelm Worringer, *Abstraktion und Einfühlung* (Munich: R. Piper & Co., 1908).

43 Peg Weiss, *Kandinsky in Munich: The Formative Jugendstil Years* (Princeton: Princeton University Press, 1979). On Endell's time in Munich, see Tilmann Buddensieg, "Zur Frühzeit von August Endell," in *Festschrift für Eduard Trier*, eds. Justus Müller Hofstede and Werner Spies (Berlin: Gebr. Mann Verlag, 1981).

44 Wassily Kandinsky, *Über das Geistige in der Kunst* (Munich: R. Piper & Co., 1912). Kandinsky completed this text in 1910, it was published in 1911, but dated 1912. In 1914, he begins work on *Punkt und Linie zu Fläche: Beitrag zur Analyse der malerischen Elemente* (Munich: Verlag A. Langen, 1926).

45 Kandinsky, *Punkt und Linie zu Fläche*, 11.

46 At Photo-Atelier Elvira, which Endell designed in 1897 (one year after Kandinsky arrived in the city), a large "free form" filled the otherwise blank surface of the front façade behind which the photo studio was situated. While clearly influenced by Hermann Obrist, the spokesperson of Munich's *Jugendstil* scene and friend to both Endell and Kandinsky, Endell's façade ornament intentionally avoided any natural references, something that Obrist still searched for. The photographers and early feminists Anita Augspurg and Sophia Goudstikker saw in Endell a companion in the struggle toward a new perception, which resulted in the commission for the design of their photo atelier. For Endell's relationship to the artistic and feminist circles in Munich, see Irene Gammel, *Baroness Elsa: Gender, Dada, and Everyday Modernity – A Cultural Biography* (Cambridge, MA: MIT Press, 2002).

47 Zeynep Çelik Alexander, *Kinaesthetic Knowing: Aesthetics, Epistemology, Modern Design* (Chicago: University of Chicago Press, 2017), 97–130. In addition, see Zeynep Çelik Alexander, "Metrics of Experience: August Endell's Phenomenology of Architecture," *Grey Room*, no. 40 (Summer 2010): 50–83.

48 While Kandinsky arrived at the Bauhaus in 1922 and stayed until its forced closure in 1933, Moholy-Nagy was active at the school for only five years, from 1923 until Gropius's departure as director in 1928.

49 László Moholy-Nagy, *Malerei, Fotografie, Film* (Munich: Albert Langen Verlag, 1925), 27.

50 Ibid., 5.

51 Walter Benjamin, "Das Kunstwerk im Zeitalter seiner technischen Reproduzierbarkeit" (1936), translated as "The Work of Art in the Age of Mechanical Reproduction," in *Illuminations: Essays and Reflections*, trans. Harry Zohn (New York: Schocken Books, 1969), 236. On the relationship between Benjamin, Moholy-Nagy, and Giedion, see Detlef Mertins, "Walter Benjamin and the Tectonic Unconscious," *ANY*, no. 14 (1996): 28–35.

52 Walter Benjamin, "The Work of Art in the Age of Mechanical Reproduction," in *Illuminations: Essays and Reflections*, 237.

53 Walter Benjamin, "Der Sürrealismus – Die letzte Momentaufnahme der europäischen Intelligenz," *Literarische Welt*, no. V (1929), translated as "Surrealism," in *Reflections: Essays, Aphorisms, Autobiographical Writing*, trans. Edmund Jephcott (New York: Schocken Books, 1986), 190.

54 Sigfried Giedion, *Bauen in Frankreich, Bauen in Eisen, Bauen in Eisenbeton* (Leipzig, Berlin: Klinkhardt & Biermann, 1928), translated as *Building in France, Building in Iron, Building in Ferroconcrete*, trans. J. Duncan Berry (Santa Monica: Getty Center for the History of Art and the Humanities, 1995), 91.

55 László Moholy-Nagy, *Von Material zu Architektur* (Munich: A. Langen, 1929), 236.

56 Giedion, *Building in France*, 92.

57 In addition to *Vision in Motion* (Chicago: P. Theobald, 1947), Moholy-Nagy explored the relationship between metropolitan speed, architecture, and photography multiple times and most explicitly in "Space-time and the Photographer," *The American Annual of Photography*, no. 57 (1943): 7–14.

58 Edward Dimendberg, "Transfiguring the Urban Gray: László Moholy-Nagy's Film Scenario 'Dynamic of the Metropolis,'" in *Camera Obscura, Camera Lucida: Essays in*

Honor of Annette Michelson, eds. Richard Allen and Malcolm Turvey (Amsterdam: Amsterdam University Press, 2003), 121.

59 Moholy-Nagy, *Malerei, Fotografie, Film*, 120. In the second edition of this publication from 1927, Moholy-Nagy included the film script "Dynamik der Gross-Stadt" as a postscript and added an introduction in which he also acknowledged films such as Ruttmann's *Berlin – Die Sinfonie der Großstadt*, which had just been released that year.

60 Walter Gropius, "Design Topics," *Magazine of Art* (December 1947). Here cited from *Scope of Total Architecture* (New York: Collier Books, 1962), 33.

61 On the relationship between Kepes, Moholy-Nagy, and the New Bauhaus in Chicago as well as for an analysis on Kepes's theories on vision and visualization, see Orit Halpern, *Beautiful Data: A History of Vision and Reason Since 1945* (Duke University Press, 2014), 79–144.

62 György Kepes, *Language of Vision* (Chicago: P. Theobald, 1944), 13–14.

63 Reinhold Martin, *Utopia's Ghost: Architecture and Postmodernism, Again* (Minneapolis: University of Minnesota Press, 2010), 55.

64 Kevin Lynch, *The Image of the City* (Cambridge, MA: MIT Press, 1960); Colin Rowe and Robert Slutzky, "Transparency: Literal and Phenomenal," *Perspecta*, no. 8 (1963); Colin Rowe and Robert Slutzky, "Transparency: Literal and Phenomenal, Part II," *Perspecta*, no. 13/14 (1971); and Colin Rowe and Fred Koetter, *Collage City* (Cambridge, MA: MIT Press, 1978). On the relationship between Kepes, Rowe, and Slutzky, see Detlef Mertins, "Transparency: Autonomy & Relationality," *AA Files*, no. 32 (1997): 3–11.

65 The 1950s saw a radial rethinking of modern urbanism by figures such as Jacob Bakema, Aldo van Eyck, Alison and Peter Smithson, and John Voelcker, who charged the older generation with "betray[ing] society in betraying the essence of contemporary thought." "Modern Architecture," for the members of Team 10, was "firmly attached to the architectural problems of around 1920," which had long since been superseded. The younger generation would shift emphasis to notions of community, user participation, and social organization. Alison and Peter Smithson, for example, saw potentials for working-class street life in the existing city by giving shape to new projects. Eventually, the generational conflicts escalated and sealed the fate of CIAM in 1959. For citations, see Aldo van Eyck, "Is Architecture Going to Reconcile Basic Values?" (1959), in *Writings*, eds. Vincent Ligteljin and Francis Strauven (Amsterdam: SUN, 2008), 202; and Jacob Berend Bakema, "What Became of CIAM?" *Architectural Review* 129, no. 770 (1961): 226.

66 Reyner Banham, "City as a Scrambled Egg," *Cambridge Opinion*, no. 17 (1959): 18–23.

67 Ibid., 21.

68 Ibid.

69 *Man Made America*, special issue *Architectural Review 108*, no. 648 (1950). Later, Christopher Tunnard and Boris Pushkarev developed the project in the publication *Man-Made America: Chaos or Control? An Inquiry into Selected Problems of Design in the Urbanized Landscape* (New Haven: Yale University Press, 1963).

70 Reyner Banham, *Los Angeles: The Architecture of Four Ecologies* (1971; Berkeley: University of California Press, 2001), 6.

71 Ibid.

72 Anthony Vidler, "Los Angeles: City of the Immediate Future," Foreword to the 2000 edition of *Los Angeles* (Berkeley: University of California Press, 2001), xliv–xlvii. In addition, Vidler's *Histories of the Immediate Present: Inventing Architectural Modernism* (Cambridge, MA: MIT Press, 2008) positions Banham's work on Los Angeles in the context of the larger spectrum of his writings and his search for a history of modernism. On Banham, see Nigel Whiteley, *Reyner Banham: Historian of the Immediate Future* (Cambridge, MA: MIT Press, 2002). For a collection of essays by Banham, see Reyner Banham and Mary Banham, *A Critic Writes: Essays by Reyner Banham* (Berkeley: University of California Press, 1996).

73 Anton Wagner, *Los Angeles: Werden, Leben und Gestalt der Zweimillionenstadt in Südkalifornien* (Leipzig: Bibliographisches Institut, 1935), 1.

74 Banham, *Los Angeles*, 229.

75 Reyner Banham, *Theory and Design in the First Machine Age* (1960; Cambridge, MA: MIT Press, 1989), 81.

76 Ibid., 330–331.

77 Banham, *Los Angeles*, 224.

78 Tom Wolfe, *The Kandy-Kolored Tangerine-Flake Streamline Baby* (1965; New York: Picador, 2009), 78.

79 Reyner Banham, "Kandy Kulture Kikerone," *New Society* (August 19, 1965): 25.

80 Reyner Banham, "Beverly Hills, Too, Is a Ghetto," *The Listener*, vol. 80 (September 5, 1968): 296.

81 Banham, *Los Angeles*, 111.

82 Ibid., 116.

83 David Hockney, postcard to John Kasmin, his dealer in London, 1964 (Los Angeles: Getty Research Institute, 2001).

84 David Hockney, quoted in *The Listener* (May 22, 1975).

85 Banham, *Los Angeles*, 233.

86 Reyner Banham, "The Art of Doing Your Thing," *The Listener*, vol. 80 (September 12, 1968): 330–331.

87 On Ruscha's work in relationship to Los Angeles, see Alexandra Schwartz, *Ed Ruscha's Los Angeles* (Cambridge, MA: MIT Press, 2010).

88 Banham, *Theory and Design in the First Machine Age*, 315.

89 Ibid., 319.

90 Banham described Moholy-Nagy's *The New Vision* as "sacred." See Reyner Banham, "The Bauhaus Gospel," *The Listener* (September 26, 1968): 390.

91 Moholy-Nagy, *Vision in Motion*, 113.

92 Ibid., 114.

93 Eric Avila, "All Freeways Lead to East Los Angeles: Rethinking the L.A. Freeway and Its Meanings," in *Overdrive: L.A. Constructs the Future, 1940–1990*, eds. Wim de Wit and Christopher James Alexander (Los Angeles: Getty Research Institute, 2013), 35. On the history of the freeway system in Los Angeles, see David Brodsly, *L.A. Freeway: An Appreciative Essay* (Berkeley: University of California Press, 1981); Scott Bottles, *Los Angeles and the Automobile* (Berkeley: University of California Press, 1987); and Allen John Scott and Edward W. Soja, *The City: Los Angeles and Urban Theory at the End of the Twentieth Century* (Berkeley: University of California Press, 1996).

94 Banham, *Los Angeles*, 5.

95 Ibid., 196–197.

96 Ibid., 195.

97 Joan Didion, *Play It as It Lays* (New York: Farrar, Straus and Giroux, 1970), 16.

98 Banham, *Los Angeles*, 197.

99 Joan Didion, "Bureaucrats" (1976), in *The White Album* (New York: Farrar, Straus and Giroux, 2009), 83. It is interesting to note that this essay was devoted to the measures that the California Department of Transportation had implemented in its attempt to streamline traffic—an attempt of which Didion was highly skeptical. During an interview with the planner Eleanor Wood, Didion realized that it was unlikely that she "could interest her in considering the freeway as regional mystery." While the planners wanted a "rearrangement of people's daily planning," Didion noted that the "rearrangement of people's daily planning might seem ... rather a great deal to want." (84) This skepticism toward planning was shared by Banham, who in 1969 had already participated in writing the Non-Plan manifesto that speculated on possibilities of suspending planning in favor of spontaneity, modeled on Los Angeles.

100 Ibid.

101 Ibid.

102 Reyner Banham and Julian Cooper, *Reyner Banham Loves Los Angeles* (London: BBC, 1972), 52 min. The film can be viewed online at http://www.youtube.com/watch?v=WlZ0NbC-YDo

103 Ibid.

104 Banham, *Los Angeles*, 121.

105 In the 1940s, Nikolaus Pevsner authored multiple essays on Townscape in *Architectural Record*, essays that were brought together in his manuscript *Visual Planning and the Picturesque*, which was only recently published as *Pevsner's Townscapes: Visual Planning and the Picturesque*, ed. Mathew Aitchison (Los Angeles: Getty Research Institute, 2010). Gordon Cullen wrote "Townscape Casebook" in 1949, which became the basis for his book *Townscape* of 1961, on which he elaborated in the book *The Concise Townscape* one decade later. Hubert de Cronin Hastings owned the Architectural Press as well as the journal *Architectural Review*, of which he was the chief editor and contributor under the pseudonym Ivor de Wolfe. For the Townscape movement, see *Architectural Review* 106, no. 636 (1949) and *Architectural Review* 107, no. 637 (1950).

106 Ivor de Wolfe (Hubert de Cronin Hastings), "Townscape," *The Architectural Review* 106, no. 636 (1949): 354.

107 For Team 10, see *Architectural Design*, no. 12 (December, 1962), special issue: "Team 10 Primer 1953–1962," ed. Alison Smithson, 559–600. In addition, see Jane Jacobs, *Death and Life of the Great American Cities* (New York: Random House, 1961); Gordon Cullen, *Townscape* (London: Architectural Press, 1961); and Bernard Rudofsky, *Architecture Without Architects: An Introduction to Non-Pedigreed Architecture* (New York: Museum of Modern Art and Doubleday & Company, 1964).

108 For a discussion on "urban context" as a generative factor for architectural and urban design, see Sandy Isenstadt, "Contested Contexts," in *Site Matters*, eds. Carol Burns and Andrea Kahn (Abingdon, UK: Routledge, 2005), 157–184. According to Isenstadt, "context" appears as a defining issue in the 1950s and 1960s "as a consequence of the critique of modern architecture." (160)

109 Reyner Banham, Paul Barker, Peter Hall, and Cedric Price, "Non-Plan: An Experiment in Freedom," *New Society* (March 20, 1969): 436.

110 Paul Barker, "Thinking the Unthinkable," in *Non-Plan: Essays on Freedom, Participation and Change in Modern Architecture and Urbanism*, eds. Jonathan Hughes and Simon Sadler (New York: Routledge, 2000), 5.

111 Reyner Banham, "Encounter with Sunset Boulevard," *The Listener*, vol. 80 (August 22, 1968): 235–236.

112 Banham, Barker, Hall, and Price, "Non-Plan: An Experiment in Freedom," 440.

113 Karl R. Popper, *The Open Society and Its Enemies* (London: G. Routledge & Sons, 1945), 140.

114 Friedrich von Hayek, *The Road to Serfdom* (Chicago: The University of Chicago Press, 1944) and *The Constitution of Liberty* (Chicago: University of Chicago Press, 1978). For a positioning of Hayek's work in the politics of neoliberalism, see David Harvey, *A Brief History of Neoliberalism* (New York: Oxford University Press, 2005),19–63. On the relationship between Non-Plan and ideological forces, see Simon Sadler, "Open Ends: The Social Vision of 1960s Non-Planning," in *Non-Plan*, 138–155.

115 Simon Sadler, "Open Ends: The Social Vision of the 1960s Non-Planning," in *Non-Plan*, 149.

116 Banham, *Los Angeles*, 226.

117 Ibid., 224.

118 Ibid., 225.

119 Banham, Barker, Hall, and Price, "Non-Plan: An Experiment in Freedom," 443.

120 Banham, *Los Angeles*, 106; and *The Architecture of the Well-Tempered Environment* (Chicago: University of Chicago Press, 1969), 271. Already in 1967, Banham wrote about Las Vegas in "Towards a Million-Volt Light and Sound Culture," *Architectural Review*, vol. 141 (May 1967): 331–335.

121 Banham, *The Architecture of the Well-Tempered Environment*, 272. For Los Angeles's fascinations with light, see Sandy Isenstadt, "Los Angeles After Dark," in *Overdrive: L.A. Constructs the Future, 1940–1990*, 48–63.

122 Reyner Banham, "Mediated Environments or: You Can't Build That Here," in *Superculture: American Popular Culture and Europe*, ed. Christopher W. E. Bigsby (London: Paul Elek, 1975), 78.

123 Tom Wolfe, "Las Vegas (What?) Las Vegas (Can't Hear You! Too Noisy) Las Vegas!!!" *Esquire* (February 1964). Here cited from *The Kandy-Kolored Tangerine-Flake Streamline Baby*, 3–27.

124 Ibid., xvi–xviii.

125 Ibid., xvii.

126 Robert Venturi, Denise Scott Brown, and Steven Izenour, *Learning from Las Vegas* (1972; Cambridge, MA: MIT Press, 1977), 18.

127 On the concept of "vision" in the book *Learning from Las Vegas*, see Martino Stierli, *Las Vegas in the Rearview Mirror: The City in Theory, Photography, and Film* (Los Angeles: Getty Research Institute, 2013); and Katherine Smith, "Mobilizing Visions: Representing the American Landscape," in *Relearning from Las Vegas*, eds. Aron Vinegar and Michael J. Golec (Minneapolis: University of Minnesota Press, 2009). On Venturi and Scott Brown's Las Vegas studio as well as the book *Learning from Las Vegas*, see *Las Vegas Studio: Images from the Archives of Robert Venturi and Denise*

Scott Brown, eds. Hilar Stadler, Martino Stierli, and Peter Fischli (Zurich: Scheidegger & Spiess, 2008); Aron Vinegar, *I am a Monument: On Learning from Las Vegas* (Cambridge, MA: MIT Press, 2008); Deborah Fausch, "Ugly and Ordinary: The Representation of the Everyday," in *Architecture of the Everyday*, eds. Steven Harris and Deborah Berke (New York: Princeton Architectural Press, 1997), 75–106; and Fausch's dissertation *The Context of Meaning Is Everyday Life: Venturi and Scott Brown's Theories of Architecture and Urbanism* (Princeton University, 1999). On the practice and writing of Venturi and Scott Brown, see David B. Brownlee, David G. De Long, and Kathryn B. Heisinger, *Out of the Ordinary: Robert Venturi, Denise Scott Brown and Associates. Architecture, Urbanism, Design* (Philadelphia, New Haven: Philadelphia Museum of Art and Yale University Press, 2001), as well as the two monographs by Stanislaus von Moos, *Venturi, Rauch, & Scott Brown: Buildings and Projects* (New York: Rizzoli, 1987) and *Venturi, Scott Brown & Associates: Buildings and Projects, 1986–1998* (New York: Monacelli Press, 1999).

128 Scott Brown was born in Zambia and raised in South Africa. She first studied in South Africa and later at the AA in London, before moving to Philadelphia to study planning at the University of Pennsylvania. There, she also taught after graduation and met Robert Venturi, with whom she began to collaborate and teach courses. In 1965, Scott Brown left to take a teaching position at the University of California, Berkeley, and shortly later was named the co-chair of the Urban Design program at UCLA, where she stayed until 1967.

129 Stierli, *Las Vegas in the Rearview Mirror*, 110.

130 Two years later, Venturi and Scott Brown taught another studio that learned from a contemporary environment; this time, they investigated Levittown. The studio was entitled, "Remedial Housing for Architects, Or Learning from Levittown." While never published, parts of the research entered the exhibition *Signs of Life: Symbols in the American City*, Renwick Gallery, Washington, 1976.

131 Venturi, Scott Brown, and Izenour, *Learning from Las Vegas*, 6.

132 Denise Scott Brown, "Remedial Housing for Architects Studio" (1970), in *Venturi, Scott Brown & Associates on Houses and Housing* (London: Academy Editions; St. Martin's Press, 1992), 51–57.

133 Denise Scott Brown, "On Pop Art, Permissiveness, and Planning," *American Institute of Planners Journal* 35, no. 3 (1969): 186.

134 Early urban photography of the nineteenth century (from street scenes to urban panoramas), for example, played a key part in the comprehension of urbanization. For the history of urban photography in the US, see Peter Bacon Hales, *Silver Cities: The Photography of American Urbanization, 1839–1915* (Philadelphia: Temple University Press, 1984).

135 Venturi, Scott Brown, and Izenour, *Learning from Las Vegas*, 20.

136 Ibid.

137 Ibid., 53.

138 Kepes, *Language of Vision*, 13–14.

139 Kepes's books were included in the Las Vegas Studio reading list and his Gestalt theory as a device to decipher visual intricacies of the city is echoed in *Learning from Las Vegas*.

140 György Kepes, *The New Landscape in Art and Science* (Chicago: P. Theobald, 1956), 69; "Notes on Expression and Communication in the Cityscape," *Daedalus: Journal of the American Academy of Arts and Sciences* 90, no. 1 (1957): 151; and Lynch, *The Image of the City*, 12.

141 Lynch collaborated with researchers and published *The View from the Road* in 1964—as the title suggests, a publication in which the experience of car travel was analyzed in large part through cinematic sequencing of images: Donald Appleyard, Kevin Lynch, John Randolph Myer, and György Kepes, *The View from the Road* (Cambridge, MA: MIT Press, 1964). Venturi and Scott Brown produced four movies during their stay in Las Vegas, seeking to come to terms with a new visual condition for a new form of urbanism.

142 The films are both independent investigations and supplements to the book.

143 Der Werkbund, *Jahrbuch des Deutschen Werkbundes: Der Verkehr* (Jena: Eugen Diederichs, 1914).

144 Venturi, Scott Brown, and Izenour, *Learning from Las Vegas*, 53.

145 Banham, *Los Angeles*, 201.

146 Venturi, Scott Brown, and Izenour, *Learning from Las Vegas*, 9.

147 Wolfe, *The Kandy-Kolored Tangerine-Flake Streamline Baby*, 8.

148 Mitchell Schwarzer, *Zoomscape: Architecture in Motion and Media* (New York: Princeton Architectural Press, 2004), 91.

149 Vinegar, *I am a Monument: On Learning from Las Vegas*, 49–92

150 In contrast to some interpretations of *Learning from Las Vegas*, it is important to note that Venturi and Scott Brown do not see the constellation of "duck" and "decorated shed" as diametrically opposed. While the "decorated shed" wins in a time of advertisements and neon signs, both are productive. See Venturi, Scott Brown, and Izenour, *Learning from Las Vegas*, 87: "We maintain that both kinds of architecture are valid … but we think that the duck is seldom relevant today." And, later on they clarify, 130: "Because this is not the time and ours is not the environment for heroic communication through pure architecture."

151 Susan Sontag, "Notes on 'Camp'" (1964), in *Against Interpretation, and Other Essays* (New York: Picador, 2001), 277.

152 Ibid., 291.

153 Venturi, Scott Brown, and Izenour, *Learning from Las Vegas*, 155.

154 Sontag, *Against Interpretation, and Other Essays*, 277, 286.

155 Ibid., 292.

156 Ibid., 291; and Denise Scott Brown and Robert Venturi, interviewed by Adam Marcus, *Museo Magazine*, 14 (Spring 2010).

2 Extrapolation

1 In the context of the German discourse alone, works by figures such as Reinhard Baumeister, Hermann Josef Stübben, Theodor Fritsch, and Martin Wagner clearly show the difference in mentality.

2 Ludwig Hilberseimer, *Großstadtarchitektur* (Stuttgart: Julius Hoffmann, 1927). I translate "*Großstadtarchitektur*" as "metropolitan architecture," but the term has recently also been translated more literally as "metropolisarchitecture." See Ludwig Hilberseimer, *Metropolisarchitecture and Selected Essays*, trans. Richard Anderson and Julie Dawson (New York: GSAPP Books, 2012). The Office for Metropolitan Architecture (OMA) was founded in 1975 under the leadership of Rem Koolhaas, Madelon Vriesendorp, Elia Zenghelis, and Zoe Zenghelis.

3 These characteristics are developed in: Karl Scheffler, *Berlin – ein Stadtschicksal* (Berlin: E. Reiss, 1910), 218. Scheffler associated Berlin with different types of cities except the traditional town: *Kolonialstadt, Kaiserstadt, Reichshauptstadt, Großstadt, Geschäftsstadt, Arbeitsstadt, Vergnügungsstadt*. This text as well as all other books and articles by Scheffler mentioned in this chapter have never been translated in full into English but have been republished in German: Karl Scheffler, *Berlin – ein Stadtschicksal* (Berlin: Fannei & Walz Verlag, 1989); Karl Scheffler, *Der Architekt und andere Essays über Baukunst, Kultur und Stil* (Berlin: Birkhäuser, 1993); and Karl Scheffler, *Die Architektur der Großstadt* (Berlin: Gebr. Mann, 1998). Translations are by the author unless otherwise indicated.

4 Karl Scheffler, *Moderne Baukunst* (Berlin: Julius Bard, 1907), 1.

5 Karl Scheffler, "Vortrag II: Das Stadtschicksal Berlin's (Lecture II: The urban destiny of Berlin)," Manuscript for Lecture Series on Berlin, c. 1920s (Staats- und Universitätsbibliothek Hamburg Carl von Ossietzky, Handschriftenabteilung, NKSche – Kasten 1 – Ts 16): 16.

6 Scheffler, *Berlin – ein Stadtschicksal*, 219. It is interesting to note that the 1935 geographical study of Los Angeles by Anton Wagner utilized the same terminology. Wagner writes: "For the current form of Los Angeles, becoming is more characteristic than being." See Anton Wagner, *Los Angeles: Werden, Leben und Gestalt der Zweimillionenstadt in Südkalifornien* (Leipzig: Bibliographisches Institut, 1935), and see previous chapter on Wagner's influence on Banham.

7 Charles Baudelaire, "The Painter of Modern Life" (1863), in *The Painter of Modern Life, and Other Essays*, trans. Jonathan Mayne (London: Phaidon, 1965), 13.

8 Scheffler, *Berlin – ein Stadtschicksal*, 12.

9 The introduction of *Berlin – ein Stadtschicksal* describes this tension as follows: "an unconditional affirmation was impossible [and] resistance to the historically given was equally pathetic" (12).

10 Manfredo Tafuri and Francesco Dal Co, *Modern Architecture* (New York: H. N. Abrams, 1979), 11, 14; Francesco Dal Co, *Figures of Architecture and Thought: German Architecture Culture, 1880–1920* (New York: Rizzoli, 1990), 53, 55; Massimo Cacciari, *Architecture and Nihilism: On the Philosophy of Modern Architecture* (New Haven: Yale University Press, 1993), 88; and Julius Posener, *Berlin auf dem Wege zu einer neuen Architektur: Das Zeitalter Wilhelms II. Studien zur Kunst des neunzehnten Jahrhunderts* (Munich: Prestel Verlag, 1979), 252.

11 Georg Simmel, "Die Großstädte und das Geistesleben" (1903), translated as "The Metropolis and Mental Life," in *Simmel on Culture: Selected Writings*, trans. David Frisby and Mike Featherstone (London: Sage Publications, 1997), 185.

12 Scheffler, *Berlin – ein Stadtschicksal*, 46: *"Der zur Formlosigkeit verdammte Geist hat sich einen formlosen Stadtkörper gebildet. Man erstaunt über den Mangel an klarer Gliederung, wenn man einen Blick auf den Stadtplan wirft."*

13 Siegfried Kracauer, "Berliner Landschaft" (1931), in *Straßen in Berlin und anderswo* (Frankfurt am Main: Suhrkamp, 1964), 50.

14 Georg Simmel, *Der Konflikt der Kultur – ein Vortrag* (Munich: Duncker & Humblot, 1918), 48.

15 Scheffler, *Moderne Baukunst*, 1.

16 Scheffler, *Berlin – ein Stadtschicksal*, 121.

17 Ibid., 19.

18 Walter Benjamin, "Das Kunstwerk im Zeitalter seiner technischen Reproduzierbarkeit" (1936). Here cited from the revised and expanded version of the first essay, where Benjamin elaborated on the notion of *"Spielraum,"* translated in *Walter Benjamin: Selected Writings, 1935–1938, vol. 3*, trans. Livingstone (Cambridge, MA: Belknap Press, 1996), 127.

19 August Schmarsow, *Das Wesen der architektonischen Schöpfung* (Leipzig: Karl W. Hiersemann, 1894); and Heinrich Wölfflin, *Prolegomena zu einer Psychologie der Architektur* (Munich: Kgl. Hof- & Universitäts-Buchdruckerei, 1886). On the concept of space in architectural history, see Harry Francis Mallgrave and Eleftherios Ikonomou, *Empathy, Form and Space: Problems in German Aesthetics, 1873–1893* (Santa Monica: Getty, 1994).

20 Karl Kraus, *Die Fackel* (December 1912): 37. For further references, see Carl E. Schorske, "From Public Scene to Private Space: Architecture as Culture Criticism," in *Thinking with History* (Princeton: Princeton University Press, 1998). More recently, Hal Foster and Anthony Vidler have investigated the term *"Spielraum"* in Hal Foster, *Design and Crime: And Other Diatribes* (London; New York: Verso, 2002), 15–17; and Anthony Vidler, *Warped Space: Art, Architecture, and Anxiety in Modern Culture* (Cambridge, MA: MIT Press, 2000), 3–5, 84–86.

21 Karl Wolfskehl, "Spielraum" (1926), in *Gesammelte Werke* (Hamburg: Claassen, 1960), 431–432.

22 Miriam Bratu Hansen, *Cinema and Experience: Siegfried Kracauer, Walter Benjamin, and Theodor W. Adorno* (Berkeley: University of California Press, 2012), 192. In addition, see Hansen's essay "Room-for-Play: Benjamin's Gamble with Cinema," *October*, no. 109 (2004): 3–45.

23 Karl Scheffler, "Die Großstadt," *Die Neue Rundschau*, no. 21 (1910): 881.

24 Walther Rathenau, *Die schönste Stadt der Welt* (1899; Berlin: Philo, 2001), 23. The essay was first published anonymously in *Die Zukunft*, no. 26 (1899): 36–48. It found wide distribution through Rathenau's collection of essays, *Impressionen* (Leipzig: S. Hirzel, 1902).

25 Ibid., 26.

26 Ibid., 23.

27 Scheffler, *Berlin – ein Stadtschicksal*, 166.

28 Ibid., 118. Scheffler and Rathenau were in frequent contact, visiting each other and exchanging ideas.

29 Mark Twain, "The German Chicago," first published as "The Chicago of Europe," *Chicago Daily Tribune* (April 3, 1892). Here cited from *The Complete Essays of Mark Twain* (Garden City: Doubleday, 1963), 87–89.

30 Scheffler read the works of Sombart, Tönnies, and Weber, and in 1917 met Sombart and Weber at a secret conference that was organized by the publisher Eugen Diederichs. For more information, see Karl Scheffler, *Die fetten und die mageren Jahre: Ein Arbeits- und Lebensbericht* (Leipzig, Munich: Paul List Verlag, 1946), 301–302.

31 Marianne Weber, *Max Weber: A Biography*, trans. Harry Zohn (New York: John Wiley & Son, 1975), 285. Weber also notes in reference to Chicago: "Look, this is what modern reality is like" (287). On Weber's impressions of America, see Lawrence A. Scaff, *Max Weber in America* (Princeton: Princeton University Press, 2011). For a study on Berlin's relationship to Chicago in the urban literature around 1900, see Ralf Thiers and Dietmar Jazbinsek, "Embleme der Moderne. Berlin und Chicago in Stadttexten der Jahrhundertwende," in *Schriftenreihe der Forschungsgruppe "Metropolenforschung"* (Berlin: Wissenschaftszentrum Berlin, 1999); and my essay "No Failure Too Great," in *Chicagoisms: The City as Catalyst for Architectural Speculation*, eds. Alexander Eisenschmidt and Jonathan Mekinda (Zurich: Scheidegger & Spiess/Park Books, 2013). For Chicago's influence on other cities, see Arnold Lewis, *An Early Encounter with Tomorrow: Europeans, Chicago's Loop, and the World's Columbian Exposition* (Urbana: University of Illinois Press, 1997); and Marco D'Eramo, *The Pig and the Skyscraper – Chicago: A History of Our Future*, trans. Graeme Thomson (London, New York: Verso, 2002).

32 Ferdinand Tönnies, "Die nordamerikanische Nation," *Deutschland. Monatsschrift für die gesamte Kultur*, no. 4–5 (1906): 577: "The American nation differentiates itself from older, more naturally and gradually grown nations through its removal from tradition and its lack of history."

33 John Wellborn Root, c. 1890. Here cited from Lewis Mumford, *The Brown Decades; A Study of the Arts in America, 1865–1895* (New York: Dover Publications, 1971), 60.

34 Scheffler, *Berlin – ein Stadtschicksal*, 194.

35 The similarities in urban development between Berlin and Chicago are striking. For example, 1871 was the year that for both cities signaled a new urban beginning; much of Chicago was erased by a devastating fire, while on the other side of the Atlantic, Berlin's emergence as the capital of the Second German Empire shifted the political, economic, and cultural landscape of Germany and Europe.

36 Scheffler, *Berlin – ein Stadtschicksal*, 194.

37 Werner Sombart, *Warum gibt es in den Vereinigten Staaten keinen Sozialismus?* (Tübingen: J. C. B. Mohr Verlag, 1906), 14. Here, Sombart rhetorically asks, "What have Nürnberg and Chicago in common?" and is quick to reply, "Nothing!"

38 Karl Scheffler, "Ein Weg zum Stil," *Berliner Architekturwelt*, no. 5 (1903): 291–295.

39 Scheffler, *Moderne Baukunst*, 1: "Only the lax and faceless (*physiognomielos*) conditions of Berlin with its willingness to receive everything that is new ..."

40 Jürgen Habermas, *The Philosophical Discourse of Modernity: Twelve Lectures*, trans. Frederick Lawrence (Cambridge, MA: MIT Press, 1990), 7.

41 Otto Wagner, *Die Großstadt: Eine Studie über diese von Otto Wagner* (Vienna: Anton Schroll, 1911), trans. "The Development of the Great City," *Architectural Record* (May 1912): 500.

42 Heinrich Tessenow, *Ich verfolgte bestimmte Gedanken: Dorf, Stadt, Großstadt – was nun?* (Schwerin: Helms, 1996), 100–101. This volume published notes and lectures from the Tessenow archive, dating back to the 1920s and including several essays on the *Großstadt* and Europe.

43 Heinrich Tessenow, *Hausbau und dergleichen* (Berlin: Bruno Cassirer Verlag, 1916).

44 Karl Scheffler, *Die Architektur der Großstadt* (Berlin: Bruno Cassirer Verlag, 1913), 172.

45 On the discourse around the German department store, see Posener, *Berlin auf dem Wege zu einer neuen Architektur*; Peter Stürzebecher, *Das Berliner Warenhaus. Bautypus, Element der Stadtorganisation, Raumsphäre der Warenwelt* (Berlin: Archibook-Verlag, 1979); and *Berlin, 1900–1933: Architecture and Design, Architektur und Design*, ed. Tilmann Buddensieg (New York: Cooper-Hewitt Museum and the Smithsonian Institution's National Museum of Design, 1987). For a more recent account on Messel's Wertheim store, see Helen Shiner, "Embodying the Spirit of the Metropolis: the Warenhaus Wertheim, Berlin, 1896–1904," in *Modernism and the Spirit of the City*, ed. Iain Boyd Whyte (London: Routledge, 2003), 97–118. For contemporary accounts of the department store, see Paul Göhre, *Das Warenhaus* (Frankfurt am Main: Rütten & Loening, 1907); Leo Colze, *Berliner Warenhäuser* (1908; Berlin: Fannei & Walz Verlag, 1989); Alfred Wiener "Das Warenhaus," in *Jahrbuch des Deutschen Werkbundes* (Jena: Eugen Diederichs, 1913), 43–54; and, slightly later, Adolf Behne, *Der moderne Zweckbau* (Vienna, Berlin: Drei Masken Verlag, 1926), trans. *The Modern Functional Building* (Santa Monica: Getty Research Center for the History of Art and the Humanities, 1996).

46 On the history of the department store, see *Cathedrals of Consumption: The European Department Store, 1850–1939*, eds. Geoffrey Crossick and Serge Jaumain (Aldershot: Ashgate, 1998); Bernard Marrey, *Les Grands Magasins: des origines à 1939* (Paris: Picard, 1979); Nikolaus Pevsner, "Shops, Stores and Department Stores," in *A History of Building Types* (Princeton: Princeton University Press, 1976), 267–270; and Joseph Siry, *Carson Pirie Scott: Louis Sullivan and the Chicago Department Store* (Chicago: University of Chicago Press, 1988).

47 Frederic J. Schwartz, *The Werkbund – Design Theory and Mass Culture before the First World War* (New Haven: Yale University Press, 1996), 46.

48 Emil Claar, "Die Welt im kleinen" (1910), in *Deutsche Großstadtlyrik vom Naturalismus bis zur Gegenwart* (Stuttgart: Reclam, 1975), 67.

49 Walter Benjamin, "Paris, die Hauptstadt des XIX. Jahrhunderts" (1935), translated as "Paris, Capital of the Nineteenth Century," in *Reflections: Essays, Aphorisms, Autobiographical Writing*, trans. Edmund Jephcott (New York: Schocken Books, 1986), 156. Additionally, see Walter Benjamin, *The Arcades Project*, trans. Howard Eiland and Kevin McLaughlin (Cambridge, MA: Belknap Press of Harvard University 1999), 10, 15, 21, 37, 40–48, 60–61. It is also interesting to note that Benjamin made frequent use of Sigfried Giedion's *Bauen in Frankreich*, which according to Detlef Mertins made a great impression on Benjamin. See Detlef Mertins, "The Enticing and Threatening Face of Prehistory: Walter Benjamin and the Utopia of Glass," *Assemblage*, no. 29 (April, 1996): 7.

50 I am here building on a trajectory that leads from Walter Benjamin via Sigfried Giedion to Detlef Mertins. See Mertins, "Walter Benjamin and the Tectonic Unconscious: Using Architecture as an Optical Instrument," *ANY*, no. 14 (1996): 28–35.

51 On the history of the Wertheim Emporium, see Robert Habel, *Alfred Messels Wertheimbauten in Berlin* (Berlin: Gebr. Mann Verlag, 2009); and *Alfred Messel: Visionär der Großstadt*, eds. Elke Blauert, Robert Habel, Hans-Dieter Nägelke, and Christiane Schmidt (Berlin, Munich: Staatliche Museen zu Berlin und Edition Minerva Hermann Farnung, 2009).

52 Walter Curt Behrendt, *Alfred Messel: Mit einer einleitenden Betrachtung von Karl Scheffler* (Berlin: Bruno Cassirer Verlag, 1911), 28–29.

53 Scheffler, *Moderne Baukunst*, 48.

54 Scheffler, *Die Architektur der Großstadt*, 141. In addition, see Scheffler's introductory text in Behrendt, *Alfred Messel*, 15.

55 Ibid.

56 Paul Göhre, *Das Warenhaus*, 12.

57 *Gebäudekunde: Baukunde des Architekten, vol. 2,* no. 5 (Berlin: Verlag Deutsche Bauzeitung, 1902), 157.

58 Posener, *Berlin: Auf dem Wege zu einer neuen Architektur*, 453–458.

59 Simmel speaks of the "appeal of the fragment" in his early essay "Soziologische Aesthetik" (Sociological aesthetics), *Die Zukunft* 17 (1896): 204–216. On the notion of "fragmentation," see David Frisby, *Fragments of Modernity: Theories of Modernity in the Work of Simmel, Kracauer, and Benjamin* (Cambridge, MA: MIT Press, 1986).

60 This cast of characters is outlined in the work of Benjamin and Kracauer as they investigated spaces within the modern metropolis—realms they called "worlds in themselves." See Siegfried Kracauer, "Die Hotelhalle" (1925, unpublished), in *Das Ornament der Masse: Essays* (Frankfurt am Main: Suhrkamp, 1977), 169.

61 Baedeker (Firm), *Berlin and Its Environs, Handbook for Travelers* (Leipzig: K. Baedeker, 1908), 12.

62 *Berlin für Kenner: Ein Bärenführer bei Tag und Nacht durch die deutsche Reichshauptstadt* (Berlin: Boll und Pickardt Verlag, 1912). Here cited from *Die Berliner Moderne 1885–1914*, eds. Jürgen Schutte and Peter Sprengel (Stuttgart: Reclam, 1997), 97–98.

63 Karl Scheffler, "Das Geschäftshaus: Der Architekt Alfred Messel" (1908), in *Der Architekt – und andere Essays über Baukunst, Kultur und Stil* (Berlin: Birkhäuser, 1993), 25.

64 Wolf Wertheim (the youngest of the Wertheim brothers), who was responsible for the building, had to pay several times 100 Goldmark as a fine to the police because of the overcrowding of locations like the staircase in the department store. Landesarchiv Berlin, B Rep. 202, no. 4110.

65 *Berlin für Kenner*, cited from *Die Berliner Moderne 1885–1914*, 98.

66 The Wertheim store expansion took place in three stages: (1) 1896–1897, (2) 1899–1900, (3) 1904–1906.

67 Scheffler, *Die Architektur der Großstadt*, 34, 38.

68 For a detailed analysis of the Altes Museum, see Barry Bergdoll, *Karl Friedrich Schinkel: An Architecture for Prussia* (New York: Rizzoli, 1994), 72–90, and Fritz Neumeyer, "Berliner Klassizismus: der entgrenzte Stadtraum," in *Das Neue Berlin: Baugeschichte*

und Stadtplanung der deutschen Hauptstadt, ed. Michael Mönninger (Frankfurt am Main: Insel Verlag, 1991), 97–107.

69 Friedrich Ostendorf, *Haus und Garten* (Berlin: W. Ernst & Sohn, 1914), 84.

70 Ibid.

71 Scheffler, *Berlin – ein Stadtschicksal*, 76.

72 Ibid., 77.

73 Franz Kugler, "Karl Friedrich Schinkel: Eine Charakteristik seiner künstlerischen Wirksamkeit," in *Kleine Schriften und Studien zur Kunstgeschichte, vol. 3* (Stuttgart: Verlag von Ebner & Seubert, 1854), 327. Here cited from Bergdoll, *Karl Friedrich Schinkel*, 203.

74 Ibid., 201.

75 Behrendt completed his doctorate in architecture at the Technical University of Dresden in 1911.

76 Alan Colquhoun, "The Superblock" (1971), in *Essays in Architectural Criticism: Modern Architecture and Historical Change* (Cambridge, MA: MIT Press, 1985), 102.

77 Ibid., 96.

78 Sarah Whiting, "Super!" *Log*, no. 16 (Spring/Summer 2009): 19–26; and "Bas-Relief Urbanism: Chicago's Figured Field," in *Mies in America*, ed. Phyllis Lambert (New York: Harry N. Abrams, Centre Canadien d'Architecture, Whitney Museum of American Art, and Museum of Modern Art New York, 2001), 642–691.

79 This reading of architecture's productive engagements with some of the more hostile conditions of the capitalist city runs counter to the predominant understanding of this early material cultivated by Tafuri, Dal Co, and Cacciari.

80 Bruno Taut, Competition Entry for the Extension of the Warenhaus Wertheim, Berlin, 1910. For more information, see Posener, *Berlin auf dem Wege zu einer neuen Architektur*, 478.

81 Peter Behrens, "Einfluss von Zeit- und Raumausnutzung auf moderne Formentwicklung," in *Jahrbuch des Deutschen Werkbundes: Der Verkehr* (Jena: Eugen Diederichs, 1914), 7–10.

82 Erich Mendelsohn, *Das Gesamtschaffen des Architekten* (Berlin: Rudolf Mosse Buchverlag, 1930), 28.

83 Scheffler hints at this kind of city in his *Die Architektur der Großstadt*, 30–43.

84 Ibid., 41: "Messel, despite his exemplary modern thinking, was still too much an academic and child of tradition, which made it impossible for him to entirely solve the great missions of our time. [After all] the most valuable characteristic [of modern building] is the impersonal and typical."

85 Ludwig Hilberseimer, "Die Architektur der Großstadt" (1914), handwritten outline on 15 folios, Hilberseimer Archive, Ryerson and Burnham Libraries, Art Institute of Chicago, box 8/3, no. 1/1.

86 Ibid., folio 11. Richard Pommer's essay, "'More a Necropolis than a Metropolis' – Ludwig Hilberseimer's Highrise City and Modern City Planning," also highlights how Hilberseimer's concept of urban planning relates to his reading of Alois Riegl's theory of "Kunstwollen," in Richard Pommer, David Spaeth, and Kevin Harrington, *In the Shadow of Mies: Ludwig Hilberseimer, Architect, Educator, and Urban Planner* (Chicago: Art Institute of Chicago and Rizzoli International Publications, 1988), 26.

87 Hilberseimer, *Großstadtarchitektur*, 21.

88 Ibid., 22.

89 Ibid.

90 Ibid., 23.

91 Ibid., 17.

92 Ludwig Hilberseimer, *Das neue Berlin 2* (1929): 39–41.

93 Hilberseimer, *Großstadtarchitektur*, 65, 55.

94 Louis H. Sullivan, *The Autobiography of an Idea* (New York: Press of the American Institute of Architects, 1924), 309, and Bruno Taut, cited in Iain Boyd Whyte, *Bruno Taut and the Architecture of Activism* (Cambridge, UK: Cambridge University Press, 1982), 17. Peter Behrens had praised Messel already in 1909 for his ability to fuse styles within a modern framework in his article "Alfred Messel: Ein Nachruf," *Frankfurter Zeitung – Morgenblatt* (April 6, 1909): 225.

95 When Root inspected a revised drawing of the Monadnock building in 1889, he was "indignant at first over this project of a brick box." Cited from Harriet Monroe, *John Wellborn Root: A Study of His Life and Work* (Cambridge: The Riverside Press, 1896), 141.

96 Sarah Whiting, "Bas-Relief Urbanism: Chicago's Figured Field," in *Mies in America*, 659.

97 Ludwig Hilberseimer, *Entfaltung einer Planungsidee* (Berlin: Ullstein, 1963), 22.

98 Hilberseimer, *Großstadtarchitektur*, 19.

99 Scheffler, "Ein Weg zum Stil": 291–295.

100 Ludwig Hilberseimer, "Vorschlag zur City-Bebauung," *Die Form*, no. 5 (1930): 23.

101 Hilberseimer, *Großstadtarchitektur*, 55.

102 Albert Pope, *Ladders* (Houston, TX, New York: Rice School of Architecture; Princeton Architectural Press, 1996), 71.

103 Hilberseimer, "Die Architektur der Großstadt" (1914), folio 11.

104 Aldo Rossi, *The Architecture of the City*, trans. Diane Ghirardo and Joan Ockman (1966; Cambridge, MA: MIT Press, 2002), 166. Originally published as *L'architettura della città* (Padova: Marsilio Editori, 1966).

105 Pier Vittorio Aureli, "In Hilberseimer's Footsteps," afterword in Hilberseimer, *Metropolisarchitecture and Selected Essays*, 340–345.

106 Andrea Branzi, *The Hot House: Italian New Wave Design* (Cambridge, MA: MIT Press, 1984), 54.

107 Andrea Branzi, *No-Stop City: Archizoom Associati* (Orléans: Editions HYX, 2006), 155.

108 Branzi, *The Hot House*, 76.

109 K. Michael Hays, *Modernism and the Posthumanist Subject: The Architecture of Hannes Meyer and Ludwig Hilberseimer* (Cambridge, MA: MIT Press, 1992), 240–277.

110 Manfredo Tafuri, "Design and Technological Utopia," in Emilio Ambasz, *Italy: The New Domestic Landscape; Achievements and Problems of Italian Design* (New York: Museum of Modern Art in collaboration with Centro Di, Florence, 1972), 394–395.

111 Branzi articulated this idea by noting that "[the] architecture of the future would emerge not from an abstract act of design but from a different form of use …," in Branzi, *The Hot House*, 60.

112 Fritz Neumeyer, "OMA's Berlin: The Polemic Island in the City," *Assemblage*, no. 11 (April 1990): 43.

113 Rem Koolhaas, "Shipwrecked," in *Small, Medium, Large, Extra-Large* (New York: Monacelli Press, 1995), 259.

114 The concept of "city repair" originated through the work of Josef Paul Kleihues, who would lead the urban renewal efforts and eventually develop the concept of "critical reconstruction." Under the overall leadership of Hans Stimmann, the IBA pursued two directions, IBA Neu with Kleihues and the less propagated IBA Alt that was organized by Hardt Waltherr Hämer. The IBA was founded in 1978, and the two directors were appointed in 1979. Early activities entailed research, conferences, and competitions while most construction took place in the years between 1984 and 1987. For more information on the history of the IBA, see Werner Oechslin, "Phönixgeburt: Die Internationale Bauausstellung Berlin – Idee, Prozess, Ergebnis," in *Josef Paul Kleihues – Stadt Bau Kunst*, eds. Paul Kahlfeldt, Andres Lepik, and Andreas Schathke (Berlin: Nicolaische Verlagsbuchhandlung, 2003); Heinrich Klotz, "Die Internationale Bauausstellung 1987: eine Bilanz," in *Das Neue Berlin: Baugeschichte und Stadtplanung der deutschen Hauptstadt* (Frankfurt am Main: Insel Verlag, 1991); and Dieter Hoffmann-Axthelm, "An Extreme Case of Urban Crisis: The Troubled History of a City of Stone," *Berlin Metropolis, A&V*, no. 50 (1994).

115 Jürgen Habermas, "Modernity: An Unfinished Project" (1980), in *Habermas and the Unfinished Project of Modernity: Critical Essays on the Philosophical Discourse of Modernity* (1980; Cambridge, MA: MIT Press, 1997), 51.

116 Rem Koolhaas, "Imagining Nothingness" (1985), in *Small, Medium, Large, Extra-Large*, 199.

117 For OMA, Archizoom presented an alternative to the rejection that architecture faced post-1968. "They were critical and projective at the same time ... a deliberate shock." Elia Zenghelis in conversation with the author, Chicago, March 2, 2015.

118 Rem Koolhaas, "The City of the Captive Globe/1972," *Architectural Design* 47, no. 5 (1977): 331. The drawing of the captive globe was originally produced in 1972.

119 Salvator Dalí, "The Conquest of the Irrational" (1935), in *The Collected Writings of Salvador Dalí*, trans. Haim N. Finkelstein (Cambridge, UK, New York: Cambridge University Press, 1998), 268.

120 Koolhaas, "The City of the Captive Globe/1972": 331.

121 Koolhaas documents these two positions in *Delirious New York* by framing Dalí as an admirer of Manhattan and Le Corbusier as the one who condemned it. See *Delirious New York: A Retroactive Manifesto for Manhattan* (1978; New York: Monacelli Press, 1994), 235–281.

122 Koolhaas, *Small, Medium, Large, Extra-Large*, 51.

123 Fredric Jameson, *The Seeds of Time* (New York: Columbia University Press, 1994), 144.

124 Ibid., 142.

125 Rossi, *The Architecture of the City*; Robert Krier, *Urban Space/Stadtraum*, trans. Christine Czechowski and George Black (1975; New York: Rizzoli, 1979); and Robert Venturi, Denise Scott Brown, and Steven Izenour, *Learning from Las Vegas* (1972; Cambridge, MA: MIT Press, 1977).

126 The examples that are discovered and analyzed in *Delirious New York* are later on explicated in texts such as "Whatever Happened to Urbanism" (1994); see *Small, Medium, Large, Extra-Large*, 971.

127 Koolhaas, *Delirious New York*, 296.

128 Oswald Mathias Ungers, with Rem Koolhaas, Peter Riemann, Hans Kollhoff, and Arthur Ovaska, *Die Stadt in der Stadt: Berlin das Grüne Stadtarchipel – Ein stadträumliches Planungskonzept für die zukünftige Entwicklung Berlins* (Berlin, Cologne: Studioverlag für Architektur L. Ungers, printed in Ithaca, NY, 1977). What began as a systematic investigation on matters of form in the contemporary city crystallized eventually as Summer School projects that Ungers led for students from Cornell University, where Ungers was teaching. The first focused on the "Block" and was based in Manhattan (1976), while the second workshop on "Urban Villas" and the third on "Urban Gardens" were held in Berlin. The publication *Die Stadt in der Stadt* grew out of the second workshop and with the help of a text that Koolhaas prepared as his contribution to the project.

129 The argument for perimeter block reconstruction was a key contribution by Robert and Léon Krier. This influenced tendencies within Berlin's International Building Exhibition (IBA) during the 1980s and ultimately spoke to popular ambitions for the reconstruction of Berlin.

130 Rem Koolhaas, "Berlin: A Green Archipelago," 6-page typescript, July 1977 (Cologne: Ungers Archiv für Architekturwissenschaft), 1; republished and translated in *The City in the City – Berlin: A Green Archipelago*, eds. Florian Hertweck, Sébastien Marot, and Ungers Archiv für Architekturwissenschaft (Zurich: Lars Müller Publishers, 2013), 12–23.

131 Ungers, Koolhaas, Riemann, Kollhoff, and Ovaska, *Die Stadt in der Stadt*, 24.

132 Michel Foucault, "Of Other Spaces: Utopias and Heterotopias," in *Architecture Culture, 1943–1968: A Documentary Anthology*, ed. Joan Ockman (New York: Columbia Books of Architecture, Rizzoli, 1993), 422.

133 It is also interesting to note that Foucault, Ungers, and Koolhaas met in 1972 at Cornell University, where Foucault was teaching and Koolhaas studied with Ungers.

134 Ungers, Koolhaas, Riemann, Kollhoff, and Ovaska, *Die Stadt in der Stadt*, 43.

3 Narration

1 Bernard Tschumi, *Event-Cities: Praxis* (Cambridge, MA: MIT Press, 1994), 12; and Bernard Tschumi in conversation with the author, New York, July 13, 2011, later published as interview in *City Catalyst: Architecture in the Age of Extreme Urbanisation, Architectural Design*, no. 219, ed. Alexander Eisenschmidt (September/October 2012): 130–135.

2 The institutionalization of *Städtebau* was already underway before 1900. The first teaching of *Stadtplanung* (city planning) was done in Stuttgart and Dresden in 1896; early lectures on *Stadtbaukunst* (the art of city building) were delivered by Theodor Goecke, Joseph Brix, and Felix Genzmer in 1903 at the Königlich Technische Hochschule in Berlin-Charlottenburg; and the first recognized academic seminar on *Städtebau* followed in the winter semester of 1907/08.

3 Patrick Geddes, *Cities in Evolution* (London: Williams & Norgate, 1915), 87.

4 Embedded in the reform culture of the late nineteenth century, the semi-public *Musée Social* in Paris, for example, saw itself first as a moderator between state and public. Here, the collection and representation of information on the city was not merely seen as an educational tool but as ground for reform negotiations between these two arenas. In 1903, Harvard University founded the first Social Museum in the US, and in 1909, the Museo Social was founded in Barcelona—organizations that during this time joined a network of museums that sought to compile information on modern urban life.

5 Geddes, *Cities in Evolution*, 87.

6 E. Hirschberg, *Bilder aus der Berliner Statistik* (Berlin, 1904), 2. Here cited from Anthony McElligott, *The German Urban Experience, 1900–1945: Modernity and Crisis* (London, New York: Routledge, 2001), 234.

7 Siegried Kracauer, "Das Ornament der Masse" (1927). Here cited from *The Mass Ornament: Weimar Essays*, trans. Thomas Y. Levin (Cambridge, MA: Harvard University Press, 1995), 75–86. Different means of representation, such as rhythmic dance or statistical investigations, gave form to what was fragmented and incomprehensible in its individual state. "Community and personality perish when what is demanded is calculability; it is only as a tiny piece of the mass that the individual can clamber up charts and can service machines without any friction. ... Like the mass ornament, the capitalist production process is an end in itself." (78)

8 Walter Benjamin, "Das Kunstwerk im Zeitalter seiner technischen Reproduzierbarkeit" (1936), translated as "The Work of Art in the Age of Mechanical Reproduction," in *Illuminations: Essays and Reflections*, trans. Harry Zohn (New York: Schocken Books, 1969), 223.

9 Ibid.

10 For an investigation on surplus information and meaning, see K. J. Knoespel, "The Emplotment of Chaos: Instability and Narrative Order," in *Chaos and Order: Complex Dynamics in Literature and Science*, ed. Katherine Hayles (Chicago: University of Chicago Press, 1991), 115.

11 Hegemann was exposed to the effective use of statistics and information arranged in diagrams during his studies under the guidance of political scientists such as Charles Gide at the Faculté de Droit de l'Université de Paris and Simon N. Patten at the University of Pennsylvania in Philadelphia, who both recognized the didactic power of statistics.

12 On Hegemann's work, see Christiane Crasemann Collins, *Werner Hegemann and the Search for Universal Urbanism* (New York: W. W. Norton, 2005) and Caroline Flick, *Werner Hegemann (1881–1936): Stadtplanung, Architektur, Politik: Ein Arbeitsleben in Europa und den USA* (Munich: K. G. Saur, 2005).

13 In November 1909, Hegemann departed from the US to Berlin in order to become the secretary-general for the exhibition. Shortly after completing his dissertation at the Ludwig-Maximilian-Universität in Munich (1908), Hegemann had returned to Philadelphia, studied the housing condition in the US, reported on exhibitions on the city such as New York's *Congestions* exhibit (for *Der Städtebau)*, and was involved in the exhibition *Boston 1915*.

14 Hermann Muthesius, *The English House* (1904; New York: Rizzoli, 1987). Here cited from Peter Davey, *Architecture of the Arts and Crafts Movement* (New York: Rizzoli, 1980), 202.

15 Max Weber, "Wissenschaft als Beruf" (1922), in *Gesammelte Aufsätze zur Wissenschaftslehre* (Tübingen: J. C. B. Mohr, 1973), 594: "*daß man, wenn man nur wollte, [alles] erfahren könne. Das aber bedeutet: die Entzauberung der Welt.*"

16 (Charles-Edouard Jeanneret) Le Corbusier, *Etude sur le mouvement d'art décoratif en Allemagne* (1912; New York: Da Capo Press, 1968), 36. Translations are by the author unless otherwise indicated.

17 Sitte's influence on Jeanneret can be detected in documents ranging from his travel to Italy in 1907 to his essay "La construction des villes" in 1910. Furthermore, Le Corbusier's shift in perspective, initiated by the exhibition, is demonstrated by the self-imposed censorship of all work that was done before. In the oeuvre of Le Corbusier, work only began to count from his now legendary *Voyage d'Orient* (*Journey to the East*, 1910/11), a trip following immediately after his stay in Germany. On Le Corbusier's time in Germany, see H. Allen Brooks, *Jeanneret and Sitte: In Search of Modern Architecture* (Cambridge, MA: MIT Press, 1982); Rosario De Simone, *Ch. E. Jeanneret – Le Corbusier: Viaggio in Germania, 1910–1911* (Rome: Officina, 1989); Werner Oechslin, "Influences, confluences et reniements," in *Le Corbusier, une encyclopédie* (Paris: Centre Georges Pompidou, 1987); Winfried Nerdinger, "Standard and Type: Le Corbusier und Deutschland," in Stanislaus von Moos, *L'Esprit Nouveau, Le Corbusier und die Industrie* (Berlin: W. Ernst, 1987).

18 No record has survived that would indicate a meeting between Le Corbusier and Hegemann during the time of the 1910 exhibition. However, both followed each other's publications closely and in 1922 Le Corbusier sent Hegemann his project of the *Contemporary City*, which Hegemann sharply criticized. It seems that a short meeting in 1926 was the only personal encounter of the two figures.

19 Apparently, a third volume was planned but never executed.

20 Werner Oechslin, "Zwischen Amerika und Deutschland: Werner Hegemanns städtebauliche Vorstellungen jenseits der Frage nach der Moderne," in *Das Bauwerk und die Stadt/The Building and The Town, Aufsätze für/Essays for Eduard F. Sekler*, ed. Wolfgang Böhm (Vienna: Böhlau, 1994), 232.

21 Werner Hegemann, *Der Städtebau nach den Ergebnissen der Allgemeinen Städtebau-Ausstellung in Berlin, vol. 1* (Berlin: E. Wasmuth, 1911), 7: "*Berlin wird augenblicklich ein internationales Sturmzentrum in dem Kampfe um die segensreiche Gestaltung der durchaus neuen Welt, auf der wir seit dem Wirksamwerden der neuzeitlichen Technik ... leben.*"

22 J. Rousseau, *Emile, ou de l'éducation*, in *Oeuvres complètes vol. IV, book IV* (1762; Paris: Gallimard, 1959), 551. Here cited from Marshall Berman, *All That Is Solid Melts Into Air: The Experience of Modernity* (New York: Simon and Schuster, 1982), 17.

23 Hegemann, *Der Städtebau, vol. 1*, 8.

24 Ibid., 128–129.

25 Ibid., 117.

26 In this trajectory, Hegemann's two-volume book *Der Städtebau* (in its relentless descriptions of the city and its unending lists of examples and relationships) shares qualities with Rem Koolhaas's essay on "Junkspace." The linguistic techniques that

Koolhaas deploys to itemize the overwhelming amount of spatial by-product as a result of replication can be seen already in Hegemann's writing. But, whereas Koolhaas deliberately speaks in a language that represents "the residue mankind leaves on the planet," Hegemann's proto-Junkspace prose is unintentional and, therefore, a raw and direct product of the metropolis. For Koolhaas's essay, see Rem Koolhaas, "Junkspace," in *Project on the City: Harvard Design School Guide to Shopping*, eds. Rem Koolhaas, Chuihua Judy Chung, Jeffrey Inaba, Sze Tsung Leong, and Graduate School of Design Harvard University (Cologne, Cambridge, MA: Taschen; Harvard Design School, 2001).

27 Nicholas Bullock and James Read, *The Movement for Housing Reform in Germany and France 1840–1914* (Cambridge, UK: Cambridge University Press, 1985), 17–70. In addition, see Brian Ladd, *Urban Planning and Civic Order in Germany, 1860–1914* (Cambridge, MA: Harvard University Press, 1990), 139–185.

28 This number is especially dramatic if compared to the density of Berlin today, with only 3,800 individuals per square kilometer.

29 Werner Hegemann, *Das steinerne Berlin: Geschichte der größten Mietskasernenstadt der Welt* (Berlin: Gustav Kiepenheuer, 1930).

30 CIAM 2 (1929) was under the heading of "Die Wohnung für das Existenzminimum" (minimum dwelling, 1930), CIAM 3 (1930) under "Rationelle Bebauungsweisen" (later also published by Karel Teige, "The Housing Problem of the Subsistence Level Population," 1931), and in 1942 José Luis Sert asked: *Can Our Cities Survive? An ABC of Urban Problems, Their Analyses, Their Solutions, Based on the Proposals Formulated by the CIAM*. Le Corbusier, *Towards an Architecture* (1923; Los Angeles: Getty Research Institute, 2007), 291.

31 Hegemann, *Der Städtebau, vol. 1*, 83.

32 Wolfgang Sonne, "Dwelling in the Metropolis: Sitte, Hegemann, and the International Dissemination of Reformed Urban Blocks 1890–1940," in *Sitte, Hegemann and the Metropolis: Modern Civic Art and International Exchanges*, eds. Charles C. Bohl and Jean-François Lejeune (London, New York: Routledge, 2009), 249–274; and Crasemann Collins, *Werner Hegemann and the Search for Universal Urbanism, 146–321*.

33 Eric Mumford, *The CIAM Discourse on Urbanism, 1928–1960* (Cambridge, MA: MIT Press, 2000), 56.

34 Hegemann focused at length on the nineteenth-century developments that were to account for the urban situation. He outlined, for example, how the Prussian three-class franchise system of 1848 indirctly fostered urban speculation by empowering the upper classes, how the early building plans (*Bebauungsplan*) of 1855 and 1858 gave way to the plan of 1862 by Hobrecht, and how the building code *(Bauordnung)* of 1887 would further contribute to the urban speculation that profited from dense, multi-story buildings for most of the city. Whereas most literature agrees with Hegemann's early assessment of Hobrecht's plan, one recent study developed a more positive reading: Claus Bernet, "The 'Hobrecht Plan' (1862) and Berlin's Urban Structure," *Urban History* 31, no. 3 (2004): 400–419.

35 James Hobrecht: "*In der Mietskaserne gehen die Kinder aus den Kellerwohnungen in die Freischule über denselben Hausflur wie diejenigen des Rats oder Kaufmanns auf dem Weg nach dem Gymnasium.*" Here cited from Julius Posener, *Berlin auf dem Wege*

zu einer neuen Architektur: Das Zeitalter Wilhelms II. Studien zur Kunst des neunzehnten Jahrhunderts (Munich: Prestel Verlag, 1979), 365.

36 Architektenverein zu Berlin, "Wettbewerbe um einen Grundplan für die Bebauung von Groß-Berlin," *Der Baumeister* 7, no. 2 (1908): 18b–23b.

37 After years of preparation and financial investments (the maps for the competition alone had cost the staggering amount of 34,830 Marks) only twenty-seven entries were filed on December 1909. The more visionary planners were certainly dazzled by the contradiction of the organizer's insistence on realistic proposals while outlining an image of a larger, more populated Berlin than it would ever be. For a full list of all participants and information on the Berlin city-building competition, see Wolfgang Sonne, *Representing the State: Capital City Planning in the Early Twentieth Century* (Munich, New York: Prestel, 2003), 343, and chapter 3: "Greater Berlin: Raising a European Capital to Imperial World Status"; Wolfgang Sonne, *Dwelling in the Metropolis: Reformed Urban Block 1890–1940* (Glasgow: University of Strathclyde, Department of Architecture, 2005), chapter 1: "Berlin and Germany"; Christine Becker, Brigitte Jacob, and Julius Posener, "1888–1918. Die Zeit Wilhelms des Zweiten," in *750 Jahre Architektur und Städtebau in Berlin: Die Internationale Bauausstellung im Kontext der Baugeschichte Berlins*, eds. Josef Paul Kleihues, Claus Baldus, and Ursula Frohne (Stuttgart: G. Hatje, 1987); Posener, *Berlin auf dem Wege zu einer neuen Architektur*, chapter: "Der Städtebau"; and Vittorio Magnago Lampugnani, "Berlin Modernism and the Architecture of the Metropolis," in *Mies in Berlin*, eds. Terence Riley and Barry Bergdoll (New York: Museum of Modern Art, 2001).

38 Architektenverein zu Berlin, "Wettbewerbe um einen Grundplan für die Bebauung von Groß-Berlin": 18b: "*Der Versuch, einen Grundplan für die bauliche Entwicklung von Groß-Berlin zu erlangen … [und] eine einheitliche großzügige Lösung zu finden, sowohl für die Forderungen des Verkehrs, als für diejenigen der Schönheit, der Volksgesundheit und der Wirtschaft.*"

39 Hegemann, *Das steinerne Berlin* (1930). Here cited from Werner Hegemann, *Das steinerne Berlin: Geschichte der größten Mietskasernenstadt der Welt* (Braunschweig, Wiesbaden: Vieweg Verlag, 1988), 207.

40 Max Weber, *The Protestant Ethic and the Spirit of Capitalism*, trans. Talcott Parsons (1904; New York: Scribner, 1952), 181.

41 Ibid., 182.

42 Berman, *All That Is Solid Melts Into Air: The Experience of Modernity, 24.*

43 While Benjamin's broadcasts addressed a wide range of topics (from the mysterious environments of Berlin to the intricate urban conditions of Pompeii, from the nomadic and boundary-defying travels of gypsies to the inventiveness of prisoners at the Bastille) the theme of the city is a common thread throughout. None of the original sound recordings have survived but Benjamin's notes and scripts of the numerous reviews, speeches, plays, and documentaries exist today. The whereabouts of the radio scripts was for a long time unclear, but they resurfaced several decades ago. Benjamin had left the scripts behind when escaping the Nazi occupation of Paris in 1940. There they only survived through acts of resistance against the Gestapo's orders to destroy the archive. In the chaos of the last years of the war, the papers traveled to the Soviet Union, from where they moved to the Central Archive in Potsdam two decades later. In 1972, they relocated again to the Academy of Arts in Berlin. In 1985,

Suhrkamp published the scripts for the first time and, in 2002, Radio Bremen launched a highly successful rebroadcasting of some. One year later these were collected for the CD release under the title *Walter Benjamin: Aufklärung für Kinder* (Enlightenment for Children) (Bremen: Hoffmann und Campe Verlag, 2003). In 2014, all of Benjamin's broadcasts as well as writings on radio were translated for the edited volume by Lecia Rosenthal, *Radio Benjamin*, trans. Jonathan Lutes, Lisa Harries Schumann, and Diana K. Reese (London, New York: Verso, 2014). This is the first comprehensive study on Benjamin's work for the radio in English. On Benjamin's work for the radio, see Sabine Schiller-Lerg, *Walter Benjamin und der Rundfunk: Programmarbeit zwischen Theorie und Praxis* (Munich, New York: K.G. Saur, 1984); Christian Hörburger, *Das Hörspiel der Weimarer Republik: Versuch einer kritischen Analyse* (Stuttgart: Heinz, 1975), chapter 8.4: "Vorläufige Bemerkungen zu Walter Benjamins Hörspielen"; *Walter Benjamin und die Kinderliteratur: Aspekte der Kinderkultur in den zwanziger Jahren*, ed. Klaus Doderer, Jugendliteratur, Theorie und Praxis (Weinheim, Munich: Juventa, 1988); Erhart Schütz, "Benjamins Berlin: Wiedergewinnung des Entfernten," in *Schrift, Bilder, Denken: Walter Benjamin und die Künste*, ed. Detlev Schöttker (Frankfurt am Main, Berlin: Suhrkamp; Haus am Waldsee, 2004).

44 Benjamin concludes his broadcast on the rental barracks by acknowledging Hegemann: "*Das steinerne Berlin* ... from which you and I have learned all that we now know of the rental barracks." Walter Benjamin, "Die Mietskaserne" (broadcast 1930), translated as "The Rental Barracks," in Rosenthal, *Radio Benjamin*, 62.

45 Walter Benjamin, "Theater und Radio" (1932), translated as "Theater and Radio," in *Walter Benjamin: Selected Writings, 1931–1934, vol. 2, part 2*, trans. Rodney Livingstone (Cambridge, MA: Belknap Press, 1996), 584.

46 Walter Benjamin, "Das dämonische Berlin" (broadcast February 25, 1930), translated as "The Demonic Berlin," in *Radio Benjamin*, 29.

47 Benjamin's "Mietskaserne" broadcast took place some time in the spring or summer of 1930. The exact date is unknown. In *Walter Benjamin und der Rundfunk*, Sabine Schiller-Lerg proposed April 12, 1930, as the date for the broadcast.

48 Benjamin, "The Rental Barracks," in *Radio Benjamin*, 59.

49 Benjamin elaborates on multiple occasions on the connection between his radio work and Brecht's epic theater. In particular, see "Theater and Radio," in *Walter Benjamin: Selected Writings, 1931–1934*, 583–586.

50 Walter Benjamin, "Der Autor als Produzent" (1934), translated as "The Author as Producer," in *Reflections: Essays, Aphorisms, Autobiographical Writing*, trans. Edmund Jephcott (New York: Schocken Books, 1986), 233.

51 Ibid., 235.

52 Walter Benjamin, "Ein Jakobiner von heute: Zu Werner Hegemanns *Das steinerne Berlin*" (A Jacobin of our time: On Werner Hegemann's *Berlin, city of stone*), September 14, 1930, in *Das steinerne Berlin* (Braunschweig, Wiesbaden: Vieweg, 1988), 4. Benjamin's review of *Das steinerne Berlin* was originally published in the *Frankfurter Zeitung* and republished on September 28, 1930, in the *Königsberger Hartungsche Zeitung*.

53 Ibid.

54 Ibid.

55 Walter Benjamin, "Über den Begriff der Geschichte" (1940), translated as "Theses on the Philosophy of History," in *Illuminations: Essays and Reflections,* 262.

56 Walter Benjamin, "Berliner Chronik" (1932), translated as "A Berlin Chronicle," in *Reflections*, 44. While written in 1932, "Berlin Chronicle" was only published posthumously.

57 Walter Benjamin, *Einbahnstraße* (1928), translated as "One-Way Street (selection)," in ibid., 69.

58 The programs were the "Jugendstunde" (Youth hour) for the Funkstunde AG Berlin and the "Stunde der Jugend" (The hour of youth) for the Südwestdeutscher Rundfunk in Frankfurt am Main.

59 Benjamin, "One-Way Street," in *Reflections*, 68–69.

60 Benjamin, "The Rental Barracks," in *Radio Benjamin*, 61.

61 Almost exactly one year before Benjamin's broadcast on the rental barracks was launched, Hegemann had already spoken at the Berliner Rundfunk (April 2, 1929) under the heading "Wie wird der Berliner der Zukunft wohnen?" (How will the Berliner of the future live). The title of Hegemann's broadcast suggests that he, as well, had the two aerial photographs in mind. His lecture was later published as "Großstädtisches Wohnungselend und die Gartenstadt" (Metropolitan housing misery and the garden city), *Deutsche Werkmeister-Zeitung* (May 3, 1929): 211–212. It is also interesting to know that the station heavily censored his radio talk, purging sections of criticism on Berlin's building policy and politics, which the article reinstalled and highlighted. The censorship, in turn, created a controversy in the press and an initiative by left-wing intellectuals, artists, and activists, who in 1933 formed the group "Das freie Wort" (The free word). I want to thank Christiane Crasemann Collins for suggesting Hegemann's radio talks.

62 Walter Benjamin, "The Rental Barracks," in *Radio Benjamin,* 62.

63 Walter Benjamin, "Die Wiederkehr des Flâneurs" (1929), translated as "Return of the Flâneur," in *Walter Benjamin: Selected Writings, 1927–1930, vol. 2, part 1*, trans. Rodney Livingstone (Cambridge, MA: Belknap Press, 1996), 265.

64 Ibid.

65 Walter Benjamin, "Erfahrung und Armut" (1933), translated as "Experience and Poverty," in *Walter Benjamin: Selected Writings, 1931–1934*, 731–736.

66 Walter Benjamin, "Der Sürrealismus: Die letzte Momentaufnahme der europäischen Intelligenz" (1929), translated as "Surrealism: The Last Snapshot of the European Intelligentsia," in *Reflections,* 180.

67 It is also interesting to note how the German Nazi propaganda machinery preferred the group reception of centralized public screenings to the decentralized use of radio in private homes.

68 Detlef Mertins, "The Enticing and Threatening Face of Prehistory: Walter Benjamin and the Utopia of Glass," *Assemblage,* no. 29 (1996): 17, 19.

69 Hilde Heynen, *Architecture and Modernity: A Critique* (Cambridge, MA: MIT Press, 1999), 116.

70 Walter Benjamin, "Karl Kraus" (1931), in *Reflections*, 247. Translating the German term *"Durchleuchtung"* into English as "radioscopy" makes connections not only to concepts of "illumination" but also to "radio."

71 Beatriz Colomina, "X-ray Architecture: Illness as Metaphor," *Positions,* no. 0, "Positioning Positions" (Fall, 2008): 30–35.

72 The physicist and early radio scientist Jagadish Chandra Bose wrote in 1894: "The invisible light can easily pass through brick walls, buildings, etc. Therefore, messages can be transmitted by means of it without the mediation of wires."

73 Walter Benjamin, "The Rental Barracks," in *Radio Benjamin*, 62.

74 Theodor W. Adorno, "Charakteristik Walter Benjamin" (1950), translated as "A Portrait of Walter Benjamin," in *Prisms*, trans. Shierry Weber Nicholsen and Samuel Weber (Cambridge, MA: MIT Press, 1983), 229: "Everything which fell under the scrutiny of his words was transformed, as though it had become radioactive."

75 During postwar reconstruction, many modern dreams of the 1920s and 1930s were implemented at a large scale. Massive building ensembles, even entire cities, were rebuilt on an unprecedented scale from Japan to Spain, resulting in the wide-reaching implementation of modern settlement patterns and construction techniques. In addition, the formation of the Eastern and Western Blocs expedited many of the rebuilding efforts on both sides. While modernist principles were prominent forces in postwar reconstruction, the dream of a unified vision (from Le Corbusier via Rudolf Schwarz to Max Bill) never came to pass.

76 René Viénet, "The Situationists and the New Forms of Action against Politics and Art" (1967). Here cited from Tom McDonough, *Guy Debord and the Situationist International: Texts and Documents*, trans. Tom McDonough (Cambridge, MA: MIT Press, 2002), 182.

77 Ibid.

78 Internationale Lettriste, "L'offre et la Demande," *Potlatch,* no. 15 (December 1954). Here cited from *Potlatch 1954–1957* (Paris: Editions Gérard Lebovici, 1985), 63.

79 Greil Marcus, *Lipstick Traces: A Secret History of the Twentieth Century* (Cambridge, MA: Harvard University Press, 1989), 393.

80 Asger Jorn, "Peinture détourné" (1959). Here cited from *On the Passage of a Few People through a Rather Brief Moment in Time: The Situationist International, 1957–1972*, ed. Elisabeth Sussman (Cambridge, MA, Boston: MIT Press; Institute of Contemporary Art, 1989), 140.

81 Marcus, *Lipstick Traces: A Secret History of the Twentieth Century*, 179.

82 Guy Debord, "Theory of the Dérive" (1958), in Ken Knabb, *Situationist International Anthology*, trans. Ken Knabb (Berkeley: Bureau of Public Secrets, 1981), 50.

83 Anthony Vidler, "Unknown Lands: Guy Debord and the Cartographies of a Landscape to be Invented," in Anthony Vidler, *The Scenes of the Street and Other Essays* (New York: Monacelli Press, 2011), 335.

84 Debord, "Theory of the Dérive" (1958), in Knabb, *Situationist International Anthology*, 50.

85 Walter Benjamin, "A Berlin Chronicle" (1932), in *Reflections*, 11.

86 Michèle Bernstein, "Le Square des Missions Etrangères," *Potlatch*, no. 16 (January 1955), 63.

87 Simon Sadler, *The Situationist City* (Cambridge, MA: MIT Press, 1998), 70.

88 Bernstein, "Le Square des Missions Etrangères," 63.

89 Guy Debord and Gil J. Wolman, "Mode d'emploi du détournement" (1956), in Knabb, *Situationist International Anthology*, 13.

90 Hal Foster, "In Central Park," *London Review of Books*, 27:5 (March 2005): 32; and Tom McDonough, *The Beautiful Language of My Century: Reinventing the Language of Contestation in Postwar France, 1945–1968* (Cambridge, MA: MIT Press, 2007).

91 Christo, "Projet du mur provisoire de tonneaux metalliques (Rue Visconti, Paris 6)," collage and typewritten text, 1961.

92 Guy Debord, "On Wild Architecture" (1972), in *On the Passage of a Few People through a Rather Brief Moment in Time: The Situationist International, 1957–1972.*

93 It is important to remember that in 1968 Paris was not the only city that experienced an intense questioning of the status quo. In fact, it was a year when many struggles coalesced around the world: demonstrations and protests by student and Black Power movements, workers strikes and revolts against existing political regimes in socialist as well as capitalist countries. Demonstrations against the Vietnam war, the use of biological weapons, and existing class and racial divisions were just as common as protests for worker benefits and educational reforms. Some of the year's most traumatic events included the assassinations of Martin Luther King and Robert Kennedy, the crushing of the Prague Spring by Soviet tanks, and the police violence against demonstrations during the Democratic National Convention in Chicago.

94 Unsigned, "Les gratte-ciels par la racine," *Potlatch*, no. 5 (July 1954). Here cited from Libero Andreotti and Xavier Costa, *Theory of the Dérive and Other Situationist Writings on the City* (Barcelona: Museu d'Art Contemporani de Barcelona, 1996), 44.

95 Constant, "Reflex Manifesto" (1948), in Willemijn Stokvis, *Cobra,* trans. Leonard Bright (New York: Rizzoli, 1988), 30.

96 Mark Wigley, *Constant's New Babylon: The Hyper-Architecture of Desire* (Rotterdam: Witte de With and 010 Publishers, 1998), 71; and Constant, "Nieuw Babylon," *Delftse School*, no. 3 (1961): 4. Both cited from *Constant's New Babylon.*

97 Ibid., 52–55.

98 Unsigned, "Critique de l'urbanisme," *Internationale Situationniste*, no. 6 (August 1961): 5–11. Here cited from Andreotti and Costa, *Theory of the Dérive and Other Situationist Writings on the City*, 115.

99 On the relationship between Constant and Rem Koolhaas, see Bart Lootsma, "Now Switch off the Sound and Reverse the Film: Koolhaas, Constant, and Dutch Culture in the 1960s," *Hunch*, no. 1 (1999): 152–173.

100 Tschumi, *Event-Cities: Praxis*, 12.

101 Anthony Vidler, "The Third Typology," *Oppositions*, no. 7 (Winter 1976), expanded in *Rational Architecture: The Reconstruction of the European City*, ed. Robert L. Delevoy (Brussels: Editions des Archives d'Architecture Moderne, 1978). Here cited from *Oppositions Reader: Selected Readings from a Journal for Ideas and Criticism in Architecture 1973–1984*, ed. K. Michael Hays (New York: Princeton Architectural Press, 1998), 14.

102 Aldo Rossi, *L'architettura della città* (Padova: Marsilio Editori, 1966). Here cited from *The Architecture of the City*, trans. Diane Ghirardo and Joan Ockman (1966; Cambridge, MA: MIT Press, 2002), 114.

103 During his internship year for the ETH in Zurich, Tschumi worked at the office of Candilis, Josic, and Woods in Paris.

104 It is interesting to note that already in 1970 Tschumi came to London to work for Price and that Tschumi later on invited Price to contribute a building to his Parc de la Villette (both collaborations did not materialize).

105 Bernard Tschumi, "The Architectural Paradox," *Studio International* (September–October 1975). Here cited from *Architecture and Disjunction* (Cambridge, MA: MIT Press, 1994), 87.

106 Denis Hollier, *Against Architecture: The Writings of Georges Bataille*, trans. Betsy Wing (Cambridge, MA: MIT Press, 1989), 47.

107 Georges Bataille, "L'Amérique disparue" (1928), translated as "Extinct America," *October*, no. 36 (Spring, 1986): 7.

108 Georges Bataille, "The Labyrinth" (1936), in *Visions of Excess: Selected Writings, 1927–1939*, trans. Allan Stoekl (Minneapolis: University of Minnesota Press, 1985), 171–177; and Benjamin, "A Berlin Chronicle," in *Reflections*, 3–60.

109 On the relationship between Benjamin and Bataille, see Michael Weingrad, "The College of Sociology and the Institute of Social Research," *New German Critique*, no. 84 (Autumn 2001): 129–161.

110 Benjamin, "A Berlin Chronicle," in *Reflections*, 9.

111 Ibid., 8.

112 Tschumi, "The Architectural Paradox," in *Architecture and Disjunction.*

113 Bernard Tschumi, *The Manhattan Transcripts* (London, New York: Academy Editions; St. Martin's Press, 1981), 32.

114 Tschumi, *Architecture and Disjunction*, 147.

115 The curvilinear pools of Los Angeles, for example, made for excellent skate parks after the drought of the 1970s—a misappropriation that not only discovered these spaces for skateboarding but changed the sport forever through the dimensions of the space.

116 Rossi, *The Architecture of the City*, 59.

117 Ibid., 60.

118 In *Architecture and Disjunction*, Tschumi acknowledged that "typological studies have begun to discuss the critical 'affect' of ideal building types that were historically born of functions but were later displaced into new programs alien to their original purpose." *Architecture and Disjunction*, 118.

119 K. Michael Hays, *Architecture's Desire: Reading the Late Avant-garde* (Cambridge, MA: MIT Press, 2010), 42–43.

120 Georges Bataille, *L'Erotisme (1957)*, translated as *Eroticism: Death and Sensuality*, trans. Mary Dalwood (San Francisco: City Lights Books, 1986).

121 Rossi, *The Architecture of the City*, 29.

122 Bernard Tschumi in conversation with the author, published in *City Catalyst: Architecture in the Age of Extreme Urbanisation*, 131.

123 Rem Koolhaas, "Eno/abling Architecture," in *Autonomy and Ideology: Positioning an Avant-Garde in America*, ed. Robert Somol (New York: The Monacceli Press, 1997), 294.

4 Conclusion

1 Félix Guattari, "Zone Questionnaire," in *Zone 1/2*, eds. Sanford Kwinter and Michel Feher (New York: Urzone, 1986), 460: "The city no longer exists as an entity. It is only a node at the core of a multidimensional network—within the spatial web of urbanization …"

2 Anthony Vidler, "The Third Typology," *Oppositions*, no. 7 (Winter 1976). Here cited from *Oppositions Reader: Selected Readings from a Journal for Ideas and Criticism in Architecture 1973–1984*, ed. K. Michael Hays (New York: Princeton Architectural Press, 1998), 15.

3 Georges Bataille, "Informe" (1929), translated as "Formless," in *Visions of Excess: Selected Writings, 1927–1939*, trans. Allan Stoekl (Minneapolis: University of Minnesota Press, 1985), 31.

4 Ibid.

5 *Formless: Ways In and Out of Form*, eds. Patrick Crowley and Paul Hegarty, (Oxford, New York: Peter Lang, 2005), 9–15.

Acknowledgments

This project would not have been possible without the support of friends, the productive criticism of readers, audiences, and interlocutors, and the backing of numerous institutions.

I want to thank the Graham Foundation for Advanced Studies in the Fine Arts, and Sarah Herda, its Director, for funding the production of the book and for the endorsement of the project. The Graham Foundation supported multiple phases of this research, starting with my dissertation and the Foundation's Carter Manny Trustees' Merit Citation. The Getty Foundation in Los Angeles provided a Library Research Residency, which gave me time to finish the final draft of the manuscript, and the wealth of its special collection was crucial in the selection of images. Special thanks go to Tracy Schuster for help with the archive and for sharing her personal anecdotes on Banham. During earlier stages of the project, the Samuel H. Kress Foundation enabled me to visit archives, libraries, offices, and buildings essential to the research of this volume.

The topic for this book emerged (now more than a decade ago) during my Ph.D. work at the University of Pennsylvania and I am most grateful to my advisors, the late Detlef Mertins as well as David Leatherbarrow. I owe a debt of gratitude to their knowledge and generosity. Furthermore, I thank the readers of that early material—David Brownlee, Hartmut Frank, Andres Lepik, Frank Trommler, Iain Boyd Whyte, and Volker M. Welter—for their insights and pointed questions. My fellow students in the Ph.D. program at UPenn, in combination with the Fisher Fine Arts Library and its unparalleled rare-book collection, made my time there most rewarding and generative. I could not have asked for a more supportive and stimulating environment.

As I wrote this book, a number of thinkers took the time to read and comment on the work. My gratitude for their diligence and generosity goes to Barry Bergdoll, Robert Bruegmann, Cynthia Davidson, Alexander D'Hooghe, John Harwood, Sandy Isenstadt, Simon Sadler, and Martino Stierli. In addition, I have benefited from many conversations, exchanges, and collaborations over the past years, for which I want to thank in particular George Baird, Aaron Betsky, Ellen Grimes, Sam Jacob, Sanford Kwinter, Mark Linder, Bart Lootsma, John McMorrough, Vedran Mimica, Albert Pope, Bernard Tschumi, Stanley Tigerman, Winy Maas, and Elia

Zenghelis. Thanks go as well to Catherine Ingraham, a mentor and friend, whose early encouragements to pursue strange topics bear fruit in this publication.

Significant parts of this book benefited from invitations to speak on my research at conferences and seminars. Thanks to Amale Andraos and Nahyun Hwang at Columbia University; Wiel Arets, Martin Felsen, and Michelangelo Sabatino at the Illinois Institute of Technology; McLain Clutter at the University of Michigan; Michael Darling at the Museum of Contemporary Art in Chicago; Martine De Maeseneer at the KU Leuven; Jes Fernie at the Royal Institute of British Architects; David Haney at the University of Kent; Janine Mileaf at the Arts Club of Chicago; Lynn Osmond at the Chicago Architecture Foundation; Michael Piper at the University of Toronto; Ashley Schafer and Eva Franch i Gilabert at the US Pavilion of the 14th Venice Biennale; Brett Steele at the Architectural Association; and David Van Zanten at Northwestern University.

Some of this text's arguments were tested in earlier versions as essays and the work has greatly benefited from comments by peer reviewers, readers, and the editors of *Architectural Design, Architectural Research Quarterly, Architectural Theory Review, Grey Room, Journal of Architectural Culture—Joelho, Journal of the Society of Architectural Historians*, and *Journal of Architectural Education*. Particular thanks go to Lucia Allais, Zeynep Çelik Alexander, Helen Castle, Beatriz Colomina, Pedro Gadanho, Andrew Leach, Gisela Moeller, Susana Oliveira, and Christiane Salge. In addition, various concepts put forward in this volume were developed through exhibitions and I would like to thank the commissioners and curators of the 13th Venice Biennale, especially David Chipperfield and Jaffer Kolb; the team at the 4th Lisbon Architecture Triennale and Fabrizio Gallanti in particular; as well as the Bi-City Biennale of Urbanism in Shenzhen and its section on Radical Urbanism by Alfredo Brillembourg and Hubert Klumpner.

In many ways, the book benefited from the unique constellation of institutions and figures in Chicago. My colleagues at the School of Architecture at the University of Illinois have only been supportive, and particular appreciation goes to David Brown, Penelope Dean, Sarah Dunn, Grant Gibson, Sean Lally, Andrew Moddrell, Clare Lyster, and Director Bob Somol, whom I also thank for reading parts of the manuscript. My excellent students at UIC also deserve mention; they often productively "détourned" the material and brought it to new places. In the final stages of the work, I received additional support from the College of Architecture, Design, and the Arts and the Office of the Vice Chancellor for Research at UIC; my thanks to Dean Steve Everett and Vice Chancellor Mitra Dutta.

At Birkhäuser, I must thank Ria Stein, who has been a champion of this project from an early stage. For editing the manuscript, I would like to acknowledge the diligent and tireless work of Elizabeth Gregory and the late Polly Koch. Thanks go as well to my dear friend and frequent collaborator, Jonathan Mekinda, whose thorough reading and intelligent questions helped sharpen early drafts.

As always, I am deeply grateful to Stefanie and Ehrfried Eisenschmidt for their endless support and for teaching me how to build, travel, argue, and discover (along with much more). Lastly and most of all, this work would never have seen the light of day without the love, patience, and inspiration of Maria Gaspar, who taught me so much about the formless and to whom I dedicate this book.

Illustration Credits

I am grateful to the many organizations and individuals who have given permission to reproduce photographs, drawings, and documents. Every effort has been made to trace, clear, and acknowledge the copyrights of the illustrations used in this volume, and I will correct any errors or omissions brought to my attention, in subsequent editions.

Architectural Design, vol. 47, no. 5, 1977, 332: 126

Architekturmuseum TU Berlin, Inv. Nr. 12587; B 3258,046; 42647: 93 (top and bottom), 97

Bibliothèque nationale de France, département cartes et plans, GE C-5316: 170

bpk Bildagentur/Kunstbibliothek, Staatliche Museen, Berlin/Photograph: Arthur Köster/ Art Resource, NY: 106

bpk Bildagentur/Kupferstichkabinett, Staatliche Museen, Berlin/Art Resource, New York: 100 (top and bottom), 143 (top)

bpk Bildagentur/Sammlung architektonischer Entwürfe, Kupferstichkabinett, Staatliche Museen, Berlin/Art Resource, New York: 105

Centro Studi e Archivio della Comunicazione, Università degli Studi di Parma: 118, 119

Courtesy of Christo and Jeanne-Claude; photograph by Wolfgang Volz/Laif/Redux: 171

Courtesy of Robert Habel. From Messel, *Der Wertheimbau* (1899), no. 26: 95

Courtesy of OMA: 122, 124, 129, 130

Courtesy of Simon Sadler: 168

Courtesy of Bernard Tschumi: 179, 183, 184, 187

Courtesy of Venturi, Scott Brown and Associates, Inc.: 64, 66 (bottom), 68, 69 (top), 75

Craig Krull Gallery, Santa Monica, California, © Julian Wasser: 55 (top)

Das Neue Berlin #4, 1929: 41: 111

D'Arcangelo Family Partnership/Licensed by VAGA, New York: 71

Deutsches Architekturmuseum, Frankfurt am Main; photograph: Hagen Stier, hagen-stier.com; © OMA: 125

Gagosian, © Ed Ruscha: 50

Gemeentemuseum Den Haag: 1025334 and 0182564, © 2018 Artists Rights Society (ARS), New York/c/o Pictoright Amsterdam: 174, 175

Inland Architect and News Record, vol. XIV, no. 5 (1889): 85

Moholy-Nagy Archive, © 2018 Estate of László Moholy-Nagy/Artists Rights Society (ARS), New York: 31, 161

The Art Institute of Chicago/Art Resource, NY, © 2018 Estate of László Moholy-Nagy/ Artists Rights Society (ARS), New York: 38

The Art Institute of Chicago, Ludwig Karl Hilberseimer Papers, Ryerson and Burnham Archives: 107, 113, 114 (top and bottom), 115

The Getty Research Institute: 66 (top)
Verwaltung der Staatlichen Schlösser und Gärten, Berlin, Schloß Charlottenburg; Eigentum des Hauses Hohenzollern, SKH Georg Friedrich Prinz von Preußen, SPSG: 102-103
VG Bild-Kunst Bonn, Bauhaus-Archiv Berlin: 32

About the Author

Alexander Eisenschmidt is a designer, theorist, and Associate Professor of Architecture at the University of Illinois at Chicago. He is editor of *City Catalyst*, among other volumes, and has curated and exhibited at venues such as the Venice Biennale.

Index